Alan Berlow
Dead Season

A Story of Murder and Revenge

A former correspondent for National
Public Radio, Alan Berlow lived in Manila
from 1988 until 1992 and reported extensively on Southeast Asia. He lives in
Maryland with his wife, Susan, and their
daughter, Maia.

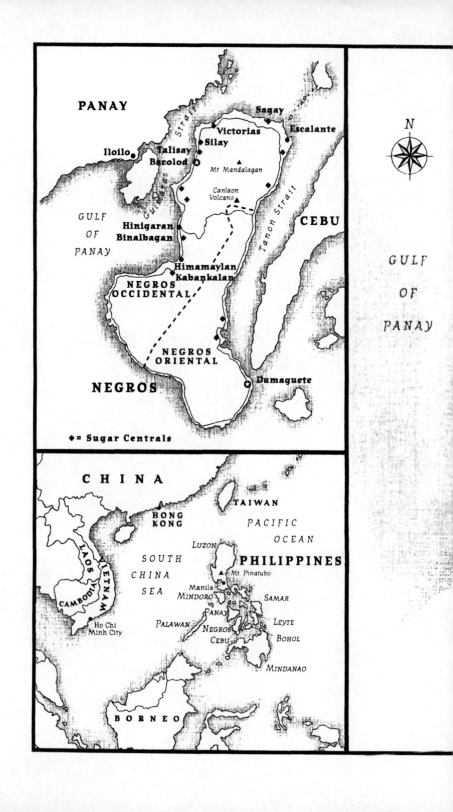

PANAY

Sagay

Victorias
Silay
Escalante

Iloilo
Talisay
Bacolod

Mt Mandalagan

Canlaon
Volcano

GULF
OF
PANAY

CEBU

Hinigaran
Binalbagan

Himamaylan
Kabankalan

NEGROS
OCCIDENTAL

NEGROS
ORIENTAL

NEGROS

Dumaguete

◆ = Sugar Centrals

GULF

OF

PANAY

N

CHINA

TAIWAN

HONG
KONG

PACIFIC

OCEAN

LUZON

SOUTH

CHINA

SEA

PHILIPPINES

Mt. Pinatubo

Manila
MINDORO

SAMAR

LAOS

VIETNAM

CAMBODIA

Ho Chi
Minh City

PALAWAN

PANAY

NEGROS

CEBU

LEYTE

BOHOL

MINDANAO

BORNEO

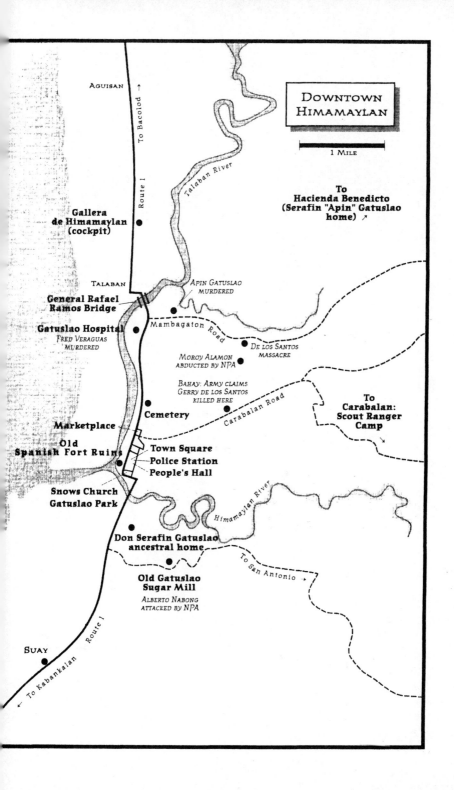

DOWNTOWN
HIMAMAYLAN

1 MILE

AGUISAN

To Bacolod

Route 1

Talaban River

To
Hacienda Benedicto
(Serafin "Apin" Gatuslao
home) ↗

Gallera
de Himamaylan
(cockpit)

TALABAN

APIN GATUSLAO
MURDERED

General Rafael
Ramos Bridge

Gatuslao Hospital
FRED VERAGUAS
MURDERED

Mambagaton Road

DE LOS SANTOS
MASSACRE

MOROY ALAMON
ABDUCTED BY NPA

BAHAY: ARMY CLAIMS
GERRY DE LOS SANTOS
KILLED HERE

Carabalan Road

To
Carabalan:
Scout Ranger
Camp
↘

Cemetery

Marketplace

Old
Spanish Fort Ruins

Town Square
Police Station
People's Hall

Snows Church
Gatuslao Park

Himamaylan River

Don Serafin Gatuslao
ancestral home

To San Antonio →

Old Gatuslao
Sugar Mill

ALBERTO NABONG
ATTACKED BY NPA

Route 1

SUAY

← To Kabankalan

Dead Season

A Story of Murder and Revenge

Alan Berlow

Vintage Departures
Vintage Books
A Division of Random House, Inc.
New York

The Library of Congress has cataloged the Pantheon edition as follows:

Berlow, Alan.
Dead season: a story of murder and revenge/Alan Berlow.
p. cm.
Includes Index.

1. Negros island (Philippines)—Civilization. 2. Murder—
Philippines—Negros island. I. Title.
DS688.N5B47   1996
959.9′5—dc20

Vintage ISBN: 0-679-74789-3

Book design by Fearn Cutler

Random House Web address: www.randomhouse.com

Printed in the United States of America
BVG 01

For Suzy

The notion of *balos* or revenge acquired such importance that if Filipinos were insulted or injured, there was no other law than the knife and spear. This condition gave the island of Negros the appearance of a population in a permanent state of war. . . . These demonstrations of violence sometimes ended in the death of a family or of someone predisposed to commit blood crimes. Fortunately, this practice has vanished from the island. It reappears only rarely and at times when the northeastern wind heats the heads of the Filipinos.

Robustiano Echauz,
Sketches of the Island of Negros, 1894

Contents

Introduction

I first heard of Barrio Mambagaton in the spring of 1988, when I was living in the Philippines and reporting for National Public Radio. I'd been sent to the island of Negros, which lies 300 miles south of Manila and had earned a sordid international reputation during the final years of the Marcos dictatorship as the place where thousands of children were allowed to starve to death while government officials and local oligarchs did nothing. Behind this seeming indifference was the dictator's disastrous decision to monopolize the nation's sugar industry and hoard thousands of tons of the commodity, gambling that the price on the world market would go up. When it instead crashed to record lows, tens of thousands of Negros plantation workers lost their jobs. In the ensuing economic fiasco, children went hungry and died, Negros became a grotesque metaphor for the thoroughgoing rot of the Marcos regime, and Communist rebels seized on the widespread misery to press a nasty little war against the island's ruling elite.

That war continued after the downfall of Ferdinand Marcos in 1986, and a few days prior to my arrival on Negros, it took the life of a young political activist who was shot dead in front of his wife and daughter by one of the faceless, predatory death squads allegedly run by the island's rich sugar planters. My assignment was to look into this murder and provide some background on the war. But while I was researching that story, I met a young boy who was hiding out from a Philippine Army special forces unit, which, he said, had recently massacred five members of his family. The boy, Joaquin De los Santos, said he came from Himamaylan town, from a barrio called Mambagaton, literally, "the place of the ghosts." He then began to unfold a grisly account of the slaying of his mother, father, and three young siblings—murders, he suggested, provoked by a cockfight.

The place of the ghosts, I quickly discovered, more than lived up to its name. Indeed, by the time I left, I felt as though I'd just stepped out of Juan Rulfo's surreal novel, *Pedro Páramo*, in which all of the characters are dead. The major difference was that in Rulfo's labyrinthine world, the deceased are still able to converse, memories persist, and thoughts, albeit frequently enigmatic and elliptical, emerge.

The dead in Mambagaton proved considerably less voluble and required far more encouragement to surrender their secrets. But their presence among the living—preserved in a skein of conspiratorial and sometimes contradictory accounts of murder and revenge— was no less haunting. That many of these tales could not be true was self-evident. Yet it was equally clear that they somehow enabled residents of Mambagaton to make sense of their world and, if nothing else, to tame their worst fears. Of particular interest to me were three individuals—a peasant farmer, a wealthy landlord, and a soldier—whose stories had become mysteriously intertwined in the local consciousness.

The first, Reynaldo "Moret" De los Santos, Joaquin's father, was a deeply religious farmer who lodged his faith with the Catholic church and an odd assemblage of animist spirits, and was enough of a dreamer to believe that he and his children need not spend their lives mired in the muck of a Negros sugarcane field. Based on everything his closest acquaintances told me, it was difficult to imagine how Moret might have posed a threat to anyone. Nevertheless, Moret's neighbors didn't seem at all surprised that the unique alchemy of Negros politics could have transformed him into a revolutionary or conspirator or that someone would have decided to have him eliminated.

Moret's friends came up with a dozen theories to explain why he was murdered, but they all agreed that the family's troubles and much of the violence in and around Himamaylan town began shortly after the assassination of the second man whose story captured my attention, Serafin Gatuslao, otherwise known as the Batman. The great-great-grandson of a Catholic priest and scion of one of the island's preeminent sugar families, Gatuslao was a militant anti-Communist, who saw the ongoing civil war as an all-or-nothing battle to reestablish the authority of the island's ruling class and preserve Negros as a bastion of paternalistic civility.

"Peace and order" was the incessantly recited mantra of elite Negros families like the Gatuslaos, even as the military and paramilitary forces they marshaled to defend their interests routinely resorted to intimidation and brutality. When the Communist New People's Army (NPA) responded in kind, the most bellicose of the landlords were among its favorite targets. Gatuslao's enemies, including some of his own workers, said he'd cheated them on their wages, committed "crimes against the people," and had gotten what he deserved. Others suggested that the NPA murdered Gatuslao because he had defended a lacquered vision of Negros past. But the most intriguing allegation to emerge in the wake of Gatuslao's demise was that his assassination by the NPA had been ordered by Moret De los Santos.

The third man whose death in Mambagaton seemed to cry out for some sort of explanation was a young soldier named Gerry De los Santos, who had joined the Army to serve his country and fight the Communists. On Negros, Gerry learned that "Communist" was a loosely defined and widely employed epithet that could be used to legitimize the murder of just about anyone. By the time of his own death, Gerry wasn't clear who the Communists were. In fact, he wasn't clear about much of anything, including whether or not he was related to the family of Moret De los Santos. The only thing Gerry seemed to have been sure about was that he was personally responsible for the De los Santos massacre and that someone was going to kill him because of it. A few days after he reached that conclusion, Gerry De los Santos was shot dead.

Moret, Serafin, and Gerry were all consumed by a conflict that was rooted in an anachronistic plantation economy, an intractable caste system, and a tradition of personal debts which had collectively ensured the impoverishment of millions of Negros citizens over the past century and a half. Because politically motivated violence was so commonplace in the Philippines and nearly always went unpunished, I was not at all surprised that the mayhem in Mambagaton had been completely ignored by the island's political leaders. At the time, I also had no reason to believe that any of these stories would reach the offices of the country's highest public officials. I did feel, however, that there was something portentous about this beleaguered little town and that the lives of these three men might shed some light on the strange world that is Negros and the problem of creating a democracy in a country like the Philippines.

Three years after my brief introduction to Mambagaton, I received a grant from the Fund for Investigative Journalism in Washington to look into the killings in that remote Philippine barrio. I was initially drawn back to Negros by its mysteries; I wanted to find out why Moret De los Santos and his family had been massacred and how or if their deaths might be connected to those of the Batman and Gerry. I was, however, also intrigued by the realization that whether or not these and other killings were in fact part of a single fabric, residents of Mambagaton *believed* that they were, had acted on those beliefs, and innocent people had died as a result. That some of these deaths were a consequence of "facts" and "evidence" generated by nothing more than fevered imagination was, for me, both inescapable and irresistible. Yet no one in Mambagaton seemed to find any of this particularly unusual.

As a journalist, I was used to dropping in on unfamiliar terrain and snatching up the extraordinary fragments of peoples' lives that constitute the news. And like many of my colleagues, I often found myself wondering what had happened to the subjects of my stories after I'd moved on to the next crisis or tragedy. More than anything, what brought me back to Negros was the opportunity to spend an extended period of time observing a society unlike any I'd ever witnessed or imagined: one with no functioning system of law or justice, where government was either absent or irrelevant, and the rules regulating everyday life were dictated by a revolving cast of vigilantes, fanatical cultists, Communist revolutionaries, private armies, and the military. The Philippines may have proclaimed itself a democracy, but on Negros almost everyone vying for power was equally committed to the subversion of democratic institutions.

The only eddy of sanity within this maelstrom seemed to be the Catholic church, whose priests spoke out, often at great personal risk, for the rights of Negros's poor and against the violence of the military and vigilantes. It was the church that had endorsed the devoutly Catholic Corazon Cojuangco Aquino against Marcos and then pressed the new president to make good on her commitment to human rights. And it was the same church that brought the De los Santos massacre and a multitude of other atrocities to Aquino's attention, exposing both her inability and unwillingness to address the country's rampant violence.

Yet the church itself was not above reproach when it came to defending the basic rights of Filipinos. On the one hand, its traditional agenda, in which the blood of martyrs is seen as "the seed of Christendom," allowed it to disregard the suffering of individuals even as it strained to exploit the latest bloody victims for its own ends. On the other hand, its refusal to condemn the wanton violence against police, soldiers, and planters like Serafin Gatuslao further undermined its moral authority and led to widespread suspicions that the priests were aligned with the rebels.

For an outsider, it was both shocking and exhilarating to see an entire community swept into the whirlwind of Negros's militant and often bizarre politics. But it was equally fascinating to observe how ordinary people managed to survive in this environment; how, like the ethereal citizens in *Pedro Páramo,* they withdrew into a kind of limbo—a dead season, as the fallow interregnum between reaping and sowing is known—in which they held on to only the most limited hopes and expectations. While the backdrop to this world, this *páramo,* or bleak plain, shifted periodically—a dictator fell, elections were held, the war escalated or subsided, feast days for the saints were celebrated—the traditional social order remained immutable. What was ultimately most striking about life on Negros was not simply the futility of its incessant habitual violence but how both rich and poor have been trapped by a system that renders the overwhelming majority of Negrenses economically and psychologically dependent on a tiny, self-serving elite.

As a reporter for NPR, I had covered the People Power Revolution of 1986 and the fairy-tale transition from Marcos's dictatorship to the democracy of Corazon Aquino. Two and a half years before the Berlin Wall came down and five years before the breakup of the Soviet Union, Filipinos floated the fantastic notion that the century's basest tyrannies might peacefully be brought to an end and that radical transformation of society was possible.

No doubt, the images of unarmed civilians massed in front of tanks and soldiers and of Catholic nuns clutching ballot boxes and rosaries to their breasts were a source of great inspiration to captive nations around the world. Filipinos called the revolution a "miracle" and found comfort in the notion that they had proved themselves capable of pulling together to fight for the common good. Those were truly heady times.

Unfortunately, nations don't shed the past like snakes their skins. A closer examination of the Philippine "model"—of the critical role played by the military in that revolution, the patrician character of the new democrats, and especially the seemingly self-destructive content of daily life in a place like Negros—might have quickly disabused Filipino romantics, as well as citizens of China, Burma, Russia, Yugoslavia, and anyone else who was watching, of the idea that democracy could be so easily sown in the poisoned soil of dictatorship.

"The victor belongs to the spoils," someone once suggested. And the daunting legacies of Spanish and American colonialism, coupled with the ruins of the Marcos dictatorship, held Negros firmly in their thrall. It is no small matter to have toppled a dictator in Manila. What the stories of Moret De los Santos, Serafin Gatuslao, and Gerry De los Santos suggest is just how difficult it is to make a true democratic revolution succeed in thousands of forgotten, out-of-the-way barrios like Mambagaton.

Part
One

Holy Week

On my knees in Quiapo till my knees ache
Lisping in prayer in Quiapo till my tongue numbs
I shall lacerate myself till I bleed
On my knees in Quiapo in the poisoned air,
Listening to hope that is not there.

—F. Sionil José, *My Brother, My Executioner*

By the time Reynaldo Parillo "Moret" De los Santos learned that someone was trying to kill him, it was probably too late to do anything about it. Nevertheless, not a few of his friends and neighbors believe that if Moret had only stayed away from the cockpit on that Easter Sunday, he and the rest of his family would still be alive. No one is passing judgment on Moret, suggesting that he should not have been at the cockpit, or that having gone there he was somehow morally responsible for the consequences. They simply made the observation, offered this conclusion, if you will, based on what the lawyers call a "preponderance of evidence," but mostly on hearsay and coincidence. Above all, coincidence. If a history were to be written, the verdict of the people of Himamaylan, preposterous as it might seem, would be that Moret De los Santos, his wife, and their three children were dead because of a chicken—a very talented chicken, but a chicken nonetheless. That's what people believe, and in a way that's all that really matters. Sometimes that is as close to the truth as people can get, or would want to get. Anyway, no one was about to demand a scientific inquiry or judicial proceeding into the facts of the matter because there was no such thing on the island of Negros, except maybe in the imagination of a few idealists. No one was going to go poking around in the mess on their own, either, because they'd probably just end up like Moret and his family: lying under a slab of cement in the paupers' cemetery with a bunch of prickly pears and twisted crotons to keep them company.

Moret had harbored more than a hunch that his time was running out, but he had discussed his fears with only a few close friends, perhaps so as not to worry his family, perhaps because it was hard to digest the idea of being hunted, perhaps because he didn't want to believe it, or because he knew there was nothing he could do about it.

He confided in Willy Villacanas, the meat vendor, and Fred Veraguas, a fisherman, but both of them were in the same predicament, more or less, and neither knew any better than Moret what to do about it. Consortia "Consoy" Perez, a lay sister at Our Lady of the Snows Church, wasn't much better off. She had an inkling of what was going on, but she looked up to *Tay* Moret—Father Moret, as she called him—as a leader and assumed he knew what he was doing. Whatever concerns Moret may have had, he hadn't shared them with Consoy. And now it was too late. The best Sister Consoy could do was to somehow square the circle of fate with faith.

If anyone should have known what was going on in Moret's life, it was Cerila, his wife, but it's a safe bet that she was in the dark, because Cerila discussed everything of importance with Jenelyn, their oldest daughter, and Jenelyn had only a glimmer of insight into what was happening. Now, Cerila is dead, so there's no telling what she knew.

Moret's second daughter, Jasmin, had a premonition of the end, but Moret only brushed it off. Jasmin was three hours into the twenty-four-hour trip from Manila to Negros, when a typhoon began to roil the sea, forcing the Negros Navigation Company steamer back to port. She waited five days on the ship for the waters to calm and, to pass the time, met several times with a fortuneteller, a balding old woman with thin wisps of gray hair who came from Sagay, at the northern tip of Negros. Jasmin paid her five pesos to read her palm, and although she couldn't remember anything else of the seer's augury, one thing stuck: The fortuneteller told her that during the next year something terrible was going to happen to her that she would never stop thinking about until the day she died.

That was it, a little nugget of fool's gold dropped in a stream of otherwise murky observations and predictions, words that might easily have been dismissed but instead rose to torment Jasmin early

in the morning the day before her father was killed. Normally, she
would have reported to work at 6 A.M. at the LNR Garment Factory,
not far from the sprawling Manila shantytown where she and her
husband made their home. But Jasmin woke up agitated, thinking
about the fortuneteller. As she paced back and forth outside her little shack, she decided she couldn't work that day. Later she recalled
the conversation she had had with Moret about the old lady and that
he had told her not to pay it any mind, that if bad luck was your destiny, it was best to just get on with your life.

Moret usually went to church several times during Holy Week.
This year he didn't go at all, however. Instead he spent the entire
Easter weekend at the cockpit. On Good Friday morning, Moret instructed Cerila to take the children to the afternoon church service
and to return home directly as soon as it was over. Jenelyn said she
didn't question her father's instructions at the time. The words of
her parents carried more weight than the word of God. Anyway,
Moret was often impulsive, abrupt, or arbitrary, and no one in the
family dared challenge his authority.

*　*　*

On Easter Sunday, the holiest day of the year in the Philippines,
you can still find a few peasants swinging their machetes in the endless fields of Negros sugarcane, toppling the tall stalks one by one.
For the most part, however, even the most despotic *hacenderos* appreciate the mystical significance attached to Holy Week and the
Resurrection. The vast majority give their workers time off, and the
best of them even make their cane trucks available to transport thousands of workers and their families to the town centers so they can
go to church and attend the local fiestas.

When Moret was growing up in Himamaylan, the Gatuslao family sponsored the fiesta and the Holy Week festivities. Then again,
the Gatuslaos pretty much ran everything in Himamaylan in those
days, in addition to owning a sizable piece of it. Don Serafin Gatuslao had five sons, and each hosted a major feast day. Agustin, who
was known as Tuting and later became a congressman, was responsible for the Feast of Our Lady of the Snows, the patron saint of Himamaylan; Miguel, known as Migueling, was in charge of the Feast
of Lourdes; and José, the Feast of the Sacred Heart. José Gatuslao,

who became mayor of Himamaylan, was known to his friends as Nanding, but behind his back people called him Mayor Coles because it sounds like *miercoles,* the word for Wednesday, which was the only day Nanding could ever be found in his office. The oldest son, Valeriano, was known as Valing and later became governor as well as the father of two of his nieces, whom he and his wife adopted from Agustin. An amiable, easygoing man, people said he was "everybody's friend," the very words that are inscribed on his tombstone in the Himamaylan cemetery, just across the fence from where the De los Santoses are buried. Valing was in charge of the Feast of San José. Leonidas, the youngest son, also had a feast day, but no one seems to remember anymore what it was.

By financing and producing the fiestas, the Gatuslaos associated themselves with the church, the soul of the community, with God, and with the church's most public and popular mission, all of which helped earn them an element of legitimacy when it came to their political operations and, perhaps, some merit with Saint Peter. Most towns in the Philippines are run this way—by one or two wealthy families who vie for political control and the veneration of their constituents.

During Holy Week, the Gatuslaos, like all good politicians, were out in force. José's wife, Trina Alvarez, pretty much took charge of the week's events, and she and the mayor had a prominent place in the procession from the church. The Gatuslaos provided food for the choir, paid to clean and decorate the church and clothe the icons, placed the flowers on the altar and the communion table, and decorated the carabao-drawn wagon that transported the image of Our Lady of the Snows and the Santo Entierro, the Dead Christ. Back then, Himamaylan was a peaceful place. No one ran around with a radical political agenda, a crusade, or some other highminded purpose. And there were no revolutionaries. People who remember those times also say just about everyone had enough to eat.

Moret De los Santos might have taken a greater interest in the church in those days had his attentions not been focused on the more immediate necessity of feeding his family. Unlike the Gatuslaos, Moret hadn't inherited either wealth or status. Moret's father, Reynaldo De la Rosa, left the family to fight the Japanese when World War II broke out, and as soon as the war was over, he abandoned his wife and Moret for a woman in nearby La Carlota. Moret was brought up by his mother, Felina De los Santos, who had Moret rebaptized with her family name. Felina lived and worked on the estate of Raymundo Tongson, a close political ally of the Gatuslaos, and as Moret grew up, he cut cane and did other jobs for Tongson. Over time, Tongson and his sons became Moret's *padrinos,* or patrons, which meant Moret could always depend on a job with the Tongsons and that they would always see to his family's basic needs. There were real limits to their generosity, however, and Moret recognized that the Tongsons weren't about to provide him a ticket out of poverty.

A grainy black-and-white photograph taken shortly before Moret's death shows a trim, muscular man with a high, ridged forehead, narrow, pinched eyes framed by rectangular glasses, and a ghost of a smile owing as much to the light in his gaze as the line of his lips. Moret seems to have been generally well liked in the community, although he was not always the easiest guy to get along with. Some found him sullen, others a bit full of himself and aggressive—the result, perhaps, of an unquenchable thirst for recognition and adulation, needs he'd tried to satisfy in high school as a boxer and later in the cockpit.

Moret's religious devotion was a fairly recent phenomenon, something he'd taken to in the early 1980s, due in part to Consoy Perez and in part to an embarrassing financial fiasco involving a former high school classmate who'd promised Moret a high-paying construction job in Saudi Arabia. Moret had been looking for an opportunity like that for years; he'd heard the stories of the big money that could be made in the Persian Gulf, of people who'd returned to Negros after a few years overseas with enough to buy land or start a little business. Himamaylan, on the other hand, was a dead end. His jobs at the highway department and as an overseer at Rojelio Tongson's hacienda barely allowed him to get by, and he was surrounded by neighbors who were out of work and hungry. The bottom had fallen out of the world sugar market, and the economy of Negros, which was largely dependent on the staple, had nearly collapsed. Even some of the middle-class landowners and planters were going bust. His classmate had taken all of Moret's savings—several hundred dollars the friend said he needed to pay a recruiting agency—

and told Moret to meet him in Manila two weeks later to process the paperwork and obtain a passport. When Moret arrived at the address his friend had given him, however, there was no recruiting agency and no friend. It was one of the oldest scams in the book, and Moret had fallen for it.

He returned to Himamaylan crestfallen, ashamed, and angry, and it was just about this time that Consoy Perez, all four feet ten inches of her, first encountered him at Tongson's hacienda. Consoy had gone there promoting the church, trying to recruit hacienda workers to the Basic Christian Community (BCC), the church's barrio organization. The BCCs had been introduced to the Philippines in the 1960s following Vatican II, a series of encyclicals issued by Pope John XXIII that committed the church to the economic upliftment of the poor, but the number and popularity of the BCCs began to surge only after they were endorsed in 1977 by the Catholic Bishops Conference of the Philippines.

BCCs initially focused on developing lay religious leaders in rural areas, as well as efforts at bringing people together for prayer meetings. Moret presided over some of these at a little chapel in Himamaylan and participated in other seemingly benign church activities such as distributing food to the poorest residents in his barrio.

Although the Himamaylan BCCs were still in their infancy when Consoy began recruiting at Tongson's hacienda, both the island's oligarchs and the Communist Party of the Philippines (CPP) could see that the BCCs had the potential to undermine the very pillars on which the local economy rested—its deeply embedded assumptions about race and class, about wealth and the presumed inevitability of poverty.

In *El Filibusterismo* (The Subversive), one of two works that inspired the Philippine Revolution of 1896, José Rizal wrote, "There are no tyrants where there are no slaves." BCC leaders promoted emancipation by giving peasants a sense of self-respect, by teaching them that they could stand up to the military and the planters and that they had a right to decent working conditions. The groups encouraged members to join the church-founded National Federation of Sugar Workers, and they initiated livelihood projects, credit unions, cooperatives, and other programs that gave people a modicum of economic power.

In 1979, an Army report described the BCCs as "the most dan-

gerous form of threat from the religious radicals." The document
stated that the BCCs were "practically building an infrastructure
of political power in the entire country. They are clear evidence
and indication of a link-up between left religious radicals and
the CPP/NPA [Communist Party of the Philippines/New People's
Army]."

Looked at from a different vantage, the BCC was engaged in the
very essence of democracy, an effort to organize the poorest Filipinos, to give a voice to the disenfranchised. It was the first step that
was often the most difficult, getting people who had no sense of
community to recognize that their situation would never change unless they were willing to work with their neighbors to address common problems.

That was Consoy's mission at Tongson's hacienda, but the last
person she wanted to proselytize was Moret De los Santos. Consoy
recalls having had a gnawing, unlucky feeling about Moret. Something about him scared her. Moreto, the "little Moro"—maybe he
was a Muslim?—with his black hair and broad nose underlined by
the shadow of a mustache, his high, pronounced cheekbones and
tenebrous, troubled look. Consoy had heard that Moret had been an
informer for the military and that he was opposed to the BCCs. It
had even occurred to her that Moret might try to kill her.

But Consoy had chosen an auspicious moment to recruit at Tongson's. One can only imagine the hopes Moret had invested in the
failed Saudi deal, how he'd built it up in his own mind, how he'd
presented it to his family and used it to impress his friends. Instead,
he'd been humiliated. Dispirited, he could see no options, no exit
from the confines of Himamaylan. Consoy and the BCC seemed to
offer Moret an opportunity—to pull himself together, stand out, distinguish himself somehow, maybe even get revenge for the injustice
of it all, his friend's betrayal, the obstinate swamp of Negros dragging him down, his abandonment by his own father.

Moret attended a three-day BCC seminar, at the end of which he
agreed to join Consoy's group and to baptize three of his children—
Joenes, Jun Jun, and Mary Joy, the same three who would later die at
his side. Moret and Cerila soon made the BCC the center of their
lives, and Consoy Perez became one of their closest friends.

By then, more "modern" priests, supporters of the BCC, had
usurped the Holy Week activities from the Gatuslaos, insisting that

the people in the barrios who were the presumed beneficiaries of all this religion should pay for it. The priests wanted to get poor people to take responsibility for their lives and to make them feel as if it was their Holy Week celebration, not something that had been given them by rich landlords to whom they then had to be grateful. Appealing to the poor for finances was also a practical decision. The priests could see that most families with money were moving out of Himamaylan, north to the capital of Bacolod or to Manila, and that eventually the church would be totally dependent on the poor rather than on wealthy *hacenderos* like the Gatuslaos. The Gatuslaos thought the priests a bit high-handed in spurning the family's generosity, but there was not much they could do about it, so they settled for running the annual town fiesta, which drew nearly as many people as Holy Week and was almost as useful for establishing the family's preeminence in the community. Nevertheless, it was a sign of a deeper schism that was developing between the church and its traditional sponsors.

*   *   *

"Holy Week," Filipino historian Reynaldo Clemeña Ileto wrote in *Pasyon and Revolution,* "was that time of the year when the spiritual and material planes of existence coincided; when, to put it in another way, the people themselves participated in Christ's passion." Ileto was describing Tagalog-speaking society on the main island of Luzon during the Spanish and American colonial periods, a culture in which the *pasyon,* the story of the suffering and crucifixion of Christ, was so firmly embedded in local tradition through week-long public readings and dramatizations that it provided both a moral framework for peasant society and a parable in which the unread and uneducated could see their own lives articulated and dramatized. Later, the *pasyon* became associated with some of the country's more aberrant and idiosyncratic Holy Week rituals and occurrences. While Moret's wife and children were attending mass on Good Friday in Himamaylan, seven people were crucified before a crowd of about two thousand in Malolos, north of Manila. The *Manila Chronicle* reported that twenty-nine-year-old Lucila Reyes, a self-proclaimed faith healer, fainted immediately when two men dressed as Roman centurions hammered nails through her palms and feet in a reenactment of the crucifixion. In San Pedro Cutud, a little farther north, the entire town was turned into a giant stage with dozens of small groups of men and women gathered in houses throughout the town singing the *pasyon* and nearly every citizen playing some role in a dramatization of Christ's final hours on earth.

Residents of San Pedro Cutud go through a similar ritual every year. As a procession of flagellants passes through the streets, their heads covered in black hoods and wreaths of thorns, blood streaming down their backs, the *pasyon* drones in the background:

> *Lagnat liping pagcagutom*
> *casalatan nang panahon*
> *patiisin natin yaon*
> *pacundangan na sa Pasyon*
> *ni Jesus na ating Poon.*

"Fever, dizziness, headache, hunger, scarcities that plague the times should all be endured now in honor of the Passion of Jesus our Lord." A gauntlet of thousands of tourists arrayed along either side of the narrow *via dolorosa* comes to witness the faceless penitents as they plod single file, whipping their hunched backs with macelike *burillos*—clusters of bamboo fingers tied together in a two-foot strand—beating out a rhythmic counterpoint to the chanting of the *pasyon*. The *burillos* make a clattering sound as they fly through the air, followed by a loud slap against naked flesh, which evokes shrieks and squeals as bystanders splattered with blood take flight from the flagellants as if from the bulls at Pamplona.

From time to time an "executioner" walks among the flagellants and presses a small paddle embedded with shards of glass against their backs, making tiny incisions that keep the wounds open. The rude line of flagellants follows on the heels of a handful of men who prostrate themselves on the ground every few yards, and they, in turn, follow a man dragging a heavy wooden cross on which he will be crucified at twelve noon. In all, four men are crucified on this Good Friday in San Pedro Cutud, nailed to crosses for about ten minutes at the top of a small mound in the middle of a dried-up rice field. The men, who have taken vows to undergo this rite, say they hope their "sacrifice" will absolve them of sins, but it's a safe bet a goodly number undergo these punishments as demonstrations of machismo. Nevertheless, religious rituals are rarely challenged in the Philippines. It is Mario Castro's ninth reenactment of the crucifixion and Rico David's fourth.

Modern Catholics would argue that no act could more completely miss the point of Good Friday than these exhibitionist caricatures of the faith, which seem to give Christ no credit for his sacrifice. Officially, at any rate, the Catholic church frowns on these extravaganzas of self-mutilation. A few years back, it convinced women in the Quiapo district of Manila that it was no longer necessary to crawl around on their knees on Good Friday as an act of penitence. The tourism ministry, meanwhile, promotes the crucifixions, which attract sizable numbers of foreigners with hard currency.

There are no tourists in Himamaylan during Holy Week. Although there is a full reading of the *pasyon* on Good Friday, the text never had the influence on Negros that it did on Luzon. Himamaylanos do, however, participate in several dramatizations that have traditionally been associated with the *pasyon*—the washing of feet, the Last Supper, the stations of the cross, and, on Easter Sunday, the reunion of the resurrected Christ and the Virgin Mother. The year before he died, Moret had played the role of Philip, one of Christ's first disciples, who was involved in the miraculous feeding of the five thousand. "He who loves his life loses it," Christ told Philip, "and he who hates his life in the world will keep it for eternal life."

It was an honor to be one of the apostles, to sit with the priests on the proscenium, where people from all over Himamaylan could see you. Having their feet washed by the priests conferred a certain added status on the participants. No one made a big deal out of it, but it was the only time during the year you saw a priest, and a white priest at that, bending down to wash the feet of brown-skinned people. Keen observers noted that the priests didn't wash both feet, just one foot of each disciple, and that they didn't really wash them, just poured some water over them. The point was the same, though. After all, the Bible just said Jesus washed the feet of the disciples, so if the priest washed one foot of each, it was probably enough; it didn't say Jesus washed both feet of each disciple. Or did it? It certainly suggests that Jesus was washing both; but the Scripture was often ambiguous, and no one was about to argue the point with the priests.

The reenactment of the Last Supper on Maundy Thursday was one of the small rewards given church leaders from the various barrios, and it was, by any account, an incredible feast, particularly in a place like Himamaylan, where ordinary people didn't normally have mounds of food heaped in front of them. Lamb was hard to find anywhere in the Philippines, but its absence was more than compensated for by the plates of pork, chicken, and beef, complemented by soup, piles of rice, several cooked vegetables, mounds of bright orange mangos, and a variety of desserts, all served to the apostles on a white tablecloth. The part of Jesus at the Last Supper was always played by the priest, and whoever took the role of Judas was invariably subjected to a bit of good-natured harassment by the other apostles, who demanded to know why he had betrayed the local pastor. Moret was invited to play an apostle again this year, but he declined the offer. Looking back, just about everyone agrees that by the time Holy Week came around, Moret strongly believed that he, too, had been betrayed.

The two elderly Irish priests, Eamon Gill and Eddie Allen, delighted in the crowds that flooded Himamaylan for Good Friday and Easter. They saw an opportunity to explain the true meaning of the holidays and to admonish the market vendors who cheated with their scales and the men who beat their wives, that if they didn't behave as Christ commanded every day of the year, they could not be redeemed simply because they came to town on Good Friday and touched the feet of the Santo Entierro, Christ in the sepulcher. The priests would look out from their pulpit on the mass of people packed into the aisles, spilling out the back of the rectory onto the little concrete apron where vendors sold yellow ice cream, candies, and coconut sweets wrapped in banana leaves. They would see the neatly groomed little boys, the girls in crinolines, their mothers with long, shiny black hair flowing over their shoulders, and hundreds of multicolored paper fans flickering before them like handfuls of confetti tossed from the rafters. The priests were struck by the rapt attentiveness of their audience, the reverential silence that seemed to greet their every word, and the old ladies clutching rosaries—pondering, trying to remember all fifteen of their mysteries—the way they would embrace the icons as though they were living beings,

talking to them, weeping over them, kissing their feet, sometimes
knocking the crown of thorns to the ground. These women would
spend hours stroking the bloodstained face of the stumbling Christ
or pressing their lips to one of the crucifixes. They would recite
prayers before the stations of the cross and beseech Jesus to save
their souls. "Cancel the sentence of eternal death deserved by my
sins," they would moan. "Give me the grace not to wound you
again."

The priests know that the message of the *pasyon* they try so hard
to impart, the homilies that flow from their lips, are often received as
though the words had been jumbled in midair and filtered through
the ears of another tradition. Most of their parishioners come to
church with their own ideas about Good Friday. Although they respect the priests and appreciate their blessings, it is precisely because they want to make physical contact with the icons that vast
numbers turn up on Good Friday as on no other day of the year.
Everyone knows it's the best day to gather *anting antings*, talismans
that can bring you good luck, make you immune from bullets, or be-
stow other preternatural powers that will protect you from enemies.

That people came to associate Holy Week with the supernatural
was hardly a mystery, given the fact that it is about the most miracle-
intensive time of the year for the church, with the restoration of the
eyesight of the spearman Longinus, Christ's foretelling his betrayal
and his death, His disappearance after breaking the bread, and the
Resurrection itself. On Holy Thursday, the priests prepare new holy
oils for confession and absolution, for anointing the dead. "Through
these oils, may you be forgiven your sins." Who would say that this
wasn't magic? If the faithful also had a hard time distinguishing holy
oils, scapulars, and crucifixes from the crocodile teeth, tree roots,
pieces of colored glass, dried snakes and lizards, and any number of
other objects that could pass as *anting antings*, who could blame
them?

On Good Friday in San Pedro Cutud, men search through the
wardrobes of young virgins and steal their panties for use as *anting
antings*. Historian Reynaldo Ileto reported that *anting antings* were
sometimes made from the remains of unchristened children or
aborted fetuses, which were placed inside a bamboo tube with a hole
at the bottom. "The liquid that slowly oozed out was collected in
a bottle and saved for Holy Week, during which time it was

sipped . . . until Good Friday." On Negros, recent years had seen a rash of grave robberies in Pulupandan and Bago City in which nothing but kneecaps were stolen. The prized objects were reportedly incinerated, pulverized, and mixed with coconut oil to produce a balm that could make the thieves invisible and ensure that their victims remained asleep while their homes were robbed.

Fishermen come to Our Lady of the Snows Church in Himamaylan on Good Friday to steal hairs from the wigs of the various Christ statues, which they weave into their nets, hoping to improve their catch. Others cook the hairs with coconut oil to make their *anting antings,* and occasionally someone will break a finger or toe off one of the images. For most of the faithful, however, it's enough to keep a piece of paper or cloth they have dipped into the baptismal font or touched to the Santo Entierro.

Moret had been one of the BCC leaders assigned to control the crowd that pressed against the glass case in which the life-size image of the Santo Entierro lay, covered neck to foot with a Lenten purple shroud. Moret would stand for hours on a raised platform, taking handkerchiefs or bits of cloths proffered by devotees, then reach through the small glass door at the side of the case, wipe them against the feet of the icon, and return them to their owners. Receiving the cloth, each supplicant would kiss or press it against his or her face, a process that continued until late into the night when the last believers had finally gone home.

It was no small matter for Moret De los Santos to stay away from the church during all of Holy Week and Easter Sunday and to spurn the offer of his friend Eamon Gill to play one of the apostles. He would not have wanted to say no to Father Gill or to make up excuses for his absence, and his decision must have been particularly difficult because if he ever felt a real need for the church, it was during those final days. Certainly he could use whatever luck it might bring him. It couldn't have hurt to have the priest wash his feet, to eat the flesh and drink the blood of Christ on Good Friday, to attend to the Santo Entierro, and to rub his feet a thousand times. But then if he participated in the rituals, a lot of people would assume he was a leader in the church. So it became a question of calculating whether there was more to gain or more to lose by being there. It wasn't just him, either. He had his family to think about. The church may have liberated his conscience and spirit, but it had also steered him onto an increasingly dangerous path with no protection other than his faith. The church could always use another martyr, but what would Cerila and the children do without him? In the end, his faith in the church was just not that strong. The church had become a liability.

The Cockpit

The Game Cock Clipd & armd for fight
Does the Rising Sun affright.

> —William Blake, "Auguries of Innocence"

Rather than pay laborers to weed their fields, sugar-cane planters often allow the fields to become dense, impenetrable webs of vegetation that can be cleared only by burning. By the time the sugarcane is ready for harvest, the stalks are engorged with sweet, wet sucrose, and their khaki-colored lower leaves are dry and brittle, combustible as paper. Normally, the fields are put to the torch early in the morning or just before sunset, when the air is calm and the fire can be controlled. A carefully planned fire will snake slowly through a field in a long, thin, crackling band of orange flame, digesting thousands of tons of vegetation, expelling thick black clouds of smoke, and leave behind blackened cane stalks still ripe with moisture, standing like a dazed, defeated army waiting to be felled by machete-wielding workers. The wind is the planter's worst enemy, with its potential to turn an entire year's harvest to conflagration in a matter of minutes. A cane fire on a rampage can easily jump across a fire break or road and destroy a neighbor's fields, and it is almost impossible to control. When that happens, there's nothing to do but pray and wait until the fire dies down.

A cockfight, like a cane field fire, is a sort of controlled combustion. A cockfight only rarely gets out of hand, usually late at night, when the cockers are tired and drunk, or, like a cane fire, when there's an ill wind.

Cockfighting is supposed to be the great leveler of Philippine society, the most democratic of institutions in a country that calls itself a democracy but is still trying to figure out what that means. The cockpit is believed to be the only place in this class-conscious culture where rich and poor men are equals, where the humble day laborer can challenge the powerful *hacendero* without fear of reprisal. The sugar planter, miller, or trader, attended by sycophantic trainers and handlers, arrives at the cockpit in a $60,000 Mercedes Benz along with his bottle of Johnny Walker Black Label; the sugarcane cutter or peasant farmer in rubber shoes comes with a fighting cock cradled in his arms aboard a pedal-driven tricycle for which he pays an eight-cent fare. Within the sanctum of the cockpit, though, the two are said to be equals, deserving of the same consideration. Their birds are weighed and matched by the same officials, judged according to the same exacting standards; the backyard breed of the peasant farmer can kill the fancy $500 hybrid import of the *hacendero* and receive the latter's blessing.

The late Louis Beltran, a popular broadcaster and one of the country's prominent breeders of fighting cocks, said he'd seen it happen. "Guys you never heard of, they breed cocks, they come up with super cocks, they go up against the millionaires, and they win." The cockpit, aficionados would have you believe, brings out the best in the Filipino. But then, sentimental views of the national pastime seem to arise spontaneously from the torrid dust- and smoke-filled pandemonium of the cockpit. There, surrounded by hundreds of shouting, sweating men placing bets with fevered gesticulations and tossing wads of money through the air, a spectator is swept up in the bacchanalian frenzy, this chaotic yet controlled drama of sacrificial suffering.

The high priests of the cockpit are the *kristos*, Christs, as the bet-takers are known, who stand within the musty, pulsing crowd, arms outstretched as if crucified, memorizing dozens of wagers at constantly changing odds—unspoken commitments consummated with the flick of a hand, a barely perceptible nod, or affirmative eye—sometimes amounting to tens of thousands of pesos, bets adhered to with a sense of honor unheard of in government or commerce or anywhere else in this society. "The cockpit is the most honest institution in the Philippines," Louis Beltran said. "You can walk into the pit and bet ten million pesos, and they'll take your word for it. But if you welch on your bet, it's very likely you will not leave the cockpit alive."

The contestants in a cockfight are splendid creatures strutting thick plumage white as snow, satin black, golden orange, or abalone, their elegant tail feathers flipped like a shepherd's crook. The fight begins when two *sabongeros,* cockfighters, at the center of the pit bring their birds face to face, allowing one and then the other to peck first at the head, then at the rump of its adversary, ensuring that both are sufficiently enraged to try to tear each other to ribbons. A pit employee known as the gaffer removes a leather sheath from the crescent-shaped blade that juts from the left leg of each bird, swabbing the spurs with alcohol to remove any poisons that may have been applied (one writer suggested that the blood of a Chinaman who died of venereal disease was a particularly potent potion) as a precaution against cheating by the rare, dishonest cocker.

As the two birds are released to battle, a hush falls on the arena and the *sentenciador,* the "sentencer" or referee, steps lightly from the path of the ostentatiously plumed gladiators. With tails lowered, angry lipstick-red faces thrust forward from flared hackles that look like little halos flecked with burning iridescent sparks. The birds collide with a hollow thud, then fly up with razored talons tearing puffs of feathers from each other, and from the impassioned crowd a startled, unisonous cry—"Whoooa!"—emerging like a single, heaving sigh. As the birds fight, either to death or exhaustion, each thrust and parry is greeted by a roar from the stands, crashing like a huge wave into the pit. Should the birds pause to rest, the hands of the *sentenciador,* sticky with blood-soaked feathers, are upon them, lifting them face to face, prodding them to carry on. The *sabongeros'* movements, brusque yet assured, are choreographed to those of the birds as if the two were tethered to a single puppeteer. Hour after hour, the blood, the money, and the liquor flow, late into the night or early morning. It is an extraordinary *danse macabre,* combining scientific breeding and ancient wizardry, that ultimately turns on the idiosyncracies of an animal with a brain the size of a pea.

* * *

The Gallera de Himamaylan, the cockpit, sits in a sugarcane field owned by John Silos—Papa Johnny, as he's known—just off the north–south road at kilometer 73 in the barrio of Talaban. This coastal barrio is technically under the control of the Tongson family, but in the political and social pecking order of Himamaylan, the

Tongsons have long been lackeys of the Gatuslaos and have served at their pleasure. Mount Kanlaon and the denuded Negros cordillera rise up to the east behind the Gallera, and you can actually see the mountains from inside the arena, through a four-foot-high opening that separates the lower and upper tiers. Serafin "Apin" Gatuslao, the grandson of Don Serafin, used to own the cockpit when it was located just up the road in barrio Aguisan. He built it with lumber from his family's logging business, which once operated in the mountains of Himamaylan. The pit proved an ill-conceived investment for Gatuslao, though, and when it failed, the entire building was bought by Johnny Silos and several of his friends, dismantled, and reassembled at its present location, which is known by the locals as Silos.

The Gallera looks like a cross between a New England barn, a tropical hut, and Shakespeare's Globe, a true theater-in-the-round constructed of raw timbers and topped by a corrugated iron roof covered with palm leaves. The cockpit is surrounded by a circular track of trampled grass and weeds about thirty-five feet wide that is dotted with merchants' stalls selling soft drinks, beer, cigarettes, and a variety of local delicacies. Crispy *lechon,* roast suckling pig, is laid out on a tablecloth of banana leaf at one booth, while at another, blackened barbecued milkfish, skewered mouth to tail by thin bamboo stakes, stand upright on a little pegboard. Shiny three-foot-tall aluminum cans advertise the sale of *balut,* fertilized, unhatched duck eggs in shells dyed a deep purple. The classic *balut,* supposedly a superb aphrodisiac, is boiled just as the chick's little beak begins to poke from its shell and is eaten in its entirety, gluey feathers, bones, and all.

To enter the Himamaylan cockpit, a visitor climbs a twelve-foot unrailed staircase—more like a ladder attached to the outside edge of the structure—steps across a threshold at the lip of the lower tier, and descends into the arena, stepping down the roughly hewn bleacher seats that lean away from the dirt fighting ring at the center. The ring, lit by a dozen long fluorescent overhead tubes, is a raised circular stage about fifteen feet in diameter and three feet off the ground, surrounded by a waist-high glass barrier. High rollers sit just outside the glass on benches that afford a bird's-eye view of the proceedings. But since the entire building is not more than eighty feet wide, no one is far from the action. Even spectators in the nar-

row balcony look as though they're close
snatch a bird from the ring by its neck. Th.
web of beams that support a domed roof,
structure the feel of a circus tent. A blackboard
cony lists the names of all of the entries: Skylark, .
Virgin, Excalibur, Hurricane, Turbo, Boy, Spartan, .
and so on. There are probably a hundred Tysons   .ne
country's cockpits on any Sunday and an equal numbe   .uham-
mad Alis.

By mid-afternoon, the Gallera's metal roof buckles under the intense
tropical sun and radiates a wilting heat down into the pit's interior,
turning it into a huge oven. The crowd, the noise, the dusty feathered air, and the faint whiff of blood carried on wisps of cigar smoke
are an unrelenting assault on the senses. Yet for aficionados like
Moret it is paradise, a perfect, private world turning on the axis of
the pit, a magical collection of Lilliputian scrimmages flashing by,
seven or eight in an hour, amid a kaleidoscopic swirl of curious and
unspeakable spectacles: the one-legged referee hobbling about, his
stump resting on a small horizontal shelf protruding from a hand-
made wooden crutch; voices of children pressing through the
bleachers selling soft drinks, candies, newspapers; pretty young girls
kneeling behind old cockers, kneading their porcine necks, massag-
ing their backs and arms, hoping for a generous tip; a *sabongero*, like
some circus geek, placing the entire head of a chicken in his mouth,
blowing air into its blood-filled lungs, trying feverishly to revive it.
Too late. Over there, drunken, boisterous soldiers armed with .45s
and M-16s packing the balcony, tossing hard-boiled eggs to their
comrades in the bleachers. At the rear of the pit, "chicken doctors"
sit with lifeless feathered clumps in their laps, tending to their grisly
chores, cleaning and stitching wounds, salvaging those they can for
another day.

The cockpit has always been primarily a male club, a stage on
which men, like their fancy birds, can strut and preen and perform
the macho ritual in which they affirm for the brotherhood their capacity for unconstrained cruelty and violence. But the cockpit is not
off-limits to women, and when Moret was fighting one of his birds,
Cerila and the children were always in the pit to cheer him on. When

, Cerila would hold on to the prize money. Later, the family would celebrate with a trip to Bacolod, where they would look at clothes at the Lopuez Department Store and eat at an inexpensive restaurant. It was Cerila's piggery that financed Moret's passion. On Negros, piggeries are the poor man's "bank." Nobody earns money raising pigs. The piggery simply forces you to save money by investing it in your animals until you are ready to cash them in. Sort of like a Christmas club. The longer you feed your pig, the bigger your bank account. To help finance the 1,500-peso entry fee and his bets in the three-day derby held between Good Friday and Easter Sunday, Cerila sold three of her pigs.

Although it might have looked as if Moret was gambling these savings—"No one makes money in the cockpit," Moret's step-brother Auelos Aminoto used to warn him—Moret didn't see it that way. He knew who the real gamblers were, men like Tota Limsiaco, a grandson of Don Serafin Gatuslao, who went bankrupt in the cockpit. Moret was no gambler, but preferred to think of himself as a "professional breeder." If the cockfight looked like a game of chance, Moret was convinced he could manipulate the odds by careful breeding, the right foods, rigorous training, and a number of other tricks he refused to discuss. This was a common conceit among *sabongeros;* all of them had their own combination of science and magic, and no matter how much money they lost, there was no convincing any of them it didn't work.

The cockpit is a veritable lyceum of experts on the arcana of rearing and choosing champion "slashers," with theories to satisfy even the most eccentric aficionados: "systems" based on feather combinations, the color of a bird's legs, the arrangement or number of scales on its legs, its scars, the shape of its beak or claws or ears. Some cockers go for green legs, others for white legs; some won't bet on a bird with yellow eyes, others don't like red eyes. If the word is out that a particular bird was stolen, some men will bet on it because, as the real insiders know, stolen birds bring good luck. Pitters can discuss the minutiae of cocking ad nauseam: the best ways to trim tail feathers, wings, and vents, the secrets of "heeling"—positioning the blade—recipes for feeds, formulas, and potions. Old-timers stuffed hot peppers up the anuses of their birds; others had them drink the cocker's own urine, establishing some sort of mystical bond between the two. Some gave their birds caffeine or amphetamine. Others would blow cigar smoke in the eyes of stags to immunize them from pain or injury, or to rid their birds of lice. Some believed having sex before a cockfight or allowing a fighting bird to be touched by a menstruating woman ensured certain defeat. More sophisticated aficionados like Moret and some of the other breeders followed news on the latest hybrids owned by the big Negros cockers, chickens costing upward of $500 apiece. Rich sugarcane planters like Juancho Aguirre, Raul Villanueva, Roberto Cuenca, Tony Trebal, Alfredo Yulo, and Enrique Gabaldon Montilla III imported these birds from the States, cross-bred them with their own stags, and fought them in Bacolod and the big pits of Manila. Millions of pesos were wagered in those fights, some of which attracted cockers from as far away as Arkansas and Louisiana. Hours were spent debating the relative merits of "grounders," birds that fight in the dirt, and "flyers," those that spring from the floor, jumping over their adversaries and attacking them from the air. There was talk of the latest power breeds from Texas—tough, unusually mindless creatures that bulldog into their opponents and tear them apart. And there were interminable discussions of "gameness," that most prized yet elusive quality of a rooster.

In the final analysis, gameness is everything to the *sabongeros*, the Holy Grail each of them pursues, the magic that makes a bird endure relentless, grueling punishments, no matter how battered or bludgeoned, and remain in the fight even to death. The most spectacular stories of gameness involve roosters who miraculously returned from the threshold of death to defeat an opponent, then stood at the center of the ring, chests heaving, exhausted and triumphant. Moret thought of the Gray as a bird like that. His favorite bird, the Gray, was a pied cock he'd pitted a half-dozen times before retiring him to sire hoped-for future champions. Gameness often revealed itself in the most tortured and excruciating contests, encounters that could make the maximum ten-minute bout seem like a marathon stretching into hours.

Cockpit rules stipulate that a fight isn't over until one of the birds is able to peck twice at its opponent without evoking a response. The victim is given three opportunities to fight back, but if it fails to do so, the winner is proclaimed. This final taunt, this gratuitous humiliation, is the prescribed denouement of the drama. It's not enough that the bird is too weak to continue, that it is about to be-

come someone's barbecue dinner. What's important is that it submit
to this superfluous indignity and acknowledge defeat—assuming,
that is, that it's still alive. Among men, such public, purposeful humiliation would be seen as "un-Filipino," but to the cocker, this act
of submission is the ultimate display of fairness and respect. A truly
game cock, lying in its blood and unable to fight, may still lift its
head and return the pecks of its tormentor until the final bell is
sounded. He may drop dead a minute later, but as long as he refuses
to accept his fate, the bout is a draw. The most perfect fight may, in
fact, have no winner. If two stags are equally matched and slash each
other to ribbons until the sound of the bell and then drop dead in a
heap, most cockers would consider it a transcendental experience.

Filipinos venerate the perfection they find in their national sport no
less than educated Westerners do the masterpieces in their muse-
ums. And it's no wonder why. Politicians paint fantastic pictures of a
coming gilded age, but none of them deliver. The priests aren't much
better. They offer compassion in the midst of chaos, which is fine as
far as it goes, but their model is remote, and if it works in heaven, it
seems to fail the test on earth; the golden rule of their game falls
apart when so few play by it. But the cockpit offers its own sublime
morality, one that delivers everything it promises. Absurd as it may
seem, in his heart the *sabongero* actually believes that if the democracy, justice, discipline, and sense of order and integrity he witnesses
in the cockpit every week could only be applied to real life, it would
be a perfect world. The cockpit is his cathedral, the cockfight his
pasyon.
     The *sabongeros* say cockfights are about breeding, which is true;
they are about the breeding of men and their power and money. A
poor man's relationship to his fighting cock is totally different from
the rich man's. The latter may own a thousand birds. They are an investment and a status symbol, whereas the poor man's bird may be
his best and only friend, the object of his affections, the only thing of
any value that he owns. If he fights it, if he bets on its life, it is a gamble far more dear than the rich man's. Entering a cockfight can be an
expensive proposition. The poor man will bring his chicken to the
cockpit week after week with no intention of pitting it, but merely to
establish his credentials as a member of the "fraternity" of cockers.
Victory in the cockpit can bring the poor man money, a degree of

fame, and entry to the enclaves of the elite, but only in the rarest, most exceptional cases. The equality he sees from gazing so long at the pit is a mirage.

The rich man doesn't stand in the bleachers with the poor man but sits in the inner circle, with his own kind. He doesn't place his bets with the *kristo* but with the manager of the pit, the *casador*. The hand signals of the *kristo* measure bets in the tens, hundreds, and thousands; the digits of the *casador* may reflect bets in the hundreds of thousands or millions of pesos. Even the chickens are unequal. The poor man's bird may, on occasion, defeat the rich man's, true enough. But over the long haul, there is no contest. The man with one or two or three birds is no match for the one who can pay a trainer to work with fifteen birds for two weeks and then select the best three to fight in a derby.

Most important, in the cockpit as well as outside, a man like Moret De los Santos always knows his place. He will address the rich men as "sir" but will be called in turn by his nickname. His dark skin and clothing will betray him, as will the tone of his voice, his posture, the way he shuffles his feet and holds his head, the way his eyes meet those of the *hacendero,* then travel away from him to the ground, and a hundred other unconscious and involuntary markers imbedded from childhood. Success in the cockpit may earn a man a degree of esteem from fellow cockers in the pit, but it won't win the poor aficionado an invitation to dine with the *hacendero.* If the cockpit was truly an expression of equality in Philippine society, it would never be tolerated. Far from embodying democracy, the cockpit is the country's clearest allegory of class and caste. It is a wonderfully absurd ruse that anchors the status quo, offering the *tao,* the Filipino common man, a picture of the prize in place of the prize itself.

*   *   *

On Easter Sunday, Moret was up early to prepare his birds for the cockfight derby. He had no plans to show his face in church that day but felt he'd be safe in the sanctuary of the cockpit, just the same. His plan was to fight three birds. A fourth, the so-called Gray, would be used to exercise the combatants and held in reserve should anything go wrong with one of the others. Moret cradled each of the birds in the crook of his arm, stroked them gently to calm them down, spread and stretched their wings, and then, with his eldest son, Joaquin, exercised the animals, sparring them with the Gray. Moret and Joaquin each held a rooster by its tail feathers and allowed it to confront the Gray for a half-minute or so to make sure it was eager to fight. When the birds settled down once again, Moret gave each a bloody piece of raw liver from a dead fighting cock, part of the secret formula he fed all of his birds on the day of a fight to give them strength and extra luck. Shortly after noon, Moret returned to his house to retrieve a small green, red, and black snake from a wooden box he kept in the second-floor living quarters. He'd discovered the snake one day when he was pumping water from the well and decided to keep it as a pet. Moret dropped the satiny smooth reptile in a sock, which he tucked inside his jacket. He believed the snake had magic powers and would bring him good fortune.

When he came downstairs, Jun Florentino was waiting with the motorized tricycle he called Arnel. Moret and Jun's father, Donato, had become close friends when they worked together at Rojelio Tongson's 200-acre sugar plantation; a similar friendship developed between their sons. Moret and the two boys loaded the birds in their tiny cages onto Arnel, climbed on board, and headed down the road toward the cockpit.

The two-lane highway in front of the Gallera was overflowing with tricycles, jeepneys (the jeep-jitneys that are the most common form of local transport), and automobiles when they arrived, the enticing hum of the Gallera floating out over them and into the muffling sea of cane fields. The birds had to be weighed by the pit's official weigher, and then Moret would have them heeled by his friend Ernesto Limsiaco, who knew exactly which knife to use for each of the unsuspecting warriors and the best way to bind it to the leg with a yard of crimson thread. Moret also needed to find his partner, Wilfredo Tendencia—Cabo Pidung, as he was known—Cabo, because he was a *cabo*, or foreman, at one of the local haciendas, Pidung being his nickname.

A squat, heavyset man with a shaved head as smooth as a honeydew, Pidung moved to a measured, arthritic cadence that was parodied in his blunt, hollow diction. Pidung had been a cop, but he lived better than a cop's salary would permit; he owned a handful of fishing boats and two houses—one in Himamaylan on a quiet street immediately behind Snows Church, another with a garden full of tall yellow calla lilies in a middle-class neighborhood of Bacolod. He

was also a part owner of the Gallera, along with several local cockers, including Rene Silos, Dising Lamason, Bukay Tongson, and
Apin Gatuslao. Moret knew all of them but was closest to Pidung,
who was a good friend of Moret's uncle, Ramon De los Santos, also
a cop. Pidung financed Moret's entry fees for the cockfights from
time to time and allowed him to hatch his chicks in Pidung's incu-
bator. When Moret won a fight, the two shared in the winnings.

Pidung had a lot less of himself invested in the pit than Moret
did. For Pidung the pit was mostly a place to pass the time, to drink,
and to bet. "I don't really pay much attention to the fights or to
who's there." His memories of that Easter Sunday, his last collaboration with Moret, were lost in a tangle of hundreds of similar week-
ends, although he did recall that it had been a lucky day, that they
had entered three cocks raised by Moret, that all three had won, and
that he and Moret each took home about 700 pesos. Pidung also recalled that the pit had been swarming with military men, members of
the local Scout Ranger unit, but he said he saw nothing unusual
about that: There were always a lot of soldiers at the cockfights, and
he didn't pay them any mind, just made a point to leave the pit by
9 P.M. "Later at night you can't avoid trouble at the cockfights, so I
always leave early."

Captain Melvin Gutierrez, commander of the Fourth Scout Ranger
Company, was the leader of a little over a hundred men based in the
foothills of Himamaylan at a place called Carabalan, five miles east
of the De los Santos home on the map and about fifteen along the
town's unpaved roads. Gutierrez's Ranger unit was one small com-
ponent of an expanding military presence on Negros, which became
the government's top priority target following the election of Corazon Aquino in 1986.

Gutierrez's mission was to make Himamaylan as unpleasant as
possible for the New People's Army, which controlled the mountains
above the town and, many officials claimed, had infiltrated the municipality and many of the local barrios. Himamaylan was strategi-
cally important because of its location at the approximate center of
Negros and at the island's narrowest point. If the military could control this natural bottleneck, the thinking was, it could prevent rebels
and their supplies from moving north to south along the mountain
range that divides Negros Occidental and Negros Oriental. But

Gutierrez had one other, unstated mission on Negros: to restore the reputation and credibility of the Rangers by avenging the lives of members of another Ranger company that had to be withdrawn from the island after it was mauled in an NPA ambush.

Although the Rangers are the Philippine Army's "elite fighting force," specializing in small-unit guerrilla operations and night warfare, they are also known for their brutality. The Ranger leadership cultivates a manly, rugged mystique, an image that is equal parts ferocity, professionalism, and what Filipinos call *palabas,* a kind of exaggerated, melodramatic theatricality or showmanship. The men wear black uniforms adorned with shoulder patches depicting a snarling black panther leaping before a white lightning bolt, which is underlined by a red caption that reads: WE STRIKE. The average resident of Himamaylan saw nothing heroic in the Rangers. They were different, yes. Unlike the other soldiers, they seemed to believe they had a mission in life, something to prove. Whenever they tried to deliver, innocent people ended up dead.

Captain Gutierrez had spent thirteen years in the Army. Subordinates honored him with the moniker Guts because he seemed to thrive in combat and, unlike many officers who fought the war from their offices, willingly joined his troops when they went out on operations. Men who served under him called him brave and service-oriented and said he kept them well supplied and well fed, something Filipino soldiers can't always depend on.

Gutierrez sported a beard, shoulder-length, jet black hair, and a triangular bronze *anting anting,* which he wore around his neck. If any of his men found this eccentric or had objections to his behavior, none ever said so. One close associate did, however, describe him as "a terror instructor," and others called him a strict disciplinarian. When his troops got out of line, Gutierrez was known to beat them mercilessly, sometimes with his bare fists, at other times with the butt of a rifle. Far from being ashamed of his pummelings, Gutierrez genuinely seemed to have enjoyed them and was known to brag about them. He was particularly proud of one beating he'd administered in which a soldier nearly died.

Moret De los Santos met Gutierrez for the first time that Easter Sunday, three days before he died, in the Gallera de Himamaylan. It was, as Joaquin De los Santos remembered it, an unnerving encounter in which Gutierrez approached Moret and demanded that he hand over his most prized possession—his ash-colored fighting cock, the Gray. Moret knew there was no way to win in an encounter with a military man. But he attempted to mollify Gutierrez without forfeiting the Gray, suggesting that the captain stop by the De los Santos house and select some other fighting cocks. It was not an offer Moret could afford, given that he had had to borrow money to buy the birds. But fear evidently convinced him it was an offer he had to make. Nevertheless, Joaquin said Gutierrez expressed no interest in any other bird and insisted that if Moret was unwilling to give up the Gray, he must "pit" it against Gutierrez's own orange game bird. Joaquin said Moret had no choice but to accept the challenge. "I feed my cock bullets," Joaquin recalled Gutierrez telling his father. "I don't know what will happen if he's defeated."

Whatever Gutierrez hoped to prove, Moret knew that it had little to do with cockfighting. But he also knew that soldiers were habitually throwing their weight around and that the encounter didn't necessarily mean much of anything. Then again, he could not easily have dismissed the fact that he'd been singled out so deliberately, or that Gutierrez had heard of the Gray, a trifling bit of information for the Ranger commander to have known. No, someone had to have told Gutierrez about Moret and about the Gray, someone who knew Moret well and was working with the military.

Moret probably had some pretty good ideas who that might have been. One likely candidate was right there in the cockpit, a disheveled little man who shuffled around in rubber slippers, his potbelly creeping out from under a soiled polo shirt, his pants ready to collapse around his ankles at any moment. Pepe Vallota is a reticent, white-haired pit official with tiny eyes and a jowly, hangdog face that makes him look like a Filipino version of Jonathan Winters. Vallota knew Moret well, although he didn't admit it, describing Moret only as "a friend in the cockpit," as if to draw a distinct border around the relationship, confining it within the make-believe world of the Gallera. Vallota was substantially better off than Moret, part of a middle-class clique that gravitated around the town plaza and John John's pool hall and got together every afternoon to play chess or gamble at cards and mah-jongg. Moret and his two best friends— Fred Veraguas and Willy Villacanas—had recently paid a visit to Vallota's tidy little home at the north end of the plaza to ask him about a hit list Vallota had supposedly given to the military, a list that included all three of their names and those of several other friends who were active in the BCC.

Moret had heard that the military planned to make a few "examples" of local BCC leaders so they would stop organizing members of the church in Himamaylan, and he wanted Vallota to somehow retract the list. But it was naive to think that this kind of genie could be put back in its bottle.

Vallota recalled the meeting well, that Moret was upset when he came to visit, and that he accused Vallota of giving information to Colonel George Vallejera. Vallota denied that there had been a hit list, then added, as if to confirm that there was, that he had had nothing to do with it. Vallota also said he'd never participated in any discussion about killing members of the BCC. Nevertheless, a week after the meeting, a hit list began to circulate in Himamaylan with the names of all three men—Moret, Veraguas, and Villacanas—as well as those of Father Eamon Gill, Consoy Perez, and several other men and women tied to the BCC.

Given the air of impending doom Gutierrez allegedly brought to the Gallera, the actual contest between the captain's bird and Moret's Gray was something of an anticlimax. Cabo Pidung doesn't even remember the fight, and Joaquin said it was fairly routine, except for the fact that when Gutierrez's bird was defeated, the soldier picked up his lifeless animal and stalked away from the pit. Since the rules of the Gallera de Himamaylan for Easter Sunday provided that the winner of a cockfight could claim the defeated animal—a custom designed to spare the loser whatever ignominy attaches to leaving the pit clutching a dead chicken—Gutierrez's behavior would have been construed as a sign of bad sportsmanship, which would have carried with it a certain loss of face.

Moret's brief run-in with Gutierrez was not the only odd encounter at the Gallera that Sunday. Earlier in the day, Joaquin had escaped the pit for a taste of fresh air when he was approached by another Scout Ranger, a twenty-five-year-old corporal named Gerardo De los Santos. Gerry was a handsome young man with long, fine fingers, a narrow face, and a thin nose, all of which would have given him a delicate, almost feminine air, were it not for a slightly squirrelly mustache. Gerry said he'd noticed the name De los Santos on the back of Joaquin's basketball jersey and wanted to know whether they might be related.

It was, on the surface, a perfectly innocuous question. Filipinos are fascinated by family connections, ties through distant blood relatives, godparents, or even links to a shared birthplace or province. Members of elite families on Negros keep elaborate genealogies that take note of the most illustrious members of the bloodline, and they drop family names like engraved calling cards proffered on a sterling tray. Even ordinary Filipinos will spend hours with complete strangers pursuing possible ties of consanguinity or geography.

If Gerry could establish a relationship to the Himamaylan De los Santoses, he would have greater entrée than other "foreigners" to the local community, contacts he might use to gather information or to impress his commanding officers. Likewise, it could have only helped Joaquin and his family to have a relative in the armed forces. However, Gerry and Joaquin grew up on different islands, speaking different languages in culturally distinct regions of the country, and the possibility of a blood link between them would probably have been about the same as that of two Smiths randomly selected from Oregon and Maine telephone directories. Nevertheless, Joaquin would have been happy to engage Gerry in conversation, since such banter is, as often as not, simply a way of making friends. But Joaquin was unable to provide much insight into his family's genealogy and suggested that Gerry stop by the house to talk to his father, who might know more about the family history. Joaquin gave Gerry directions, and the two parted.

Mambagaton

A man might live twenty years in Manila and know less
about the Filipinos than by a few weeks' residence in
Himamaylan.

—John Roberts White, *Bullets and Bolos*, 1928

Due east over the cordillera, the sparkling stars of the
scorpion hung upside down like an elegant earring dangling from
the face of a nearly full moon. In the mountain barrio of Carabalan,
a team of Army Scout Rangers rolled out of its base camp in three
trucks and headed west toward the center of Himamaylan. The
rough road ran parallel to the Himamaylan River, through two deep
rice paddies and miles of silky sugarcane spikelets. An occasional
peasant shack or nipa hut appeared only as silhouette. Below, in the
Gulf of Panay, the Rangers could see the soft yellow glow of
kerosene lamps bobbing with the pontooned wooden sailing *bancas*
of night fishermen on the moon's silver waves. The Rangers had been
ordered to prepare for combat, and as they were carried along in the
night, they must have smoked their cigarettes, clutched at their rifles,
grenades, scapulars, and amulets and thought about whatever it is
men think about when they're sent to kill people they've never met.
This particular group of Rangers had been lucky since its arrival on
Negros; only one of the comrades had been felled by a rebel, and
everyone seemed to agree it was due to his own recklessness.

The men, specially trained for night combat, knew that when they
got to their jumping off point, they would have to move fast. Surprise was essential. Most of them didn't focus on the background
noise, the rationale for all these raids: the so-called peace and order
situation, defeating the Communists, democracy, and so on. Other

people could worry about politics and debate what it all meant. Tonight's mission was somewhat vague, though the Rangers had the raw outline, which was all anyone really needed: "intelligence reports" of a rebel gathering somewhere in the barrio called Mambagaton, Ilongo for "the place of the ghosts."

How the barrio got this peculiar name is something of an enigma. According to one account, it derives from an incident in which a man was murdered during a rainstorm, which ignited the phosphorous in his blood and incinerated him. Another, tamer explanation has it that, before the Gatuslao logging operations chopped them all down, Mambagaton had been covered with tall *balete* trees, the most popular sanctuary for ghosts. All the men in the trucks knew was that Mambagaton was what the military called an "NPA-infested area," a "Red area," which meant the Army might claim control in daylight, but at night the terrain belonged to the NPA.

The Rangers reached the Himamaylan marketplace at the paved two-lane coastal road around 4:30 in the morning. It was market day, and vendors were unpacking merchandise, laying it out on the ground, setting up their little booths. The Rangers aroused little curiosity. Soldiers seemed to be everywhere those days.

Just south of the market, the priest was preparing for the early morning prayer at Our Lady of the Snows Church. It was the third day of Easter, so he would be reading from Luke 24, in which the two Marys arrive at the tomb of Jesus at dawn. "Why do you seek the living among the dead?" they are asked. The Rangers weren't allowed to worship at the Snows Church; Captain Gutierrez forbade it. He said the priests were Communists. Anyway, the church wasn't on their itinerary this morning.

The convoy turned right and headed north from the center of town, passed by Transloading, Bangat Trece, and the Gatuslao Hospital, then turned right onto the unpaved Mambagaton Road and proceeded slowly, cautiously, across the old cane railroad tracks just below the Gatuslao's prawn farm. It was not a particularly welcoming stretch of road, despite the cool, loamy smell that rose up into the truck and embraced its occupants. A long irrigation ditch ran alongside the south side of the road in front of a field of sugarcane culms waiting to be harvested, a field so dense that a man a dozen

feet inside it would disappear from view. Six months earlier, New
People's Army rebels hiding in that field and in those same trenches
had murdered Serafin "Apin" Gatuslao and his two bodyguards, the
Giconcillo brothers. Gatuslao had been the wealthiest landlord in
Himamaylan, a close ally of the Army, and one of the most strident
anti-Communists on Negros.

Overhead, the last wisps of luminous rain clouds hurried past the
moon and off the coast toward Palawan and the South China Sea.
The Rangers had their weapons loaded and at the ready. They continued east past the prawn farms, where little paddle wheels churned
up patches of white in the otherwise still, black ponds, then slowed
before a tall, rounded stone bunker that crowded the deeply furrowed road, narrowing it to less than a single lane. Yards of olive-
green nylon webbing were draped from the top of the bunker to
deflect hand grenades and gave the bulky structure the appearance
of a dumpy old woman seated behind a dark veil. The trucks
squeezed by her and rumbled on, past the JMJ convenience store,
Tongson's Hacienda Pacita, Crusher Crossing, more prawn farms,
and then pulled to a stop beside a grove of *ipil-ipil* trees and thickly
armored *buri* palms at a tiny *sitio,* or neighborhood, called Aton-
Aton.

Aton-Aton. The name is like a "No Trespassing" sign pounded
into the ground on a stake, a warning to strangers to "Keep Out," a
sort of declaration meaning "This belongs to us!" or "This place is
ours!" Although the name suggests that there might be something
valuable there, something residents were vowing to defend, the
moonlight streaming through the clouds' ragged holes illuminated
nothing more than a cluster of small houses and nipa huts huddled
just below a shallow bluff ridged with sugarcane. A collapsing, lat-
tice fence with red hibiscus and copper bougainvillea poking
through it marked the edge of the road.

The largest building was an unpainted two-story structure of sun-
bleached wood, its first floor and sliding windows covered with rectangular tin plates, mottled and gray, like lichen-covered boulders
along a mountain trail. Moret De los Santos had originally built the
house on a small lot set aside for him at the sugar plantation of his
employer, Ernesto Tongson. But when Negros *hacenderos* became
convinced that they could make a fortune growing prawns for export to Japan, Tongson decided to take back the lot, and Moret was

forced to dismantle the house. Tongson provided him a new lot in Aton-Aton, where Moret pieced the house back together.

From the second floor, where the De los Santoses slept, three windows looked north over a hand-operated water pump, Cerila's piggery, and a few disconsolate banana trees that slouched in front of one of Tongson's rice fields. The ground floor was taken up by a kitchen with a crude charcoal stove, a small living area, and a storage room filled with sacks of rice.

Five acres of paddy owned by Tongson and farmed by Moret gave the De los Santoses all the rice they needed. Moret cultivated, planted, and harvested the rice and split the yield fifty-fifty with his boss. Moret was superstitious about rice, probably because he knew firsthand what it was like to do without it. He had vowed that his own family would never relive his experience. When he planted his rice, Moret prayed for rain, and when the rain came, he would slaughter a chicken. When the rice was harvested, he made a small offering of seeds to the spirits; some of these were left in the rice field and some at the little altar he'd built in the house for his Christian saints. Three times a day, when the De los Santoses ate their rice, there was to be no quarreling, only conversation to lift the spirits, and no one was allowed to leave a single grain uneaten, since doing so might bring a curse on the whole family.

On what turned out to be his last full day on earth, Moret had expected to finish the rice harvest, and in the evening the family planned to celebrate with a small party. As was his custom, Moret had invited friends who had helped with the harvest, and Cerila had pounded and roasted the first rice of the year to make *pilipig*, a traditional delicacy. This year's harvest party would be special because it was also to be a farewell celebration for Joaquin, who would be leaving for Manila the following week. His plan was to move in with his sister, Jasmin, enroll in one of the city's computer schools, get a technical degree, and then apply for admission to the prestigious Philippine Military Academy. Joaquin had just graduated from the Himamaylan High School with good grades, and was first in his class in the Citizens Army Training program. He and Moret both thought he had a good shot at eventually being admitted to the PMA, a significant achievement for the son of a poor man like Moret.

What was to have been a joyous day got off to an inauspicious start when Moret went to check on the fighting cocks he kept at

Tongson's fishpond and found most of them dead. Wild dogs had gotten into the shed where the birds were kept at night. Moret couldn't tell whether someone had left the door open accidentally or deliberately. Then, in the afternoon, a fierce rain forced Moret to postpone the harvest and dissuaded Joaquin's friends from coming to the party. Moret stuffed his dead fighting cocks in a rice sack, took them home, and told Cerila to prepare all of them for dinner. Jenelyn protested that it might not be safe to eat them, but Moret insisted; the birds were simply too expensive to waste. For the moment, the enormity of his loss consumed all of Moret's powers of concentration, and he wouldn't brook any argument. The family ate its last meal together in silence. Then, before going to sleep, they prayed together, all of them, that is, except the two little ones who were too young to pray but would listen and make the sign of the cross.

The arrival of the Rangers was heralded by the howls of a dozen local mongrels, who stole the last minutes of sleep from the barrio's farmers. The soldiers were given hasty orders, alighted from their trucks in the damp morning air, and fanned out through the *sitio* as the dogs, continuing their warnings, slinked back in retreat. One group of Rangers positioned itself beside the hut of Dan Galagpat, Moret's stepbrother, another near the home of Rudi Garcia. All of them trained their weapons on the home of Moret De los Santos.

Joaquin was already awake, listening quietly to a small cassette player, when he heard the dogs howling. Dressed only in his green basketball shorts, he slipped out of bed, cracked open a wood jalousie window, and peered into the charcoal shadows of the lingering night. Less than fifty feet away he could barely make out a group of six men in fatigue uniforms and the outlines of M-16 and M-14 rifles. He watched a second group of five men as they jumped from the back of a transport truck. In all, he counted more than a dozen men, most of them wearing knitted masks with a single circular opening for the eyes, nose, and mouth that made them look like a flock of enormous owls.

The dogs woke Moret, and he also went to explore what all the commotion was about. Joaquin heard him sliding open one of the heavy tin-covered window frames and caught a brief glimpse of his father as he looked outside. "Lie down," Joaquin whispered as he began moving toward him. But his words had no sooner left his lips than they were interrupted by the explosion of a rifle bullet that slammed into Moret's forehead, toppling him to the floor and killing him instantly. As Joaquin reached his father's side, a barrage of gun-fire began to shred the thin wooden walls of the De los Santos home.

Joaquin raced around the two small upstairs rooms, trying to con-struct barriers against the gunfire, using trunks, furniture, and a sack of rice, to little avail. After Moret, six-year-old Mary Joy was the next to be hit. Joaquin picked up the little girl and was placing her beside his father when he heard fourteen-year-old Joenes cry out for help. Later, Joaquin would recall seeing a look of pained horror in Joenes's face and then noticing what he thought were his brother's intestines spilling out of him. An autopsy would report that a bullet entered Joenes's lower back and exited from his stomach, that another bullet hit him in the side of the face and exited through his left eye, and that parts of both feet had been shot off.

Joaquin said his brother was still conscious as he reached down to comfort him. "He said to me, '*Toto,* you're not wounded. You should jump out and try to escape.' But I told him, 'I can't, because they've surrounded the house.' And when I laid down his head, he was also dead." Joaquin put Joenes with his dead father and Mary Joy, whose wide-open but lifeless eyes gazed at the ceiling, then flat-tened himself on the floor, in the red welter of their remains. A rocket-propelled grenade exploded inside the house with a deafen-ing roar, followed by two more grenades and what seemed like hun-dreds of rounds of rifle fire. Occasionally, one of these shots would hit the lifeless body of his father or brother or sister, and Joaquin would feel the concussion as the corpses, like bags of sand in front of a bunker, absorbed the round. As Joaquin lay there, expecting to die but hoping that daylight and the crowing cocks would wake him from his nightmare, he felt sick thinking that the bodies of his father and the children were saving his life.

The Rangers' assault continued. Bullets tore apart the family's simple furnishings—a tired old couch, a mirror, drinking glasses, plates, a painted plaster crucifix, the dictionary where Moret pressed clippings from the children's first haircuts (to impart wisdom), a

framed photo of Cerila, and the little glass-fronted altar Moret inherited from his grandfather. Images of Santo Niño, the country's
patron saint, San Vicente, Joseph, and Our Lady of Fatima—the omnipresent symbol of the anti-Communist elite on Negros—were all
reduced to dust. Joaquin moved again to one of the windows to see
whether there was any way of escaping but froze when he spotted a
soldier directly below him, then watched as the blue steel of the
Ranger's rifle locked onto him as if drawn by a magnet and in the
same instant announced itself with the dull metal "click" of a misfire.
Joaquin realized instantly that it was the sound of survival, that the
gun's magazine was empty. "It was at that moment that I thought to
myself, 'God is really going to save me.' "

Captain Gutierrez had stationed himself behind the De los Santos
house, where the rocket grenades were fired into the home, a curious
bivouac inasmuch as there were no windows on that side of the
building, no way for the commander to see any movement of people
or to ascertain the extent, if any, of gunfire coming from inside. He
was dug in just outside the hut of Rudi Garcia. Garcia, the father of
twelve children, was a truck driver for Roger Tongson, and knew the
faces, if not the names, of many of the locally based Rangers whom
he'd picked up hitchhiking along the road to Carabalan. Because the
men were wearing masks and had torn their name patches from their
uniforms, Garcia said he could recognize only two of those involved
in the shooting: Gutierrez and Gerry De los Santos. The astonishing
thing about Gerry, Garcia recalled, was that throughout the lengthy
bombardment, he never lifted his weapon, never fired even a single
shot, but just sat on the ground in a daze, as if transfixed by something above or beyond the events erupting in front of him.

Garcia said he was perplexed by Gerry's behavior. Whereas all
the other soldiers behaved as if they were in some arcade shooting
gallery competing to see who could use up the most ammunition,
Gerry was totally disengaged. The Rangers' visit to Mambagaton had
given Garcia a lot to think about, and in the days that followed, he'd
completely forgotten about Gerry. It was only two weeks later that
his observations of Gerry came back to him with the sickening taste
of a poorly digested meal. Gerry De los Santos was dead, Garcia
learned, and the word in Mambagaton was that he'd been murdered
by Captain Gutierrez.

To Garcia there was absolutely no question that Gutierrez was in
charge of the assault on the De los Santoses or that he had come

looking for Moret. Although the captain would later file a report claiming that the Rangers just happened on the site in the course of a routine patrol, Garcia vividly remembered Gutierrez examining a map of the area—a photocopy on which he'd circled the De los Santos residence. "Gutierrez was giving the orders. At around five thirty, during a pause in the firing, he turned to me and asked if this was the house of Reynaldo [Moret]. But he only spoke to me after they'd shot up the place for a half hour. Of course, by then, they [the De los Santoses] were already dead." Garcia confirmed for Gutierrez that it was indeed Moret's house, at which point Gutierrez gave an order to stop firing and told two soldiers to enter the premises.

Joaquin, bathed in the blood of his family, moved to block the door with an iron bar but was spotted immediately by one of the Rangers. "There are still people alive!" Joaquin heard him shout, and as he turned to look for a hiding place, he was struck in the back by a single bullet that broke his collarbone and exited through the front of his left shoulder. As Joaquin collapsed to the floor, the Rangers smashed through the upstairs door and entered the living quarters. "You'd better search the house for firearms," one of them said, but the other came up with nothing more than a pair of Army fatigues and combat boots Joaquin had used for his high school military training. The Ranger suggested that the clothing must have been taken from a dead soldier in an ambush, but he also seemed disturbed by the carnage laid out in front of him. "There were supposed to be a lot of people here," he said, "but the only ones I see are this family."

As the soldiers went about their work, Joaquin said he could hear the men nibbling on pieces of Moret's barbecued fighting cocks from the previous night's dinner:

> I was on my stomach pretending I was dead. But I could see the men as they moved about the room. My four-year-old brother Jun Jun was still alive and he began pleading with them. "Have pity on us," he said. "We are innocent. We have done nothing against you; we have done no wrong." He was crying the whole time. And I heard one of the soldiers say in Tagalog, "Leave him alone, he's only a child."

Joaquin said it was at this point that he recognized the voice of Corporal Alex Bayle. "I knew him because we played basketball to-

gether. Bayle came over to me and he put his foot on my head."
Bayle's companion warned him that Joaquin was still alive and could
escape, but Bayle insisted Joaquin was already dead. Bayle disappeared shortly after the events at the De los Santos home. His
friends said he had gone AWOL, but members of his family never
heard from him again, and there were rumors that he was one of several Rangers murdered by Gutierrez. Joaquin says he doesn't know
whether Bayle genuinely believed Joaquin was dead or deliberately
saved his life.

As the two soldiers left the house, they grabbed Joaquin's combat
boots, a pair of shoes he'd bought for his graduation, his tape
recorder, and 3,500 pesos from a pair of Moret's pants, money Moret
had planned to use to enter an upcoming cockfight. As soon as the
two men were outside, Gutierrez shouted another order: "Finish
them off. Only two men will fire." Moments later, the shooting resumed from the ground floor with a spray of bullets that splintered
the bamboo-slat floorboards. When the firing ceased, the Rangers
began to question Rudi Garcia and some of the others. "They asked
me to identify the neighbors. They wanted to know if one of them
was the daughter of De los Santos, and I said, No, because I was
afraid if I told them the truth, they might kill her." Nevertheless,
three Scout Rangers entered the hut where Moret's daughter Jenelyn, her two children, and her little sister had been confined. Jenelyn
was so afraid she could barely respond to their questions. "A masked
soldier kicked open the door and pointed his rifle at me. Then he
asked me in Tagalog if I knew the De los Santoses. I said I didn't.
And he asked me where my husband was. I told him he was working
at the fishpond. And he said to me, 'If your husband isn't home, you
should keep the door closed,' and then he left." Her two infants and
her sister Juvi, who stood by her side, said nothing. As the Rangers
departed from the tiny barrio, one of them shot and killed Ernesto
Tongson's carabao, which Moret had used for plowing.

Inside the De los Santos house, it was finally quiet. The only sound
Joaquin heard was his own breathing, the only smell, the coppery
perfume of blood. Quarter-inch spaces separated the brown bamboo
floor slats where Joaquin lay, and he could see the white plastic rice
sacks stored in the room below. Staring down at them, he noticed

that they were spattered with blood and realized that it was dripping from his wound. Joaquin felt dizzy as he raised himself up and looked around the room. All the elements of his life were there before him, familiar and personal, but transformed into something distant and incomprehensible. Everything was changed, and he was seeing it for the first time, through new eyes that couldn't cry. He saw his father in a bloodied white polo shirt and silly red underpants with little white polka dots, his brains scattered on the floor, his wounded sister and brothers, a blood-smeared cabinet, and everywhere white pillow feathers floating about and settling on the remains of his family. It was as if he'd awakened inside some macabre plastic snow globe. "Souvenir of Mambagaton," it would say on its tacky plastic base, "the place of the ghosts."

Suddenly, Cerila stumbled in from the adjoining room, although she was no longer the Cerila Joaquin had known for seventeen years. This Cerila was bleeding from her breasts and from her stomach, and the lower part of her face had been turned to a dark red maw. "When I looked at my mother, I could see that her mouth had been shot away," Joaquin said. When he went to help her, Cerila tried to speak, but emitted only faint, indecipherable gurgling sounds. Joaquin helped her to sit down on the edge of a bed, and Cerila signaled limply with her hand that she wanted to write. The boy looked around the room but could find neither a pen nor pencil, and Cerila, impatient with what remained of her life, dipped her index finger into the red well of her mouth and began to write on the little wood box in which Moret caged his magic snake. Slowly, deliberately, she wrote the letter M on the box, then returned her finger to her mouth and back to the box, wrote an O, and repeated this gesture like some grotesque being tasting its own bloody flesh. Finally, she'd inscribed her message: MOROY.

Joaquin screamed for help.

Easter Wednesday

God falls—down, down God goes—
not an angel at his beck,
mankind astride his neck.

—Nick Joaquin,
"The Fourteen Stations of the Cross"

When the Rangers left, people began to crawl out
from beneath their houses or from behind whatever barricades they
had found as panic wrenched them from the dark into the lucidity of
survival. Now they congregated outside the De los Santoses' home.
Some were crying, but most just stared at the splintered bullet-
pocked walls and the three gaping black holes where the rifle
grenades had entered. Jenelyn De los Santos approached her parents' house tentatively, holding tight to the hand of her sister Juvi.
She heard Joaquin's cry for help but couldn't force herself across the
threshold and up the single flight of stairs. Moret's stepbrother Dan
Galagpat and several other neighbors brushed past her into the
house and helped Joaquin, Cerila, and Jun Jun downstairs, where
they were placed in two pedal-driven tricycles.

It takes about ten minutes to drive the two miles from the De los
Santos residence to the Gatuslao Hospital, but on a tricycle the trip
along the rocky Mambagaton road takes closer to a half-hour. Hospital records indicate that the De los Santoses were admitted to the
small, white, single-story facility at around 6:30 A.M., that Jun Jun
was dead on arrival, and that Cerila was just barely alive. No doctor
was present, but the nurses inserted an IV and attached a bag of
saline to her. Cerila again signaled for something to write with and
was given a pencil and a child's notebook in which she scribbled in
Ilongo, *Moroy nagpatay sa amon.* "Moroy killed us." Since Moret and
the children had clearly been killed by the Scout Rangers, the mean-

ing of her note was not immediately obvious. But it was impossible to question Cerila, who would die a few minutes later. Filipino parents customarily bid farewell to their children before they die. But according to Jenelyn, Cerila's last words to her were a request that her brother-in-law Dan seek revenge. Dan remembers it a bit differently. He says Cerila merely asked him to look after the family. And although he says he would have liked nothing better than to avenge the killings, that he dreamed of revenge, he regrets that he didn't have the means to do it and had to flee Negros shortly after the massacre because he was concerned for his own safety.

The death certificates filed by the Gatuslao Hospital with the municipality of Himamaylan provide only the most perfunctory description of each victim's wounds. One curious omission appears at line 12 on each of the documents, which asks the attending physician to characterize the cause of death by checking one of four boxes: homicide, suicide, accident, or other. In each case the line was left blank.

As Dan was leaving Mambagaton to bring his brother's family to the hospital, Jenelyn entrusted her two babies to Juvi, instructing her to take them to the hut by Tongson's fishpond, where Jenelyn's husband worked. Juvi hurried the children down the Mambagaton road and was approaching the JMJ *sari-sari,* or neighborhood store, about a half-mile from her home when Igmedio Alamon came out of the shantylike structure and began walking toward her. Juvi had known the Alamons and their four children since she was old enough to remember. They lived only a few hundred yards from the De los Santoses in a tiny house that floated like a small island on the green sea of a Gatuslao sugarcane field. Mr. Alamon, who worked for the Gatuslaos, was one of her father's closest friends, his *kumpare,* and Moret was the godfather of the Alamons' youngest daughter, Maria Cecilia.

Juvi was not surprised to see Alamon at the JMJ store; it was owned by his son, José Maria, and Alamon hung out there most of the time when he wasn't working. Juvi's thoughts were on her sister's instructions, on the safety of her niece and nephew. Her mind had settled by then in a place somewhere beyond fear, and she barely gave Alamon a moment's notice until, suddenly, he was towering above her, blocking her path. Angry and agitated, Alamon leaned toward her, looked the tiny twelve-year-old straight in the eye, and muttered, "You will be the next to die." Then, having leveled his threat, he just as quickly turned on his heel and walked away.

What Alamon meant and why he made his remark was not at all apparent to Juvi, but when she told members of her family, they had a pretty good idea what was going on. Over the next day people in the area were talking a lot about Alamon and his relationship with the De los Santoses. Mostly they discussed Cerila's dying words and "Moroy," which was how Igmedio Alamon was known to everyone in and around Mambagaton.

Moroy Alamon didn't attend the funeral of his friend Moret De los Santos, although his wife, Prescilla, did go to the De los Santos house the day of the killings to pay her respects. By the afternoon on the day of the massacre, word was already circulating that the surviving De los Santoses believed Moroy was responsible for the killings and that they would seek revenge, so Moroy and Prescilla decided to leave town. Moroy believed that his friend Moret had ties to the New People's Army, had even accused him of working with the rebels, and he knew that the NPAs could exact revenge if they wanted to. The morning after the massacre, Moroy and his wife took a bus from Himamaylan to Bacolod, made their way to the Bonago wharf, and bought second-class tickets on the next boat to Manila.

*   *   *

The center of Himamaylan is only two miles from Aton-Aton along a direct line of sight, so anyone who wasn't up and about by 5 A.M. almost certainly was by the time all the shooting had stopped. Although no one knew exactly what had happened, by mid-morning, as trucks, jeepneys, motorcycle taxis, and tricycles discharged a steady stream of customers, speculation was already swirling through the marketplace like so many dust devils. At first, conversations seemed preoccupied with "the firefight," "the encounter," or "the ambush," but as more and more information percolated through the stalls, people began to talk about a "massacre," and on the massacre the discussion stayed, spreading out like a tangled vine of morning glories, turning to every nuance of light and shadow until by noon, when business began to slow down, everyone had his own richly garlanded version of events to take home to the barrio.

At one of the market stalls, the severed heads of fleshy pink pigs hung from rusty finishing nails, their faces frozen like masks in the same ridiculous smile, as if they couldn't have been more pleased to be there. A man wearing a blood-splattered T-shirt and jeans hooked thick slabs of pork and beef beneath a hand-painted sign picturing a buxom girl in tight shorts and sneakers, walking along a brown road beneath the smoking peak of Mount Kanlaon. WILLY MEAT STAND, the sign reads in bold red letters across the top, and in the lower right-hand corner, like the signature of an artist, WILLY VILLACANAS PROPRIETOR.

Willy didn't yet know that his friend Moret was dead, but he'd heard the gunshots from the direction of Mambagaton, and something told him he wasn't going to be getting good news. The arrival of the Scout Rangers, who often came into town on Wednesday for the open market, did nothing to improve his spirits. Willy had been having trouble sleeping the past few nights. He'd been contacted by a friend who was a member of Rodolfo Tongson's private army, a band of thirty-five or so heavily armed men that operated as a sort of security or vigilante force, depending on what the boss wanted at any particular moment. The friend reported that Tongson was trying to have him killed, and had offered 30,000 pesos (about $1,200) to kill Willy. Given the fact that Willy was active in the Basic Christian Community, whose members were frequent targets of right-wing planters and their friends in the Army, it was not the kind of warning, whether true or not, one could take lightly.

The butcher's fears mounted when he heard the news later in the morning about the De los Santoses, and again that afternoon, when another friend came by to say that Willy's was the next name on a list of BCC leaders who were to be killed. This, combined with the rumor that Tongson wanted him eliminated, was enough to convince Willy that his life was in real danger. That night a group of soldiers came looking for the butcher at his home. Luckily, Willy wasn't there. When he heard about the visit, he knew it was time to leave town. Too many people had been picked up by the military and were never heard from again. Willy fled to Cebu, the island due east of Negros.

*   *   *

Father Eamon Gill, the parish priest of Himamaylan, is a leading champion of the Basic Christian Community in southern Negros.

Born in Mayo, Ireland, in 1923, Gill's first assignment as a priest in 1951 was on Negros, and he's made the island his home ever since. Fluent in Ilongo, Gill is a gentle, unassuming man with watery blue eyes, and glasses that are perpetually sliding down the veined slope of his nose.

Gill recognized that in a town like Himamaylan it was impossible for only two priests to be in regular contact with the barrios, where most of the people lived. Himamaylan was only 142 square miles, about the size of Hartford, Connecticut, but there were no paved roads into the mountains, no roads at all into many of the communities, no telephones, no reliable transportation, and no real police force outside of the town proper. If the priests visited each barrio once a year, it was a lot. The idea of the BCC was to give the church a full-time presence in the barrios by training local community leaders. At the most elementary level, BCC leaders were taught how to conduct prayer meetings, but they were also taught a simple philosophy of self-help, which stressed the concept of building local communities in which people looked after one another. This meant providing food to those who had none, assisting those in need of medical care, and organizing people to stand up against organizations and individuals that attempted to seize their property or otherwise intimidate them, be they exploitative landlords, the military, the vigilantes, or the New People's Army.

Although Father Gill insists that the BCCs were essentially religious in nature, an integral part of the church's mission on Negros, he never shied away from the charge that the groups were "political." "Everything we do on Negros is political," he once said. Generations of fear stood in the way of any effort to bring people together, and there was more fear now than ever before. The Himamaylan BCCs never did mature into an effective political organization, but they were a start, and it was Gill's promotion of them that earned him the enmity of many local planters, including Moret's *amo,* or boss, Ernesto Tongson, and his brothers, Rodolfo and Rojelio.

Behind his back, the planters called Eamon Gill "Demon Gill," and they organized demonstrations against him. One anonymous leaflet accused Gill of training NPA rebels in the mountains. Ernesto Tongson said he and his friends boycotted Gill's church services because they disliked the priest's involvement in politics. "We'll go back to it when it's in the hands of Filipinos who are opposed to the Communist insurgency." Ironically, Gill himself was a vigorous anti-Communist, a member of the Order of Columbans, which was expelled from China after Mao Zedong's takeover in 1949. Nevertheless, the planters viewed him as a "Red," and his name would periodically crop up on the lists of various death squads as a target for assassination.

Gill had arrived on Negros unprepared for the mystical and animist trappings the island's common people appended to their Catholicism, but came to appreciate that there could be a fine line between myth and religion. He learned quickly that when he went to bless a fisherman's boat, a peasant's hutch, or a merchant's store, his sprinkling of holy water was, more than likely, preceded by the sacrifice of a chicken, pig, goat, or dog. Sometimes a group of young boys would corner a stray dog to be used in one of these rituals and pelt it to death with stones. Gill's parishioners knew better than to explain these rites to him—how they would pour the animal blood on or near whatever object he had come to bless, to protect it from any number of local forces of darkness—but the priest periodically stumbled on the evidence. Although the church frowned on these practices, most of the priests were content to let them pass as long as they weren't invited to dine on a sacrificial dog.

Some of the priests might discreetly suggest that the blood be smeared in the sign of a cross, satisfying themselves that this was at least a step in the right direction. Others simply explained these phenomena as a byproduct of ignorance and poverty. In a country where ordinary people as well as members of the clergy report finding images of Christ in the rose petals of one famous convent, seeing icons crying tears or blood and women giving birth to snakes and fish, it would be futile to take a stiff-necked position against all reports of otherworldly phenomena. "When you're hungry, you see visions," Jaime Cardinal Sin, the archbishop of Manila, once said, explaining away widely reported sightings of the Virgin Mary dancing in the sun. "My first advice is, 'Eat.'" But although the church has a policy of deflating reports of miracles, the bishops also maintain a Commission on Visions and Phenomena to investigate them, just in case.

For his part, Father Gill did his best to provide some perspective on these events but was careful not to appear overly dismissive, since his own experience on Negros had taught him that the world did not always operate according to the laws of science or normal expectations. Gill did not toss the word "miracle" about lightly; he himself had seen things he could not explain in any other way, such as the time he'd "flown" his motorcycle across the widening yawn of an open drawbridge and landed safely on the other side. Then there was the case of a woman named Marietta, whom he'd met shortly after his arrival on Negros. Marietta, who had been having an adulterous affair, announced to Gill that she was going to die and asked to be given Holy Communion. The priest told her he thought she appeared perfectly healthy and would soon feel much better, but Marietta persisted, and although the church forbade Communion for an adulteress, Gill agreed to perform the rite if Marietta promised to mend her ways as soon as she recovered, a commitment she assented to without hesitation. According to Gill, when he finished his prayers, Marietta thanked him for his kindness, looked him straight in the eye, announced, "Now I'm going to die," closed her eyes, lay her head back on her pillow, and immediately expired.

A messenger brought word of the De los Santos massacre to Father Gill at Our Lady of the Snows Church shortly before 7 A.M., and Gill left immediately for the Gatuslao Hospital, grabbing his Bible and the recently consecrated holy oil he needed to perform the last rites. The priest had a reputation for being more than a little disorganized; a close friend remarked that Gill had three files, "letters, miscellaneous, and other." Nevertheless, Gill was passionate about his work and about documenting as best he could the ongoing conflict on Negros, which was claiming as its victims a growing number of his parishioners. As he left his quarters, he also grabbed a small camera.

The priest was horrified by the carnage that awaited him at the hospital and recalled that he "could hardly recognize Mrs. De los Santos as a human being." It was too late to take Cerila's confession or to offer Communion, and although there was no indication that Cerila had given any thought to repentance in her final hour—quite the contrary—Gill bent the rules, offered a "conditional absolution" pardoning her sins, and prayed for her soul. He also spoke at length with Joaquin De los Santos, who, as the principal witness, feared that the soldiers would soon try to come after him. The priest assured Joaquin that the church would protect him and arranged to have him moved to the island's main hospital in Bacolod. Gill then had the bodies of Joaquin's family members taken back to their home.

Gill himself drove to Mambagaton a short while later and found a large collection of family, neighbors, and friends milling around the De los Santos house, among them twelve-year-old Juvi, who was standing with her sister, staring wide-eyed, as if in shock. The white-haired priest mingled briefly, speaking with various witnesses to learn the basic details of the incident, and was walking toward the house when Juvi appeared at his side and took his hand. Together Gill and the little girl entered her home, ascended the wooden staircase—where Moret had put each of his children's first fingernail clippings so they would grow up strong—and entered the living quarters under the rippled tin roof that creaked each morning as the sun began to heat it up. Sand-colored geckos with sticky paws shaped like little stars found shelter in the rafters, so Moret had put the children's baby teeth there, reasoning that since the lizards' teeth were straight, the children's would grow that way as well.

Gill was unprepared for the scene that confronted him. "When I got to the house, the fluff from the pillows was still floating around. It was the first thing that impressed me when I entered. It was like a storm had blown through the place." In a space cleared from the debris, Juvi's mother and father, her little sister, and two younger brothers were laid out on the floor. The priest and the little girl stared at the faces of Cerila, Moret, Mary Joy, Jun Jun, and Joenes; they just looked from one to the other and back again without a word. Finally, Juvi turned to Gill and said she would like to have her picture taken with each of them. The priest, overcome by the scene before him, found himself incapable of any response and proceeded to honor her request.

Juvi moved to her mother's side and posed rigidly while Gill lifted the small automatic camera to his face, framed the two of them, and pressed the button, igniting a white flash that lit up the dark room and sent little blue stars floating in front of Juvi's eyes. Juvi kissed her mother, moved to her father, then stared back without expression at Father Gill, who silently raised his camera and flashed another picture. She then stepped to the side of tiny Mary Joy, who, save for her haunting, vacant eyes, looked like an angel in her white

nightgown with her head propped at the center of a large pillow that
extended out beyond her shoulders like little wings. Gill mechani-
cally captured the scene on film, then repeated the process two more
times until Juvi had been photographed with each member of her
family and had kissed each of them good-bye. When the pictures
were developed, each had a little line of yellow numbers along the
bottom—88-4-6—indicating the date they were taken.

The next day, Gill felt he had to return to Mambagaton to reassure
his parishioners, but he didn't want to go alone this time, so he
asked Fred Veraguas, Moret's close friend and fellow BCC leader, to
see whether he could pull together a group of people to go with him.
Desmond Quinn, another Irish priest, agreed to join them. Quinn
had spent thirty years in the Philippines and was no stranger to the
horrors Negros offered up from time to time. His friend Rudi del
Carmen had come to him with torture marks on his feet, fingers, and
testicles shortly before he fled to the mountains, where the military
hunted him down and shot him. Like Gill, Quinn believed cases like
Rudi's should be documented with grotesque exactitude and prevailed on del Carmen's widow to delay the funeral so a doctor could
perform an autopsy. The autopsy found that the soldiers fired more
than a hundred bullets into del Carmen's body.
    When Gill, Quinn, and the others arrived in Mambagaton, they
were surprised to find the little community completely abandoned.
Residents of the eight or ten homes had all left the previous evening,
when Scout Rangers returned briefly to examine the site. The De los
Santos survivors had by then removed most of the salvageable possessions from the house. Curiously, they had not taken the family
altar with its seven icons. What was most unusual, though, was the
fact that the bodies had been left completely alone, something almost unheard of in Philippine culture, where relatives stay with the
deceased constantly until the body is laid to rest. Filipinos typically
observe an uninterrupted vigil with family and friends gathered
around the coffin, eating, talking, playing cards, or sleeping—anything so the deceased will not feel abandoned. Rather than leave
them alone, Father Gill decided to bring the bodies to the church.

                              *   *   *

The sun was just reaching over the horizon when the Rangers pulled out of Mambagaton the morning of the massacre. They retraced their route back to the center of town. Cane trucks passed them heading north to the Binalbagan sugar mill, belching thick clouds of diesel exhaust and scattering cane cuttings in their wake. The air was fresh; the sky was brightening; it was going to be a sunny day.

Most of the Rangers got out at the Himamaylan market, near Peachy's Restaurant, one of the numerous Negros establishments where the Añejo Rum girls reside. The girls, in their Victoria's Secret fashions, are uninhibited, wanton, what the locals call "bold," and available to anyone with a little imagination. One of them has silky *café latté* skin, gleaming black hair, wet pouty lips, and wears a diaphanous pink negligee, which she has just begun to remove. "*Manamit gid . . . sa tanan,*" the best for all, the poster bearing her picture says. Most of the Añejo Rum girls seem to be just getting started, waiting for you to get pissed on a bit of their rum and take them on, although, occasionally, one of them seems to have just finished. You can tell because the only thing she wears is a beatific smile. The Añejo Rum girls are omnipresent. You even find these beauties in the mountains, taunting the New People's Army fighters with their prudish morality, seducing them from their rigid orthodoxies, teaching them a thing or two Mao neglected to mention in his little book.

The food at Peachy's is kept in a glass case to keep the flies away until you get it to your table. Then the idea is either to eat fast, using one hand to shoo the flies away, or, if you're lucky, someone will stand behind you with a rainbow-colored plastic pompom and rustle it above your head until you're finished. The glass case holds plates piled high with rice, a beef stew, fried mackerel, fried milkfish, fried pork, fried chicken, and fish heads floating in a swampy green broth. This fish head soup, *sinigang*, is as common in the Philippines as the Añejo Rum girls and could conceivably be the national dish. It takes a little getting used to, though, that eye looking up at you each time you dip your spoon to eat.

The Rangers bypassed Peachy's and headed for a little coffee shop owned by the father of Joeri Gimotea. Joeri was like a brother to Joaquin De los Santos. The two boys were almost always together, and Joeri often spent the night with the De los Santoses. In fact, he'd planned to stay there the night before because of the farewell party for Joaquin, but the heavy rain had kept him away. Joeri had no idea what had just occurred at his friend's home. He said the Rangers sat at a little table smoking cigarettes, ordered a round of San Miguels, and talked in hushed voices. The only thing he could discern from their conversation was the word "massacre." The Rangers, it seemed to him, were reassuring themselves that it hadn't been their fault.

The arm of the law on Negros is short and the palm is slick. Laws against murder are rarely if ever applied when the victims are poor, and fewer than a handful of cases have been brought against members of the armed forces. And that's in civilian courts. The military's justice system is worse than a bad joke. Under Marcos and Aquino, massacres routinely went uninvestigated and unpunished. The Scout Rangers knew that violence against civilians could be committed with impunity. Only a few weeks earlier, paramilitary forces had slaughtered Luciano Garlet and his four children in Carolan in broad daylight—the Army said the family was murdered by members of the NPA disguised as pro-government vigilantes—and that incident had nearly been forgotten already. Then an Army patrol killed twenty-three-year-old Liza Obero and her three daughters in Candoni, and you didn't see anybody hanging from a tree because of that. The soldiers could feel confident that there would be no serious repercussions from the carnage in Mambagaton.

Even so, for the "elite" Scout Rangers it didn't look good to kill a mother and three children. So the morning's events might be hard to explain, and for some of the soldiers at least, they weren't all that easy to swallow, either, the dead children and all. Then again, if they were honest, they would have to admit that, at the time, they were having a lot of fun shooting up the place, more fun than they'd had in a while, that there was something invigorating in blasting things apart, even if it wasn't something you wanted to admit out loud. Maybe the whole thing was an accident, a mistake, a terrible misunderstanding. Was it really possible that there were no rebels in the house, only the family? The Rangers pondered these questions. Maybe some of the victims were actually rebels. And maybe the Rangers actually thought there were shots coming from inside the family's living quarters. It is also fair, however, to ask how long these highly trained professional soldiers could have gone on believing their fire was being returned without hearing the whistle of a single bullet above their heads, the ricochet off a rock, or the thud of lead striking the ground or one of the buildings. Two minutes? Five? Certainly not a half-hour. And with all that gunfire, was it really possible that not a single one of their men had been wounded, that there were no bullet holes in the homes where the Rangers were gathered? Who were they kidding?

The Rangers weren't supposed to have doubts. They were supposed to be a team—cohesive. They had done what they were told. It wasn't their idea to get up in the middle of the night and go out hunting goddamned NPAs. These patrols rarely produced much of anything, anyway. The Rangers were there because the regular Army troops did anything necessary to stay out of combat: went on "patrols" close to base, rolled in the mud, fired a few shots, filed the paperwork on the "encounter," the phony body counts, got shit-faced, fucked some whores, and went to sleep. To a man, the Rangers felt they were carrying more than their fair load. But then, everyone knew this war wasn't going anywhere, that you couldn't beat the NPA on the battlefield. It was nice to hear your commanders assure you that your little victories made a big difference, but it was hard to see any sign of progress. And now this. Considering the number of shots that had been fired, it was logical to conclude that everyone inside the De los Santos house was dead. There should be no witnesses, not that anyone would testify against them. If they did, the Rangers would just deny everything. On the other hand, the Rangers hadn't actually bothered to find out whether anyone had survived, and the two who had entered the building knew that at least one child was alive when they followed the order to "finish them off." Perhaps he'd survived. Maybe they could have saved him, could have stopped the massacre right then, could have told Gutierrez there was a little boy alive. If the boy was dead now, it would be hard to claim that that was a mistake. Unless everyone kept his mouth shut.

While his troops stewed over the morning's events, Captain Gutierrez made his way around the town plaza to the two-story People's Hall, which houses the mayor's office and a small police station with a single-cell lockup guarded by two or three ornery-looking canines. Gutierrez's truck was parked in front of a row of empty cement flower boxes, each inscribed with the name of one of the town's venerable ladies: Doña Alicia, wife of former Congressman Gatuslao; Doña Trining, wife of former Mayor Gatuslao; Doña Linda, wife of former Governor Gatuslao; and Doña Esperanza, widow of Serafín "Apin" Gatuslao, who had been shot dead in Mambagaton six months earlier. The captain's mission at the People's Hall was damage control. Gutierrez spoke briefly with the mayor, although he probably hadn't intended to. He'd been in Himamaylan for more than a year, and this was the first time he'd met Mayor Providencia "Daisy" Silverio, so it was unlikely he would have chosen this particular occasion to pay a courtesy call. More likely, he ran into her when he was on his way to see the chief of police, Celestino Guara. When it came to the war—the "peace and order situation"—the military was, for practical purposes, answerable only to itself, or more accurately, its fractured selves, since it was often difficult to say who, if anyone, was in charge. So Gutierrez would have felt no compulsion to justify his actions to the civil government, and certainly not to Silverio, who would never presume to question a military man anyway.

Police Chief Guara was a different matter. Since their arrival, the Scout Rangers had had an uneasy relationship with the police; "matters of jurisdiction" would be a polite way of describing it. More precisely, the police felt the Rangers were walking all over them, that the Rangers had expropriated police responsibility for dealing with the NPA, that they were unpredictable and were actually making the "peace and order" situation worse. More and more policemen were becoming targets of NPA Sparrows, or hit men, and Himamaylan had become a focus of NPA operations.

Unlike the ostentatious special forces under Gutierrez, the police were inclined to cut their deals with the rebels and work things out. The poorly paid police had enough trouble working their illegal businesses, shakedowns, and extortions, and few had any pretensions of ridding the world of the Communist menace. The Rangers, on the other hand, were outsiders; they didn't speak the language, had no long-term commitment to Himamaylan or to Negros, and, from Guara's point of view, were too damned gung ho. But their arrival had been inevitable, as had the diminished role of the police. The rich planters were growing weary of the military's refusal to vigorously prosecute the war, tired of the extortion, the burning of their sugar fields and equipment, and the killing. So they'd increased the size of their own private armies and demanded more Army troops until Negros had become the country's biggest battlefield.

Gutierrez knew that the police had pretty much been sidelined, but he also knew they could create problems. Ordinary day-to-day killings were easily explained, but the incident in Mambagaton could be blown up by the press; it could call unnecessary attention to Negros, embarrass the island commander, and raise hackles in Manila. It could damage Gutierrez's reputation. Lieutenant Guara would almost certainly be asked to make some sort of inquiry into the massacre, however perfunctory, and his report would inevitably go up the chain of command, back to the captain's superiors at Fort Bonifacio in the capital.

Experience told Gutierrez that there would be protests from the church, that he would be accused of so-called human rights violations. He was used to that. He also believed that these claims were merely nuisances, if managed intelligently. Although Communists in Aquino's government occasionally raised a fuss, there was little danger that the military would lose control over the matter, and military authorities rarely if ever acted on these complaints. What was important was to get the story straight. Any story. For that, Gutierrez needed Guara on his side.

For the next two days, the massacre would be the lead story in the *Visayan Daily Star,* the island's only paper at the time. In the first report—COUPLE, CHILDREN KILLED IN STRAFING: MILITARY BLAMED—the Rangers didn't look so good. Xenia Tupas of Task Force Detainees, the country's principal church-based human rights group, was quoted as saying the killings were done by the military. As far as the military was concerned, Tupas and the TFD, in which Moret was also active, were both part of the insurgency; their credibility was zero, even when they happened to be right. But the *Star* report also gave Captain Gutierrez his say, quoting from a statement he'd issued claiming that there had been a firefight and that three NPA rebels had been killed. Army headquarters at Task Force Sugarland also issued a statement saying the De los Santoses were all members of the New People's Army, although the brief comment didn't specify whether or not that included the four-year-old. A second report in the *Star* quoted Gutierrez as saying that armed rebels had been conducting a meeting in the De los Santos house and that the Rangers had recovered the body of a dead NPA rebel.

The same day's edition of the *Star* carried three other interesting items: an unsigned letter complaining about church interference in politics; a report that an Army soldier had been abducted and killed by NPAs in Himamaylan; and a tiny, page-one story headlined: UNIDENTIFIED MEN GUN DOWN PLANTER, which noted that Florencio Henson, forty-five, the father of three, living in the town of Murcia, was killed by a single bullet. *Star* publisher and chief editorialist Ninfa Leonardia had no comment on any of these killings but wrote instead about International Non-Smoking Day and an upcoming fiesta in La Carlota. Leonardia was apparently preoccupied with preparations for a tenth-anniversary edition of the *Star* that would come out at the end of the week filled with congratulatory advertisements, including one from the regional military command. Neither the De los Santos massacre nor the Henson murder was ever mentioned again in the *Star*. There was, however, one lengthy opinion piece in the paper two days after the massacre, written by an anonymous planter. Right-wing columnist Primo Esleyer graciously turned over his space in the paper so that the unidentified author could attack the church for "intervening in matters temporal and exclusively political"—in particular, for supporting an agrarian reform bill that proposed turning over a tiny fraction of the country's agricultural land to landless peasants. "The intervention is divisive, pitting the landless and the landowner against each other. . . . The church has adopted a policy of 'preferential option for the poor.' Are the 'non-poor' second-class Catholics? Or is it a sin to be rich or 'non-poor'? Must the landowners now seek other churches, since it is practically sinful to be a Catholic landowner?"

Lieutenant Guara filed his official report on the massacre almost immediately after his meeting with Gutierrez, a mere two and a half hours after the shooting stopped. The single-paragraph statement says that the De los Santos house was fired on "by unidentified armed men," and it names the victims. Of course, Guara knew perfectly well who the assailants were and that they were commanded by Gutierrez. Not only was it common knowledge in Himamaylan by the time people took their afternoon siestas, but Guara had gotten the story—or a version of it—from Gutierrez himself. Guara deliberately neglected to mention the Rangers in his report. "We worked out a compromise with the Scout Rangers," Guara acknowledged, although the "compromise" was more nearly a capitulation. "Gutierrez told us, in effect, to keep our hands off this investigation, to let higher authorities handle it, to let Cardones investigate it."

If he was contemplating a coverup, Gutierrez couldn't have picked a better man for the job than his close friend Colonel Reynato Cardones. Cardones, a native Negrense, was a soldier's soldier and no more likely to come up with damaging information on Gutierrez than on his own mother. Handsome, engaging, and articulate, Cardones had all the trappings of a "professional" Filipino soldier, right down to the affected air of complacent indifference, which even the most sordid allegations failed to unhinge. Cardones knew that horrific atrocities were committed under his command, but he was always prepared to provide a snappy denial or the appropriate exculpatory context.

Thus, violations of the rules of war by his men or flagrant abuses, such as the burning of 180 homes in Carolan, south of Himamaylan, were routinely dismissed as "Communist propaganda." Cardones just as easily explained away the beheading of Norberto Gallines, a twenty-eight-year-old member of the Basic Christian Community. After vigilantes hacked out Gallines's liver, ate part of it, and then presented the head—a photo shows a boyish, pockmarked face, long eyelashes, and a slightly perplexed expression due to the fact that Gallines died biting a slightly swollen lip—to the Army's "Charlie Company" hoping for a reward, Cardones affected a sympathetic smile, explaining that he appreciated how naive outsiders might be upset by such "anomalies," but that they simply didn't understand the local culture. "These are basically tribal communities. If they kill an enemy, they behead him. It's part of the ritual."

What outsiders call human rights violations, Cardones construed as a form of local justice; where abuses by the military or paramilitary forces occurred, he said it was necessary to keep them in perspective. The military should be seen as a sort of watchdog and the abuses as nothing more than a nuisance. "It's like a dog with fleas; sometimes the dog has more fleas, sometimes less. The people complaining about human rights want to kill the dog because it has some fleas. But the purpose of the dog is to guard the house. The issue is its role in counterinsurgency. You can find abuses anywhere."

Thus, it came as no surprise that Cardones had a ready justification for the events at the De los Santos home, arguing that there had been a "legitimate encounter" in which NPAs had fired on Gutierrez's men from inside the house. Moret, far from being some innocent choir boy who liked to conduct prayer meetings, was actually a die-hard member of the NPA who worked with several front organizations. "He was a member of the revolutionary movement; that was common knowledge where he was working in the district engineer's office. He was a member of the organizing committee of Mambagaton. Whether he was the chairman, I don't know." Most important, however, Cardones charged that Moret was responsible for the murder of Serafin "Apin." Gatuslao, Himamaylan's most prominent landowner and an outspoken anti-Communist. "Our intelligence showed that he was the one who decided that Gatuslao was to be liquidated, and eventually Gatuslao was liquidated. That was initiated by this guy De los Santos."

Now, one might ask—and people did ask—why, if Moret De los Santos was a suspect in the slaying of the landlord Gatuslao, hadn't the military arrested him? Six months had passed since Gatuslao's murder, and Moret hadn't been hiding; he could easily have been picked up at his job any day. Why send a combat patrol to his house in the dark of night? Even if he was guilty, did that justify murdering his wife and three children? The particulars of the allegation linking Moret to Gatuslao were fuzzy. But it didn't really matter. Merely raising the possibility that Moret had killed Gatuslao sufficed to legitimize the massacre in the minds of the island's military and political authorities.

Tsismis

The *tsismis* rose from the body of Moret De los Santos even before his soul had a chance to escape. As if from some fetid substance that had been accumulating inside him, *tsismis* seemed to gush from Moret's wounds, an acrid, sulfurous vapor whispering through Mambagaton and Himamaylan, infecting its people. *Tsismis:* stories, intrigue, lies, gossip, speculation. Gathered up like rice in a basket and tossed in the air, sending husks to the wind, leaving behind kernels of truth. Truth and half-truths, anyway, or private truths, mixed together, folded into one another, became the gruel of life. *Tsismis* sorted out the mysteries, pieced together conspiracies, created "facts," and made sense of the madness. Tales of the murders traveled from witnesses to friends to enemies to the fish hawker in the marketplace, to the lady selling amulets, to Willy the meat vendor, and from them emerged multiple antinomies, contradictory explanations, epitaphs that gave voice to the ineffable. *Tsismis.*

Moret went to seminars given by NPA guerrillas in the mountains. He channeled funds to the NPA through the church, collected taxes for the NPA, distributed rice to the NPAs from his house. The NPAs had used Moret's house to store weapons. They held meetings there; had a conference there the night before the massacre; drew up plans there to kill the wealthy landlord Serafin "Apin" Gatuslao—the Batman; hid their weapons there the night before they liquidated the hacendero. *Moret had just come from the cockpit when he guided the rebels to the ambush site, showed them the best place to lay in wait for Gatuslao. Oh, and yes, it was Moret who killed Remetio Ban a week before the massacre. Ban was a military informant.* He was also a convicted murderer; served time in a Manila prison. He'd gone to a dance to hunt down Moret, got into a fight, and stabbed another man. Someone shot Ban in the head when he left, and Moret's friends weren't talking. "After dark, all cats are gray," they'd say. Well, now the military had taken its revenge, and Moret was dead. Tsismis.

Tsismis of romance, sex, and petty rivalries, the *tsismis* of everyday life, gave way to the *tsismis* of the night, of horror and death, the kind of death most in need of *tsismis:* death by the untouchables, by the military, the NPA, the vigilantes, the death squads, the fanatical cultists; death that precludes justice, that invites only forgiveness or revenge. *Tsismis:* garbled echoes of events posited as questions, returning as answers. *Tsismis*—a missing link, a smoking gun, the connective tissue of random events—draws together a still life of mayhem. Titillating, exasperating, soothing, obvious yet opaque, a koan, a paradox. *Tsismis.*

A lot of people seemed to be dying in the weeks and months following the De los Santos massacre, and there were a lot of theories. Naturally, some people pondered whether the deaths might be related; others insisted that they were. Four members of Moroy Alamon's family were killed. So was Rex Villacarlos—right along the Mambagaton Road, near Ernesto Tongson's fishpond, where he worked with Moret's son-in-law, near the place they murdered Gatuslao and his bodyguards. *Villacarlos was with the Scout Rangers at the De los Santos massacre, along with several civilians.* Which civilians? Well, nobody seems to know. Rex's death made no sense to his neighbors. Rex, for God's sake, never hurt anyone; he mostly sat around and knitted with the girls! What was the point of killing him? *He was a military informer, hung out with paramilitaries, vigilantes.* Strangers, not from Negros, speaking Kiniraya, shot him, and the boys who were with him wet their pants. Joeri Pagontalan almost fainted. William Taylor, the Australian who married a Filipina and ran a rice mill in Himamaylan, was also killed. The wife pleaded for his life, begged them not to kill him, but the NPA said Taylor worked for the CIA; they shot him in front of her, and she wept for him. Father Gill was supposed to have lunch with Taylor that day. He wasn't sure of Taylor's religion, but his wife asked him to perform last rites, which the priest did as he'd done for De los Santos and Gatuslao before him, as he would for Fred Veraguas and others. CIA PUNISHED, the headline read, quoting from the NPA statement. "It is clear William Taylor intervenes in the Philippines by giving information to the CIA in the province." *The military didn't make a move without orders from the CIA, from the U.S. military. The United States still ran everything.* Common knowledge. Part of the theology. *Tsismis.*

Then there was Gerry De los Santos, the Scout Ranger who couldn't bring himself to fire a single shot during the entire De los Santos massacre. Gerry died multiple deaths just days after the massacre. *He was killed in an ambush by the NPA at Bahay, near where Gatuslao was killed; shot with a handgun; with an M-16. He was killed on orders of Gutierrez because he was going to blow the whistle on the massacre. The Rangers all got drunk after the massacre and Gerry told Gutierrez he was going to report the incident to his superiors. "You know, this De los Santos was a good man," Gerry told him. Right to his face. Gutierrez just blew him away. Like that. Had to stop it right there, show his men who was boss, before things got out of hand. Shot Gerry in the back; shot him because he was related to the De los Santoses; had to get rid of the survivors; because Gerry would have had to avenge the massacre: a matter of honor. Shot him in self-defense. Killed him because he didn't fire a shot during the massacre; because after the massacre he refused to participate in Scout Ranger operations. Insubordination. Couldn't be tolerated.*

Gerry also killed himself. His gun went off accidentally. He committed suicide because he was so afraid; went crazy and shot himself in the head, in the mouth, in the chest; went crazy because he was so ashamed that he'd betrayed his own family; led the Rangers to the house; sinned against his own blood; didn't realize what he'd done; that he'd been tricked by Gutierrez to locate the De los Santos home. And Gerry wasn't the only Scout Ranger killed. There were three in all. They also protested the killings. One of them told Gutierrez he was going to tell Cory Aquino what happened. Boom! Dead. All were shot dead on orders of Gutierrez; shot personally by Gutierrez; shot by his top aide, Alan Arrojado; shot to keep the lid on the massacre, as part of the coverup; shot in Gutierrez's own office; shot in their nipa huts, in the military camp at Carabalan. Tsismis.

Gutierrez had gone to Mambagaton to steal Moret's fighting cocks.

Went after Moret because of the cockfight, because he was insulted, humiliated; because Moret refused to give him the Gray, failed to show the proper respect. The massacre was engineered by Rodolfo Tongson to avenge the killing of his close friend, Serafin Gatuslao. Gutierrez had given Moret a chance to save his family. The Scout Rangers told the De los Santoses to give up, to come out of their house. But Joaquin shouted back, "If you want to kill us, we'll all die together." The NPAs fired first. The Rangers had no choice. Self-defense. They hadn't even come looking for Moret but for Moroy; they thought Moroy was an NPA. When they questioned him, to save himself, Moroy fingered Moret.

Moroy Alamon was a paid informant of the Scout Rangers; paid to monitor Moret's movements; to get even with Moret. Moroy had told the Rangers there were NPAs at the De los Santos house, because Moroy had quarreled with Moret; because he was jealous of him; because Moret got a job he wanted; because Moret wouldn't give him water for his rice field. Moroy was told to leave town and never return; was killed by someone in the De los Santos family; by Joaquin; by Moret's stepbrother, Dan. He was shot by the NPAs. One of the Rangers put a gun in Cerila's mouth and asked her if she knew Moroy; when she said she did, he blew her face off. Another slashed her breasts with a samurai sword. Tsismis.

The De los Santoses were dead, Gerry De los Santos was dead, and so were Serafin Gatuslao and Moroy Alamon. A bunch of peasants, a soldier, and a planter. Killed in Mambagaton. And only *tsismis* to explain it.

Sugarland

O let us love our occupations,
Bless the squire and his relations,
Live upon our daily rations,
And always know our proper stations.

—Charles Dickens, "The Chimes"

The Roman goddess of agriculture would enjoy the view from her namesake, Ceres Bus Liner, which travels Negros Route 1, the island's coastal road and passes through some of the richest alluvial farmland in all of the Philippines. Negrenses call this place Sugarland or Sugarlandia, and it doesn't take long to figure out why. The western plain of the boot-shaped island, located 300 miles southeast of Manila, is a vast silver-green expanse of sugarcane plantations that stretch from the Gulf of Panay, across gentle foothills, and on up to volcanic mountains, the source of more than a dozen rivers. Even in the capital city of Bacolod, vacant lots are planted with the tall hard grass, the island's principal source of revenue.

People have been planting sugarcane here so long, they can hardly imagine planting anything else, even though a lot of *hacenderos* admit it doesn't make much sense. They can, after all, harvest only one crop a year, and the price of sugar is subject to extreme fluctuations. But the people who run the island's big plantations and the mills have sugar in the blood and sugar on the brain, and the commodity so dominates the local economy that most planters probably believe the island would blow away if it weren't anchored to the ground by millions of rods of sugar.

The Ceres Liner is a big diesel-belching transport that sometimes looks like Noah's ark. It's not unusual to see it roar by with a sure-footed goat tethered to the top like some giant hood ornament and its interior filled with squealing pigs stuffed into sacks and shoved

under the seats, or bundles of live snipes or chickens bound together
by their feet and lying on the floor in feathery heaps. The bus follows
an assigned route, but you can flag it down anywhere along the way,
and you can disembark wherever you want. You can also pack it to
the gills with all the junk you can carry and travel from one end of
the island to another for a few pesos. The Ceres bus is largely un-
adorned. A weaving across the top of the windshield says, GOD BLESS
OUR WAY, and a small shrine to Santo Niño sits on the dashboard
with one of those flickering copper-colored electric candles. A sign
warns passengers to BEWARE OF PICKPOCKETS.

Route 1 was known as the Calle Real, the Royal Road, under the
Spaniards, although it was, in those days, more an idea than an actual road. Even when the Spaniards were booted out in 1898, following the Spanish-American War, it was nothing but an unpaved
wagon route that was almost impassable for more than short dis-
tances. Today the two-lane blacktop is the only paved highway on
Negros, and there are still long stretches in the south that have yet to
receive their first slathering of macadam. Passengers who ride the
Ceres Liner there wrap their heads in towels or T-shirts and clasp
handkerchiefs to their faces to keep from suffocating in the squall of
dust, and when the bus makes its periodic stops, they beat at their
clothing as one might an old rug in spring cleaning.

The fifty-mile stretch of highway from Bacolod to Himamaylan,
located at the "ankle" of the boot, is a collection of idyllic vistas that
could have been lifted from a child's storybook. A chocolate-colored
road cuts off from the highway and weaves its way through the lus-
cious green valley of ten-foot-high cane stalks in orderly rows three
feet apart, past a solitary farmhouse and the freestanding stone
smokestack of an antique sugar mill, then disappears below majestic
Mount Kanlaon, whose smoking 8,000-foot summit peeks out above
a thin necklace of clouds. Dense groves of coconut palms shelter coffee beans from the blistering sun, and regal white egrets strut about
emerald rice paddies that flicker like mirrors as the Ceres bus roars
by. Along the coast, women and little children net *bangos* (milkfish)
fingerlings from tangles of mangrove roots to sell to wealthy fishpond owners. Elegant twelve-foot fishing vessels with triangular sails
stitched together from pastel pink, blue, or green rice sacks skip
across the Guimaras Strait, while pontooned fishing *bancas*—
Mediterranean blue, mustard yellow, and crimson—rest on beaches
below huts roofed with dried fronds of the nipa palm. In the aisles

of the Ceres Liner, boys no older than seven, eight, or nine sell little
bags of quail eggs, peanuts, cigarettes, and fragrant, floral necklaces
of white *sampaguitas.*

If such mementos existed, these would be the picture postcards
of Negros Occidental. But the windows of the Ceres bus also frame
ghostly images of machete-wielding men covered in black soot, their
heads swaddled like mummies, felling tall stalks of sugarcane one by
one, stripping them of leaves, and loading them onto ancient, rusted
trucks. Women in tattered clothing plod silently through the fields,
ripping weeds from between the rows of sugarcane while the razor
leaves of the sugary stalks tear mercilessly at any exposed flesh.
Nearby, parchmentlike remains of yesterday's harvests are consumed
in the crackle and roar of deep orange flames, fires that creep across
the plain, generating choking clouds of pewter-gray smoke and a
searing heat that penetrates the vehicles of fleeting travelers. By late
morning, the sun is merciless, squeezing out the last drop of life
from the cane cutters, just like the giant cane crushers in the sugar
mills. The mills, the so-called centrals, are the signature structures of
Negros Occidental: huge, hulking collections of rhomboid blocks in
a dozen shades of rust, dinosaurs of the Industrial Revolution that
loom over the countryside. During milling season, miniature iron-
horse rail cars, *vagones,* work around the clock delivering ton after
ton of brown cane stalks, smokestacks belch black soot from burning bunker fuel and white steam from processing, and, all around,
the sweet, sulfurous perfume of molasses lingers in the air.

The Ceres Liner speeds past rice mills and their perpetually burning mountains of discarded husks, past tiny oases of bamboo,
patches of cactus, snake plants, blood red poinsettias, and stark silk-
cotton trees with their exploded kapoks waving like dishrags from
naked, leafless branches. At Hinigaran, the sullen brown river is
clogged with illegal fish pens that make boat traffic impossible. The
river used to be filled with crocodiles, and the town was famous
for the twenty-foot specimen, one of the last of the reptiles seen on
Negros, that was caged on the town square until it died a few years
back. Hinigaran is also home to Colonel Cardones's Task Force
Sugarland, the headquarters of the Negros Island Command, and a
sand-bagged bunker stands threateningly beside a once-paved and
now deeply rutted section of the coastal highway. Just beyond it, a
small, unmanicured parade ground is littered with tanks, jeeps, and
armored personnel carriers in varying states of disrepair. Weather-

beaten tropical shacks and open-air concrete buildings pass for offices, and goats, chickens, and dogs are more in evidence than soldiers, who have the good sense to find refuge from the scalding tropical sun. Although it would probably be unfair to leap from the appearance of Task Force Sugarland to generalizations about the commitment or capabilities of the men assigned here, such associations are tempting.

Binalbagan, the next town on the road, got its name, which means "roadblock," from a gigantic snake that once blocked the highway there, preventing anyone from passing. Today, the only roadblocks are the piles of sugarcane sheered from overloaded trucks by the overhanging girders of the Magsaysay Bridge. Bands of children stage gleeful raids on the heaps of sugar as soon as they're knocked from the trucks. During harvest season, the highway is littered with cane stalks that ferment in the sun and fill the air with their vinegary smell. Much of the cane is headed for the Binalbagan-Isabela Sugar Company, the largest sugar mill in Southeast Asia. BISCOM is the hub of a cane railroad, where the *vagones* and a seemingly endless line of overburdened trucks wait for as long as three days to get their cane into the mill.

Negros, the country's fourth largest island, is only 112 miles top to bottom, covering an area about the size of the state of New Jersey. But the odometer on the Ceres's dashboard and the humbling presence of Kanlaon only hint at the dimensions of a place where mountains, an impenetrable rain forest, and a lack of roads so completely separated the eastern and western plains for centuries that the two populations continue to speak mutually incomprehensible languages. An Ilongo-speaking native of Himamaylan traveling a mere fourteen miles east to La Libertad on the opposite shore would not be able to understand a simple conversation among its Cebuano-speaking residents.

Route 1 reaches the outskirts of Himamaylan at Barrio Aguisan, where the Ceres Liner stops briefly at a tin-roofed waiting shed that can accommodate perhaps a dozen people, its walls covered with the red, hand-lettered names of men who sponsored this innocuous little project—pillars of Himamaylan society such as Roberto Gatuslao, Tony Gatuslao, José Gatuslao, and Serafin Gatuslao, the man Moret was accused of murdering. The waiting shed is by no means the Gatuslaos' most significant contribution to the town, but many people will tell you there have been precious few others, despite numerous reminders of the prominent family, among them, the Governor Valeriano M. Gatuslao Hospital, the Don Serafin Gatuslao Elementary School, a disheveled park known as the Congressman Agustin M. Gatuslao Memorial Center, and the Doña Julita M. Gatuslao Memorial School.

The volcanic peak of Mount Canlusong comes into view just before the hacienda of Papa Johnny Silos, the *sabongero*. In his cane field sits the cockpit, the Gallera de Himamaylan. Papa Johnny's handsome white house sits about a hundred yards from the highway behind an iron gate adorned by a thick patch of red, orange, and pink hibiscus. Papa Johnny fancies doves, and a dozen or so of the snow-white birds fly up and flutter about a three-tiered birdhouse. The birds are pampered and docile and never roam very far. The shanties of some of Papa Johnny's servants sit along the driveway to his home. In the deeply furrowed field beside the dirt road, a barefoot man, his wife, and two little children are planting sugarcane, a mound of "cane points" close at hand. The cane points, hard, white, foot-long sticks from last year's harvest, will become the roots of this year's crop. They are also an hourglass for eight-year-old Rebecca's life. Like many children on Negros, she doesn't go to school but works with her parents. Her mother walks through the field, cradling a woven basket filled with cane points, and drops two of them every few feet along the neat rows. The little girl squats on the ground, her feet and hands caked in mud, and forces the stiff rods into the moist, receptive, sweet-smelling earth, one at a time, three per minute, 180 per hour, 10,000 per acre. As she goes about her work, she is careful not to soil her pretty yellow dress.

Across the road in a grove of mango trees is Papa Johnny's clubhouse, which looks out on fifteen rows of concrete tepees, three-foot-high shelters for his more than 150 fighting cocks. Any planter worth his salt will have a clubhouse. Papa Johnny's is a place to relax with friends, away from the women, to smoke cigars and cigarettes, drink his Johnny Walker Black Label—always Black Label—while maids in white bring them cool yellow mangos.

There are two bridges into the town of Himamaylan, the new Talaban Bridge and the old long-abandoned Ramos Bridge, named after

General Rafael O. Ramos, the leader of the southern Negros rebels
in the very brief war against Spain in 1898. It is perhaps fitting that
the bridge has fallen into disuse, a reminder both of a successful revolution abandoned, or, many would say, betrayed by the island's
sugar barons and of a prominent family that has fallen from power.
Before the Gatuslaos, the Ramoses were the most influential people
in Himamaylan, and when General Ramos accepted the surrender
of the Spaniards, his family was the town's largest landowner. The
Ramoses (no relation to Philippine President Fidel V. Ramos) are de-
scended from a Spanish friar by the name of Agustin Olmedillas del
Carmen, one of many priests who secretly raised families on Negros
in the nineteenth century. Olmedillas was appointed parish priest of
Himamaylan in 1848, which made him the town's top religious and
political agent of the Spanish ruling powers. He went on to become
one of the most influential leaders of the Catholic church in the
Philippines and played a major role in the economic development of
Negros during the period of its most rapid growth. Olmedillas died
in 1870, after an argument with his Negrito houseboy, who stabbed
him with a knife, and his property passed on to his three sons—José,
Martin, and Rafael—who had taken the family name of their mother,
Maria Ramos.

Many of the island's elite were obsessed with land, but the Ramoses seemed to go to extremes, insisting that their children marry
within the family to prevent any dilution of their steadily growing
estate. Thus, José Ramos's daughter Gregoria married her cousin
José II, the son of Martin Ramos; José's daughter Engracia married
Martin's son Timoteo Ramos; and Martin's son Agustin married his
cousin Paz, the daughter of Rafael. Over time, the Ramoses developed a reputation for siring children one descendant described as
feeble-minded and others describe as stark-raving lunatics. Everyone
blamed it on the inbreeding, except in the case of Dolores "Lolita"
Ramos, who married José's son Francisco, a man, as his priest put it,
with "numerous sweethearts." It was one of Francisco's mistresses,
Maria Tragico, who supposedly put a hex on Lolita and drove her in-
sane. Family members say Lolita was "bewitched" and was kept in a
locked room until the day she died.

In reality, there was not enough incest within the Ramos clan to
prevent the dispersion of its land, and intermarriage finally had less
to do with the decline of the Ramoses than did politics, which they

and other rich Negrenses pursued with no less lust than they did their mistresses. Father Olmedillas's son Agustin had an addiction to politics and served at one time or another as mayor of Himamaylan, congressman, and provincial governor. Campaign debts eventually forced him to sell a huge tract of Himamaylan land stretching from the old Ramos Bridge south to what is now the Gatuslao Park. The buyer was Don Serafin Gatuslao.

Land and politics go hand in hand on Negros—all important political offices are controlled by men and women with large holdings of sugar land—so when the Ramoses sold their land to the Gatuslaos, the latter picked up political control of Himamaylan as part of the spoils. The Gatuslaos have fought to hold onto that political base ever since.

Just after the Ramos Bridge, the road enters Crusher Crossing, one of dozens of places in Himamaylan named for things that used to be, places that don't exist on any map or signboard but only in the mental gazetteers of their residents. Crusher Crossing used to have a rock crusher that made the gravel when Route 1 was being built; a place called Planing Mill used to have a sawmill owned by the Gatuslaos that turned the logs from their logging operations into lumber. Transloading got its name because the Gatuslaos used to bring the timber from their logging operations there to be shipped off to Panay, Bacolod, and even Japan. Since then, the forest has been cleared away, but the names Transloading and Planing Mill remain as its memorials. The Gatuslaos made a lot of money selling ice along the highway at a place called Ice Plant, but you can't buy ice there anymore because the ice plant is gone. A Church of Jesus Christ of Latter-Day Saints stands at Ice Plant now. Like all the other Mormon churches on the island, with their austere design, white cement, and stunted steeples, this one has a fully paved basketball court beside its entrance. The only one in Himamaylan—and with netted rims, no less—it's an almost irresistible enticement to local boys with few places to play. The basketball court is nearly always empty, though, because Catholics forbid their children to play there lest they feel any sense of obligation that might make it difficult to resist the Mormons' earnest proselytizing.

The neatly groomed missionaries in their black slacks, white shirts, and uniform white-on-black plastic nameplates arrive in Himamaylan on the Ceres Liner, comfortable in their deeply held convictions, exuding self-confidence, and knowing little or nothing about the people they have come to convert. So far, Nephi, Moroni, Omni, Zeniff, Ether, and the other prophets of Joseph Smith's inspiration have not gained much of a foothold in Himamaylan. But then there's a lot of competition for local souls. The Catholic clergy is deeply suspicious of the Mormons, more so since they went around asking for all the genealogical records on the island. Some of the priests are convinced that the Mormons are part of a CIA-backed conspiracy.

When people mention Himamaylan, they are usually referring to the *población,* the center of town, which covers less than 1 percent of the municipality, and not the rural and mountainous areas where 85 percent of the people live. An American visitor at the turn of the century described it as a depressing place, and time has done little to enhance its appearance or to distinguish it from hundreds of other falling down towns of dusty one- and two-story wooden buildings with rippled metal roofs and peeling paint. Himamaylan has no sidewalks, and the stores are built right to the edge of the highway, nearly all of them identified by look-alike signs: white, capital, block letters on faded forest-green backgrounds, with square medallions to the right and left of each shop's name advertising Coca-Cola or San Miguel beer. Most are *sari-saris,* convenience stores that sell canned meats and fish, sachets of laundry soap, shampoo, aspirin, and other household necessities. Kate Fresh Inn, Babette's Bake Shop, Libo-an Store, and Malou Sari-Sari Store are all identified by the bookend signs, as are the RMV Store, Fely's Store, Triple M Store, Hurry Wholesaler, Rising Sun Hardware, and Peachy's Restaurant.

The aesthetic redundancy of Philippine provincial towns probably has less to do with poverty than with the country's limited notion of community and the plutocracy's contempt for the general public. There are probably few countries in the world that devote less money to public spaces. In the capital of Manila, a city of 11 million people, there are only a handful of public parks, far fewer even than a city as overcrowded as Calcutta. Most of the larger green spaces, such as the Polo Club and the golf courses, are reserved exclusively for the elite or the military.

Small towns, on the other hand, typically radiate from a church and public plaza. Himamaylan boasts a substantial plaza—perhaps forty by eighty yards—with a bandstand, basketball court, and flagpole. Coconut palms, acacia, and rubber trees shade little benches, and old frangipanis with gnarled arthritic trunks spread their stumpy branches like the fingers of an amputee, each tipped with its own fragrant, electric pink blossom. Facing the People's Hall at the center of the plaza on a concrete tripod is a bust of national hero José Rizal, the father of the country, who was executed by a Spanish firing squad for inciting the Philippine revolution. This Rizal is just like a thousand others in an equal number of town plazas, monuments that fail even to hint at the complexity of the medical doctor, painter, and novelist whose books inspired the revolution he himself condemned. In recent years, the Rizals have had to compete with life-size statues of a more recent martyr, Benigno "Ninoy" Aquino, Jr., late husband of the president, who is usually dressed in a perma-pressed cement suit that makes him look like a traveling salesman.

Himamaylan's *población* is small enough that people living there all know, or at least .ecognize one another, and they know about one another's business and personal affairs as well. Although it would be hard to find any rich residents, a few are wealthy enough to own automobiles, large homes, and businesses, to have multiple servants, and to send their children to college. These people have little in common with the majority of the population of rural Himamaylan, whose "quality of life" ranges from destitute to impoverished. Elite families like the Gatuslaos had all but abandoned Himamaylan years ago, although some still maintain homes or cottages so they have a place to stay when they visit their haciendas. People with money began moving out of Himamaylan in the 1960s and 1970s so their children could attend better schools and because there was no sign of economic development in southern Negros. The last of the elite were driven out in the 1980s by the Communist insurgency. Most relocated inside Bacolod's walled enclaves, where they are protected by private security guards; the wealthiest moved to Manila.

Himamaylan is a lazy town. There's never been much to do there. Serafin Gatuslao used to own a bowling alley, but it closed years ago. A lot of the men spend their days at John John's Recreation Center shooting pool, playing mah-jongg, blackjack, chess, and poker. They'll stand in front of John John's with their sweaty T-shirts rolled up and perfectly balanced on dark brown nipples, sipping San Miguels. Occasionally they'll press the cool condensation from the bottles against their bloated bellies as they watch the traffic on Route 1 and the comings and goings in the marketplace.

A local history of indeterminate authority reports that the name

Himamaylan comes from conjoining the word for a plague called *hima*—which some Spanish friars contracted—with the word *baylan*, referring to the native priests who were able to cure the disease. Whatever the derivation, Himamaylan was not much of a town in 1790, when the capital of Negros was transferred there from Ilog and a sizable fort built to protect it at the mouth of the Himamaylan River. In 1845, when the capital was moved from Himamaylan north to what is now Bacolod, the Spaniards ordered the fort destroyed. The brief town history reports, "There was found [in the fort] a small leather box in good condition," which contained a twenty-four-page history of the town, and "eight books of what pagan Indians called *anting anting.*" The priest ordered these books destroyed because they were considered "pagan charms." The history also seems to have been destroyed or else disappeared.

Although most people are unaware that a fragment of the ruined fort still exists, everyone knows about the huge *aya* tree with its spreading web of roots that seems to have sprung from the Spanish structure and consumed it. An old fish seller, Feliciano Garche, says the tree once stood in a corner of the fort's prison yard. "Nobody dares chop down that tree because they say the *engkantos* [evil spirits] living there will break your neck." A little boy supposedly died shortly after he cut branches from the tree, and people say Agustin Gatuslao was killed after he ordered another large *aya* tree cut down in front of Snows Church, apparently unaware that the tree was inhabited by spirits.

Our Lady of the Snows Church is a minute walk inland from the *aya* tree. Nobody is exactly sure where the church got its name, although people will tell you it had to do with a snowstorm sometime during the Spanish colonization, an implausible event, given that Himamaylan is only ten degrees from the equator. Stranger still—and a stroke of good fortune at that—the storm began just as Moro pirates were preparing to attack the town, a not uncommon occurrence along the Negros coastline until well into the nineteenth century. In 1785, Himamaylan and neighboring Binalbagan had been attacked by forty-three Moro vessels; both towns were razed to the ground, and 110 people were carried off as slaves. Fortunately, on this next occasion, a woman in the white church bell tower sighted the Moros and began pulling furiously at the bells to warn the townspeople. As the bells clanged, the clouds miraculously began to gather, the sky turned black as lead, and a beautiful girl with long shimmering white hair emerged from behind the dark curtain, radiating an intense light as snow fell all around her. On seeing that, the pirates had the good sense to flee for their lives, and the people of Himamaylan rejoiced, giving thanks to Nuestra Señora de las Nieves. Later they named the church in her honor.

Father Eamon Gill has heard numerous versions of this story but doesn't believe any of them. He thinks the name derives from the great Cathedral of Santa Maria Maggiore in Rome, built on instructions from the Virgin Mary herself at the site of another miraculous snowfall during an August heat wave in A.D. 342. Gill suggests that an image of Our Lady of the Snows, the patron saint, was probably brought to Himamaylan from Europe by one of the early Spanish priests.

The current Snows Church is a stolid, unpretentious, white concrete building with a detached bell tower as graceful as a tall refrigerator carton. Bob Gatuslao built the church according to a sketch given him by the priest at the time, and the Gatuslao family paid for most of its construction. They provided wood from their lumber company for the frame and for the tongue-and-groove ceiling, imported an old brass bell from a church in Rome, and donated several thousand gold leaf tiles, which form a glittering backdrop for the fifteen-foot-tall crucifix that hangs at the front of the nave. The only other architectural flourish is a rose-shaped window of clear glass set above the main entrance.

For a brief time, during the construction of the present building, Himamaylan actually had two churches. To avoid any interruption of the liturgical calendar, the new Snows Church was actually built around the older, eighteenth-century stone edifice, which was then dismantled from inside its successor. It was as if the one had given birth to the other.

The spacious, naturally lit interior of the Snows Church has a self-conscious austerity imposed by priests wary of any ostentation or embellishment that might offend people praying for something to eat. Two long rows of wood pews run the length of the church below a clerestory of jalousie windows. To the right of the chancel, an electric candle flickers before a lace-draped tabernacle shaped like an old-fashioned radio, which parishioners no doubt wish it were at times, given the none-too-uplifting music typical of church services here. Sentimental and sometimes lachrymose, the music of the Negros church is, more often than not, parched, listless, dyspeptic, and monotonous. On the wall, immediately to the left of a wooden speaker's podium, a digital clock marks the precise time. Below it stand a small shrine to the Virgin and a two-foot-tall image of the Santo Niño, the Christ child, dressed, as is traditional, in a flamboyant red cape, gold blouse, and white knickers. Cherubic, pink-cheeked, a gold crown on his head, he holds in his left hand the world, a golden globe, with a cross poking from the North Pole like the flag of a triumphant explorer.

The original Santo Niño came to the Philippines in 1521 with the country's European discoverer, Portuguese explorer Ferdinand Magellan, and has since become the unofficial patron saint, although educated clerics often dismiss him as a weak "child God" or some sort of primitive idol. This condescension never seems to have bothered Filipinos like Moret De los Santos, who venerated the Santo Niño and asked him daily to perform miracles.

Magellan didn't fare nearly as well as the Santo Niño. He was sailing under the Spanish flag, looking to fulfill Christopher Columbus's dream of discovering a westward route to Asia, when he became the first European to stumble onto the archipelago and, according to his official chronicler, its "tanned, fat, and painted" people with black hair down to their waists and pierced ears a man could pass an arm through. No sooner had he landed than did Magellan set about converting the natives and murdering those who resisted, setting the stage for the next 300 years of Spanish rule. Alas, Magellan didn't make it out alive but was murdered by Lapu-Lapu, a native chief whom nationalists have given new life in recent years; as the first Asian to successfully thwart a western invasion, he has become a symbol of anti-imperialism and anticolonialism. *Lapu-lapu* is also the name of the national fish, a type of grouper.

On any normal day, the Ceres Liner passes through Himamaylan in less than a minute on its way to Kabankalan, the largest town in southern Negros. Just about the only time the liner stops is on Wednesday, when the marketplace becomes a colorful quilt of fresh fish and meats, zucchinis, watermelons, spiny yellow-green jackfruits the size of a full-grown pig, stinky durians, mangosteens, rambutans, and other tropical miracles. Mounds of new and used clothes, carabao harnesses, ropes, rusting tools, and impossible-to-identify machine parts are all laid out under a square block of corrugated iron roofs that keep off most of the sun and significantly less of the monsoon rains.

Whether or not they have something to buy or sell, people come to the market. Rosy-lipped women with teeth stained dark red sell betel nuts, a stimulant chewed with lime that is popular in the mountains, and hand-rolled cheroots. Friends socialize and exchange gossip at raw wood tables, drinking from gallon jugs of rusty-orange palm wine, oblivious to the pungent odor of dried fish and shrimp paste spread out on newspapers around them and soon to be oblivious to just about everything else.

Modern medicines are largely unaffordable, and a sizable percentage of the population doesn't believe in them, but there are ample supplies of traditional remedies for sale at a half-dozen tables. An elderly woman with zebra-striped hair runs a small pharmacopeia of seeds, grasses, barks, leaves, and oils—herbal potions she says will take care of just about any ache or ailment, cold, or fever. She sells tiny bird's nests to cure chicken pox, teas for spider bites, gray egg-shaped seeds from the *dalugdog* tree to boil for stomachaches, and incense that will supposedly make your homing pigeons less susceptible to capture. Also arrayed on the table is a large collection of *anting antings* in all shapes and colors, including odd, amoeba-shaped *anting antings* for children—lizard skin or plastic stitched around bits of paper with a few words of Latin. "They keep the spirits away and keep children from getting sick," the zebra-haired lady says. But there are *anting antings* for grown-ups as well, talismans that confer great powers and protect them from enemies. The zebra-haired lady lifts a tarnished .45 caliber bullet from her collection of charms and holds it up for examination. "If you're new in this place, you should have one," she says. "So the *engkantos* won't harm you."

*   *   *

There is no *anting anting* to forestall the dead season, when tens of thousands of sugar workers are unemployed. *Tiempo muerto*, or *los muertos* runs from May to September, overlapping with the monsoons, and the mixture of rain and want of income can be a lethal brew. Sugar workers with little or no money feed their children less or not at all, making them more susceptible to respiratory infections and diarrhea, which, in their weakened condition, are often fatal. During the dead season, funeral processions with mourners following tiny coffins are a common sight. Some people refer to this period as *tiempo tinggulotom,* starvation time.

Moret De los Santos and Serafin Gatuslao both grew up on sugar plantations. Serafin, of course, never worked in the sugar fields, whereas Moret was cutting cane as soon as he was strong enough to wield a machete, and lived his entire life surrounded by sugar workers. Like them, the horizon of his universe, indeed his entire identity, was defined by the hacienda. Even today workers will say, "We are from Paco," referring to the Ramos hacienda, or "We are from Benedicto," one of the Gatuslao haciendas, rather than naming their town or barrio. Sometimes the hacienda actually takes the place of a town and may include a church or chapel, a school for the children, and stores that sell essential provisions.

Cane workers, some of them hung over on "one-year-old," the local sugarcane rum, enter the fields at sunrise on a stomach of boiled rice, a bit of cooked greens, and perhaps a small piece of dried, salted fish. A man working in a normal cane field will dress in jeans and a T-shirt. Working a burned field is another matter. Row behind row, a burned cane field looks like an endless prison of blackened upright bars, each oozing a thick, viscous gum and covered with a fine silken ash. Men working in burned fields swaddle their heads in towels or rags and the rest of their bodies in thick denim, leaving only their faces exposed. At the end of the day they emerge from the fields looking like overgrown tar babies.

Sometimes the *hacenderos* can be seen driving along the dirt roads that run through the cane fields, tossing up a choking fog of light brown dust that seems to hang suspended behind them, then settles like a heavy tarpaulin over their workers, blotting them out. Cutting cane in temperatures that reach 120 degrees is back-breaking, monotonous work, the most difficult job available on Negros. A skilled laborer can cut up to two and a half tons of sugar in a single day. All of the island's cane is harvested by hand, all of it by men. They work in teams of ten, fifteen, or twenty, cutting one stalk at a time with curved *bolos* or machetes shaped like long, wide-blade meat cleavers with a blunt forward end and a wood handle smoothed to a black ebony luster from constant use. The whoosh of a machete in the hands of an experienced cutter is followed by a dull thunk or sharp ping as the blade passes through the stalk at a forty-five-degree angle no more than three or four inches above the ground.

Planters can be extremely fussy about how their cane is cut— there is money in every inch that is lost—and the precision of the cutters lends a certain unexpected tidiness to the process. As each eight-foot stalk is felled, its leaves are stripped away by sweeps of the machete and are left on the ground in a thick green wake behind the advancing cutters. From the remainder of the stalk, the top ten inches or so are cut and thrown onto a pile of "tips," rootstock for next year's planting.

The leaves of the cane plant, rough, hairy, and razor sharp, cut narrow incisions in the hands, arms, and face. More serious injuries, the loss of an eye to a sharp cane leaf or a machete wound, are common. Gnarled, stunted fingers on heavily callused hands are signatures of the job. Hacking wounds and deaths from fights among workers are reported regularly. The cutters wear rubber thongs, the only shoes most of them own, although a significant number go barefoot, their feet so leathered that they are resistant to most hazards.

To a migrant sugar worker, one cane field is pretty much like the next, but working conditions may vary. Housing and relationships with overseers range from acceptable to abysmal. Workers are often billeted in barracks, many with no beds, blankets, or mosquito nets, no sinks and no toilets. Human waste may be left for the dogs or placed in an old newspaper and tossed onto a pile of garbage; "flying saucers," people call them. Cooking is done over wood or charcoal fires. Water is normally available at a pump or from a single spigot, which may be shared by a hundred or more people. The stench inside these barracks can linger for weeks after the last worker has moved on to the next hacienda. The minimum wage law is largely irrelevant to cane workers, not only because most planters ignore it but because nearly all of them pay on a piecework basis. The more a work crew harvests, the more it earns. The planters say nothing would ever get done if they paid an hourly wage.

The "Sugarlandia" of the upper-class imagination is captured in

the oil paintings that adorn its homes and offices: scenes of cane
fields and rice paddies where simple, diligent farmers labor with dignity, like their plodding, obedient water buffaloes. In the background stand the sugar mills—the overarching symbols of Negrense
power and achievement—the quaint dwellings of peasants, tiny cabins with roofs of nipa palm or cogon grass, and the great volcano
Kanlaon. It is an abundant province; the markets are great cornu-
copias overflowing with fruits and vegetables. "You can grow anything on Negros," the planters tell you proudly. In the oil paintings,
the soil is always dark and rich, the sun shining, the people clean, ro-
bust, and neatly groomed.

Franklin Fuentebella, a sugar broker who leases sugar land in
Himamaylan, has one of these icons in his office, a scene rendered
in soft pastel hues, depicting rugged, handsome cane cutters wield-
ing sparkling machetes against a forest of cane, a range of majestic
mountains behind them. The focus of the painting is a beautiful
woman with long shiny hair, delicate hands, a thin nose, oval face,
and other strangely European features, the kind of beauty who
might be spotted by a talent scout and swept off to Manila to become an instant movie star and, in her spare time, a model in shampoo ads for a multinational corporation. The people in this and
similar paintings are not smiling, but neither are they stoic or angry
or in any way threatening. One curious omission: You will never find
the planter or his wife and children in these paintings. Maybe it's just
harder to romanticize the planter's position. Or maybe it's necessary
to romanticize poverty in order to live beside it every day. Then
again, no one actually believes that these images accurately reflect
the reality of workers' lives on Negros—certainly not Franklin
Fuentebella, whose cane fields were periodically burned by the New
People's Army because of his so-called crimes against the people.
Still, the paintings are fair depictions of the Sugarlandia myth, which
endures despite the insurgency and the violence and the banal,
everyday poverty.

*   *   *

Hacenderos such as Serafin Gatuslao and Moret's boss, Ernesto
Tongson, believed Sugarlandia worked—that the economy provided
for people because employers like themselves personally took the

time to look after their workers' needs and treated them as though they were "members of the family." The planters speak of their haciendas as mini-welfare states in which employees are given "cradle-to-grave" care. Some even boast that their servants dine with them at their own table. This paternalism, this sense of *noblesse oblige,* is a point of pride, the legacy of their parents, grandparents, and great-grandparents, the pioneers of Negros, a sort of Christian charity with its own built-in absolution. "If they're sick we give them medicine. If they have no food, we give them rice," says Serafin's cousin Bob Gatuslao. "I've given my workers ten hectares [twenty-five acres] just so they can build their homes." Serafin's wife, Esperanza Uy, known as Panching, insists her husband "did more than his fair share of helping these people. He paid all their hospital bills, he built schools for them, he helped the teachers and paid the tuition of the students from grade one up to college." Other planters, such as Moret's boss, provide small patches of land where employees can grow their own food. Eduardo Suatengco, the manager of a 2,000-acre family farm inherited from his grandmother, says paternalism is what binds Negrenses together. "The planter is like the father, and the farm and the laborers are like his children. He takes care of them, and he sees to it that they are provided for. That has always been the system since as far back as you can go."

Another *hacendero,* attorney Leon Moya, describes a similar sense of obligation. "We do act as fathers to our men. We do the things a father should do to protect his workers. We take care of the burials, the marriages, and we counsel them; if there is a killing, before they go to the police, they come to us." In addition to the so-called thirteenth-month bonuses—an extra month of pay at the end of the year, which is required by law and which a few planters actually pay—many provide loans to help families through the dead season. Like politicians, *hacenderos* are besieged with requests for financial assistance—for baptisms, fiestas, weddings, and so on—and many see these expenditures as a moral obligation. Some say they don't expect these loans to be repaid. If other planters were only half as generous, they tell themselves, Negros wouldn't have so many problems.

Tadeo Villarosa thinks of his hacienda as a family corporation: "We look at our workers as part of the corporation. When we talk about, let us say IBM, you don't talk about the stockholders as a separate entity from the executives and the workers, no? We're one. We all belong to one company. It just so happens that I own all the shares and my workers don't own any, but it's one company, you know? So when you help the firm, you help not only the stockholders, you help also the laborers."

As long as anyone can remember, this is how the planters have come to explain their way of life, in stories and anecdotes of family and business that form neither a philosophy nor a concrete set of values but nonetheless sustain their pastoral vision of Sugarlandia. The *hacenderos* feel they have provided for many of these workers since they were toddlers: the maids, cooks, and laundresses, the *yayas* or nannies, servants-in-waiting all in clean white cotton uniforms, the gardeners, the guards, the sugar workers. The *amo* calls them all by their given names, a:id they in turn address him with the respectful *Toto*, or "Uncle." They are always there for him, never challenging or questioning his authority, responding metronomically—"Yes, sir," "Yes, ma'am"—to every order, greeting the most inconsequential kindness with an appreciative "Thank you, sir," and "Thank you, ma'am." Perhaps the *hacendero* reads too much from these responses, but it is almost all he ever hears from "his" people, except when they come humbled and downcast, ashamed, really, to appeal for help, which he, in turn, dispenses judiciously, reminding himself not to spoil them through overindulgence. Like children, you could ruin them to the point that they would take advantage of you.

Unlike his natural children, however, it is the planter's design that his workers never grow up. He tells himself it isn't in their nature, they are uneducated and, sadly, unintelligent, their mental abilities woefully limited. Doctors attribute the learning disabilities to childhood malnutrition. Whatever, the *hacendero* doesn't blame himself. But he can definitely see the problem in the woodenness of their responses, their hollow voices, their failure to follow the simplest instructions, their inability to recall a sequence of more than two commands. It is only a small step to conclude that they are really too stupid to do anything but weed or cut sugar. A planter can easily satisfy himself that they are uniquely suited to the work, like their bovine companions in the fields; that it is all God's will; and that the same divine judgment ordains that the *hacendero* receive the bounty that is his due. When children were dying of starvation all over Negros during the 1980s, most of the elite denied there was any hunger on the island. They would point to a banana or papaya tree and insist that there was food growing everywhere. Eduardo Suatengco blamed what hunger there was on bad eating habits. "The majority of these laborers, they buy a lot of junk food. They buy a lot of Coca-Cola, and they smoke a lot. That's why they become malnourished. Basically I think the majority of the problem is that. Lack of education."

The sugar planters discuss their workers' shortcomings among themselves incessantly and suffer them all with the balm of contempt. Always aloof, they force their "children" into a mold of solicitousness and passivity, degrade them thoroughly, then stand back and wonder how anyone can have so little self-respect.

The class society cultivated by the Negrense elite leaves workers removed from slavery by only a few degrees. Placed in an American context, the sugar worker's life at its worst might resemble that of a black sharecropper during Reconstruction. Men and women are free to leave a hacienda to try to find work elsewhere, but for practical purposes, many are owned, body and soul, by their masters. And they are often the lucky ones, far better off than workers who are cast adrift, having no permanent affiliation with a hacienda, reliant solely on income as day laborers. "In such a system," planter Suatengco says approvingly of the haciendas, "you [the *hacendero*] control the community, because everybody is dependent on you, and you have a say in everything they do."

Suatengco's view of the plantation at the end of the twentieth century suggests that little has changed on Negros since the century's start, when John Roberts White, an officer in the U.S.-created Philippine Constabulary, described a "feudal" hacienda system in which the *hacendero* was "overlord," where living conditions for workers were like "our own South before the war, when slavery fostered brutality. . . . Even the laborers, men, women and children . . . might be said to belong to the *hacendero,* for they were usually so deep in his debt for the clothing and food advanced that escape was well-nigh impossible. And the *hacendero* would tell you that unless the peasants were in his debt, they would not work."

Today, debt is still the coin of the realm in Sugarlandia. A simple debt may be an obligation to repay a loan of money or an advance of rice. Loan shark loans, *cinco por seis,* are the most common. A worker is given five pesos and is expected to repay it with six at the end of the month—an annual interest rate of 264 percent.

In its most ruthless incarnation, the hacienda is a complex maze of debts that, like the narrow corridors of cane in which workers pass their lives, offers only fleeting glimpses of escape. Like the American sharecropper, a worker may have to purchase provisions at a hacienda store at ridiculously inflated prices, or borrow money for food at usurious rates. He may work at the mercy of an unscrupulous overseer who misrepresents the amount of cane he's cut, and he may find at the end of the cutting season that he has earned almost nothing and is still in debt.

A more important, pervasive, and often more insidious form of debt known as *utang na loob* lies at the heart of the paternalistic system and is often described as the glue that binds Filipino society together. Frequently translated as a "debt of gratitude" or "lifelong debt," it is literally an "internal debt," the debt, *utang,* being tied to *loob,* a person's "inner being" or "inner self." The debt is typically an unspoken understanding reached without lawyers, paperwork, or even a handshake, by accepting a "gift": a job, money to deal with a medical emergency, or a favor granted by someone with political power. The debtor may be expected to attempt to repay such a gift, but more often such debts are like those owed one's parents, guilt-laden obligations which both parties understand can never be fully repaid. *Utang na loob* carries an ontological weight that is tied up with the debtor's sense of honor, self-esteem, and basic morality.

A worker for Serafin Gatuslao might incur a series of simple debts, which neither party would expect to see repaid. Some workers might look at these loans of rice or money or medicine as their due and might even resent Gatuslao for having reduced them and their families to such penury. More likely, though, and particularly as the list of gifts mounted without any prospect of repayment, the worker would feel a combination of shame and inferiority, as well as a sense of obligation and loyalty to Gatuslao, his *amo,* provider, and savior. Without him, a child might be dead, or the worker's family might go hungry. And although there is a sense of mutual responsibility, the one side typically pays but a few pesos, while the other often pays for the rest of his life. In some cases, the sense of obligation is even passed on to a succeeding generation.

Moret De los Santos carried just such a sense of lifelong obligation, a profound sense of *utang na loob,* toward the Tongson family. Raymundo Tongson, Sr., had looked after Moret's mother when her husband abandoned her; he had provided Moret with work, a place to build his house, a small piece of land on which to grow food for his family. The Tongsons had paid for Moret's high school education, for his children's schoolbooks, and had come to his family's aid in various emergencies. When Joaquin went to the Raymundo Tongson High School, Raymundo Tongson, Jr., paid his expenses.

Raymundo's sons all looked after Moret in one way or another. Rodolfo Tongson employed Moret at his hacienda (until they had a falling out), Rojelio Tongson employed him in the highway department, and his brother Ernesto hired Moret to farm his rice field. The Tongsons employed Moret's son-in-law at one of their fishponds and gave Moret's crazy half-sister Wilma, who never recovered from having been raped as a young girl, a job collecting the dried cane leaves during the harvest. In return, the Tongsons expected Moret's services but, more importantly, his fidelity. If they had a job for him to do, he did it without equivocation. If one of the Tongsons needed to know whether or not to hire someone or whether or not he could trust one or another of his workers, he consulted Moret. Moret was the family's eyes and ears in the hacienda, their pipeline to the working class. The Tongsons relied on Moret to remain informed about possible troublemakers, and they might even use him and his presumed network of contacts to communicate with the NPA if, for example, the rebels demanded "taxes." Because Moret was poor, he had greater credibility with the rebels and could assure them that the Tongsons were fair to their employees, or that damaging Tongson properties would hurt the poor people who worked for the family. If someone in the Tongson family was running for office, or if the Tongsons were campaigning for the Gatuslaos, they might turn to Moret to make sure all of their employees and the people in Moret's little community knew whom to vote for. To the extent that Moret had been able to pull his family out of poverty, he was deeply indebted to the Tongsons. The Tongsons empowered Moret. They had given him a certain stature in the community. And they never let him forget it.

In turn, the Tongsons had their own deep sense of *utang na loob* toward the Gatuslaos. Like any powerful family in the Philippines, the Gatuslaos had pieced together a network of relationships that allowed them to hold onto wealth and prestige. The Tongsons were their obedient satraps and were rewarded by the Gatuslaos with titular control over Talaban, the narrow, coastal barrio due west of Mambagaton, as well as with patronage and construction contracts.

The Tongsons' status was a longstanding gift of the Gatuslaos. The Tongsons, Chinese mestizos like the Gatuslaos, came to Himamaylan at the turn of the century from Iloilo, shortly after the arrival of Don Serafin Gatuslao. Raymundo eked out a living selling *tuba*, the palm wine he collected from the coconut trees at the Gatuslaos' and other haciendas. Later, José Hernando Gatuslao, the mayor of Himamaylan, made him his chief lieutenant and the foreman at his logging concession. "He was a very trusted man," recalled Bob Gatuslao, José's son. "My father needed someone he could rely on when he went out of town. In return for his loyalty, my father gave him protection." Protection meant work, a livelihood, and that no one would dare cross Raymundo Tongson without worrying first about having to answer to José Gatuslao. It meant the Tongsons would always be provided for. "It is well known in the Philippines that one needs a godfather for everything," Rizal wrote, "from the time one gets baptized to the time one dies." The Gatuslaos were godfathers to the Tongsons, as were the Tongsons to the De los Santoses.

The haciendas survived because people who had every right and reason to revolt lacked the means and the leadership to undertake such a risky endeavor. But in the 1970s and 1980s, both the economics and the culture of sugar began to change, and as thousands of hacienda workers found they could no longer depend on the system that had provided a safety net for their parents and grandparents, they began to seek help beyond the haciendas' perimeters. Some found it in the church, some in the unions, and others in the New People's Army.

The Church, the Dictator, and the Communists

No matter how long the procession, it always comes back to the Church.

—Popular saying

The church that buried Moret De los Santos, his wife, and their three children was very different from the one sustained by the Gatuslao family, which had its roots in sixteenth-century Spain and was, for most of its three hundred years in the Philippines, practically indistinguishable from the government. The latter was a church born of the Counter-Reformation, resistant to the more modern ideas of the Enlightenment, and guided by a theology that subordinated the temporal sufferings of man to the imagined rewards of the afterlife. The church of the De los Santoses, on the other hand, was one that emerged from its medieval cocoon in the 1960s, only to find itself face to face with a government that was equally indifferent to the most basic issues of human survival.

The Isla de Negros got its name from Spanish explorers, who were fascinated by the island's dark-skinned aborigines, whom they labeled Negritos. At the time, Negros's tiny population consisted of people of Malayan heritage who farmed rice along the coastline, and the Negritos, a nomadic people who wore G-strings and lived in the upland forests, where they hunted, cultivated root crops, and supposedly hung their dead in trees. The explorers came away from Negros with a grim view of the island, but nowhere near as dark as that recorded by the priests the Spanish crown sent to colonize it; they described Negros as a brutish, inhospitable place, "a territory immersed in scandalous misery." This view was not altogether unwar-

ranted, considering that the priests were under constant assault by
Moro pirates, the physical elements, and members of the native population, who were understandably resistant to the alien Christian
faith and the church's campaign to forcibly relocate families along
the Negros coastline "under the bells of the church."

The Philippine provinces were technically run by Spanish *corregi-
dores,* or military governors, but in 1583 King Philip II gave the
church primary responsibility for administering the country's rural
towns and hamlets, and in places like Negros, the friars remained
the paramount influence throughout the Spanish occupation. The
Catholic church divided the islands among five competing monastic
orders—Augustinians, Dominicans, Franciscans, Jesuits, and Recollects—assigning priests to far-flung villages, where they learned the
native dialects and struggled to spread the Word and build local
communities. In their zeal to make the archipelago a "showcase of
the faith," however, the Spanish friars also obliterated much of the
local culture. Negros was a case in point.

The Negros friars viewed the local populace as racially and
morally inferior, as having what one writer called "a primitive intelligence . . . impervious to logic." To save the natives' souls, the Spaniards collected and burned icons, musical instruments, charms, and
amulets, beat and tortured idolaters, and destroyed the shrines
where the *Indios,* as they called the Filipinos, worshiped. By the time
the Europeans were forcibly removed from the Philippines at the
end of the nineteenth century, the Negrito people who had inspired
the island's name were nearly extinct. Whether they had an oral,
mythic history, a Genesis or Popol Vuh or *Ramayana,* is not known.

The despotism of the friars, more than any other single factor, led
to the Philippine revolution against Spain in 1896 but did not actually come to an end until the United States seized the archipelago
two years later in the Spanish-American War. That short-lived affair
was followed by a Philippine revolt against the new would-be colonizers, one of the bloodiest and least-known chapters in American
history, which resulted in the deaths of more than 200,000 Filipinos
and carnage that rivaled anything perpetrated by the Spaniards. U.S.
military officers, their hands bloodied in the recent wars against
native Americans on the Great Plains, were equally savage in putting
down the Filipino rebels. The American colonizers who followed
proved as patronizing as the Spaniards in their views of the Fil-

ipinos—their "little brown brothers," as William Howard Taft, the
first U.S. civilian governor in the islands, once called them.

Nevertheless, the Americans were determined to distinguish their
regime from that of the hated friars, convinced that they could create a "showcase for democracy." The "mission of the United States
is one of benevolent assimilation," President McKinley said. And although both the benevolence and the degree of assimilation continue to be subjects of endless controversy, there is no question that
the Americans became the country's new missionaries, evangelists
for democracy and hard work.

During their first twenty years in the Philippines, the Americans
built roads and ports, invested in irrigation and hospitals, and made
improvements in health care that contributed to a doubling of the
population. The U.S. government also dispatched more than a thousand schoolteachers to the islands, wresting education from the
hands of the priests for the first time in three centuries and, between
1900 and 1920, raising the literacy rate from 20 percent to 50 percent, then the highest rate in Asia. On Negros, Americans, Spaniards, and the wealthiest Filipino planters—responding to an act of
Congress giving Philippine sugar duty-free access to American markets—invested heavily in state-of-the-art mills and processing plants,
which radically transformed the island's principal industry. The
sugar boom that followed saw a massive increase in the acreage
planted and reinforced the island's addiction to the commodity. The
boom also created thousands of new jobs, and in the 1930s it inspired the first, largely unsuccessful, efforts to organize workers.

Throughout this period of intense economic growth, the Catholic
church on Negros was preoccupied with defending its turf. Filipino
nationalists who opposed the return of the Spanish friars and the appointment of an American bishop fomented a schism within the
church that saw thousands of Negrense Catholics leave for the newly
created Philippine Independent church, with its Filipino priests and
hierarchy. At the same time, the Catholic church felt besieged by
American Baptist and Protestant missionaries, who not only prosely-
tized directly but also won control of most of the island's secular
schools, which were the most visible public service provided under
U.S. rule.

It was only in the 1950s that the Catholic church made its first
serious forays into what might be called social activism, when an

Italian Jesuit priest, Hector Mauri, attempted to organize sugar workers around wage and benefit issues. Between 1958 and 1961, Mauri and the church-created Federation of Free Farmers launched a series of strikes against the largest haciendas. The planters and the government responded with violence and mass arrests, and the church backed off, disassociating itself from the union and withdrawing support from Mauri.

The first truly sustained attempts by the church to address the island's pervasive poverty came only after the Second Vatican Council, the ecumenical conference held between 1962 and 1965, which encouraged priests to address the socioeconomic concerns of their parishioners. It was this more worldly church that would eventually attract Moret De los Santos and alienate families like those of Serafin "Apin" Gatuslao. By the time Moret became involved with it in the early 1980s, a church identified with the plantation owners, millers, and traders only a decade earlier had come to be known as a church of the poor and, in some quarters, a church of the Communists.

*   *   *

The increased social involvement of the Philippine church tracked closely both the career of Ferdinand M. Marcos and the rise of the New People's Army. Although Vatican II had set the church on a more progressive course, Marcos deserves much of the credit—or blame—for the increasing radicalization of many of the priests in the 1970s and 1980s. When Marcos was first elected president in 1965, most of the country's one hundred or so bishops were staunchly conservative and either pro-Marcos or apolitical. Twenty years later, the Catholic church, led by the archbishop of Manila, bore much of the responsibility for the nationwide movement that brought Marcos down.

Murder in the Philippines is, to paraphrase Clausewitz's oft-quoted maxim on war, "an extension of politics by other means," a rational instrument of policy, albeit, like war, less than an exact art. The political career of Ferdinand Marcos was baptized in the blood of murder—as a young man he was found guilty of murdering his father's chief political opponent by firing a single .22 caliber bullet into his back—and his career was brought to its end because of the murder of Marcos's chief political opponent, Benigno "Ninoy" Aquino, Jr.

Although a murder conviction would not normally be a prescription for a successful political career, Marcos, who had graduated at the top of his law school class, was able to use the public spectacle of his trial, in which he argued his own defense, to establish a national reputation. He was sentenced to serve ten to seventeen years in jail, but the conviction was overturned less than a year later at the instigation of José P. Laurel, chief justice of the Philippine Supreme Court and father of the man who would later be Corazon Aquino's running mate in the election that unseated the dictator.

Marcos capitalized on his vindication to win a seat in the House of Representatives. He spent three terms there, was elected to the Senate, and finally to the presidency. In his inaugural address, Marcos promised that "every form of waste, conspicuous consumption, and extravagance shall be condemned as inimical to public welfare" and called upon Filipinos to "join hands with me in maintaining the supremacy of the law." But by the time he was reelected in 1969, Marcos was already wallowing in the corruption that would be his most enduring legacy. His reelection campaign had been oiled by an estimated $50 million campaign chest, much of it paid out as bribes to local officials who stuffed ballot boxes on his behalf. Then, in 1972, to get around a constitutional two-term limit on the presidency, Marcos alleged that Communists were "waging an armed insurrection" in order to overthrow "the duly constituted government" and imposed martial law. Newspapers and radio and television stations were closed, public demonstrations were banned, and six thousand political opponents, including Ninoy Aquino, were arrested.

In reality, the New People's Army consisted of no more than 1,000 armed men at the time Marcos declared martial law. Over the next decade and a half, however, Marcos's repression, his destruction of the national economy, his use of the military and police to hold onto power—and finally the murder of Ninoy Aquino, which Filipinos overwhelmingly blamed on the dictator—progressively undermined Marcos's public standing, radicalized a growing segment of the clergy, and nurtured the rebel movement. By the time Marcos fled, the rebels had 20,000 armed fighters, and the Communist party was operating guerrilla fronts in all but eight of the country's seventy-three provinces.

*   *   *

Midway through Marcos's first term as president, a new bishop, Antonio Yapsutco Fortich, was appointed in Bacolod and began a slow political and spiritual awakening that would eventually make him the island's most powerful voice for change and one of the dictator's most despised critics. Fortich was born in 1913 into a wealthy, Chinese mestizo, sugar-milling family, which, as he tells the story, believed that work developed character, a philosophy the future bishop admits he did not then share. "In my family, they wouldn't give you money for candy unless you worked for it. So I had to gather up the dry leaves of the sugarcane to get just twenty centavos a day. It's very itchy, very itchy work, and for twenty centavos only!" But it didn't take Fortich long to figure out a way to escape his chores; as he recounts the experience, "I got into a little corruption." Fortich came up with a simple plan that allowed him to get paid for not working, a practice Negrense *hacenderos* refined into an entire life-style. Since there were always plenty of impoverished, unemployed laborers around, Fortich hired one to do his work, paid him ten centavos a day, and pocketed the other ten himself. Fortich says it took years before he began to see the dark side of Negros and to realize that he himself was part of the problem.

A joyful man with a wry wit and an ever-present cigar, Fortich had been welcomed with open arms by the Bacolod elite, who, at the time of his investiture, presented him with a new Mercedes Benz. But his honeymoon with the elite was short-lived. Only months after he became bishop, Fortich made his first venture into politics with a pastoral letter that stunned his friends and supporters in the ruling class. "I find it necessary to speak out because of the conditions and problems existing in the plantations in the diocese," he began. Trying to be evenhanded, Fortich condemned those who "seek to destroy our society by violence and subversion" as well as "irresponsible labor groups," comments that should have endeared him to the *hacenderos*. But Fortich reserved the brunt of his fury for the island's wealthy landlords, whom he accused of stealing land from peasant farmers.

"It is with deep sorrow that I hear of these attempts to take away the land which has been lived on and developed by the poor. Such actions in utter disregard of the rights of the weak and powerless are a grave offense against Christian charity." The bishop went on to condemn planters who exploited the legal system to legitimize their thievery, and he attacked them for abusing their employees and servants. "By refusing to allow their workers to live as befits their dignity as sons of God and brothers of Jesus Christ, they debase not only the laborers whom God has put under their responsibility but also themselves. They sacrifice their rights to be respected as Christians: and their communions and pious acts do not edify but rather scandalize those who should be living by their example."

It was pretty strong stuff coming from the bishop, a bit more, in fact, than a lot of his wealthy friends could stomach. Fortich almost seemed to be slamming the doors of the church in the face of the elite. The Fortich letter, it turned out, was written by his close adviser, Luís Jalandoni, a young priest and scion of one of the island's wealthiest sugar families, who would soon be advocating "a struggle for national liberation." When Marcos declared martial law, Jalandoni went underground. He later became a member of the Communist party's Central Committee.

Jalandoni was one of several radical, activist priests influenced by the work of Gustavo Gutiérrez, a Peruvian theologian whose book, A Theology of Liberation, published in 1971, circulated widely in the Philippines. The book's Marxist analysis, its explicit condemnation of capitalism as the root cause of dependency and servitude, and its tacit endorsement of "just violence" as a remedy for political and economic oppression all found a sympathetic audience among many Negros priests, particularly after the imposition of martial law.

Another work, a short monograph published in 1971 by a Filipino priest, Arsenio Jesena, circulated widely on Negros in mimeographed form and had an even greater impact in shaping the thinking of the Negros church. "The Sacadas of Sugarland," an eye-opening tract on the lives of Negros's itinerant cane cutters, or sacadas, stands out as probably the single most damning indictment of the island's plantation system. Jesena described how landlords employed what was tantamount to slave and chattel labor, and he contrasted the lives of workers earning 5 pesos (about 50 cents) a day with that of a well-known hacendero who blew 120,000 pesos in a single cockfight and kept "a regular harem of teen-age prostitutes in his Bacolod office." After living and cutting cane beside the sacadas through a harvest season, Jesena delineated a catalogue of schemes the hacenderos and their contractors and managers employed to cheat their workers, leaving many penniless and deeply in debt at the end of the harvest season. "I saw the injustice of it all, and I began to understand why the Communists are Communists," Jasena wrote. "I asked these downtrodden *sacadas,* 'If the Communists come, will you join them?' They said, 'Yes.' I asked further, 'If they tell you to kill the *hacenderos,* will you do it?' And they said, 'Yes.' "

Bishop Fortich described Negros as "a social volcano" that was "waiting to explode" and predicted a bloody revolution unless at least some of the island's agricultural lands were given to the poor. Fortich focused relentlessly on the land issue but found that the landowners resisted even the most moderate reforms, such as payment of the minimum wage. Nearly two decades after his first blast at the planters, after Marcos had already fallen, Fortich was still attacking them for paying workers less than a dollar a day. "Can you imagine a family surviving on that with, say, three children?" he fumed in one interview: "On top of that, the haciendas have the annual dead season, when they hardly pay anyone anything. You go around on the haciendas, you ask if there is any mother who can afford to buy a can of milk. If you're only receiving twenty pesos a day, do you think a family can afford to buy a can of milk? So, you say, breast feeding. It's true, the mother is trying to do that. But she is also undernourished. So where is the milk from the body of the mother? . . . Everyone should know that the people on the farms are really suffering."

On an island where payment of a survival wage was considered radical and communistic, it was only natural that Fortich and some of his more outspoken priests would be characterized as some sort of renegade band. The ideas they promoted, though, including the demand for land reform, had all been endorsed by the conservative Catholic Bishops Conference in Manila. The bishops had responded to Vatican II by mandating Social Action Centers in every diocese in the country, church-financed offices that were to focus on issues of "justice and peace." On Negros, the Social Action Center became involved in cooperatives and livelihood programs for subsistence farmers. More important, it created the National Federation of Sugar Workers (NFSW)—which launched a series of strikes at large haciendas in the early 1970s for payment of the minimum wage and better working conditions—and the Basic Christian Community, which would become the largest grass-roots organization the island had ever seen. For people like Moret De los Santos, who had grown up in a church devoted entirely to the salvation of the soul but lived in the world described by Father Jesena, the BCCs offered a fresh perspective that for the first time brought the church down to earth and into their daily lives.

Fortich gradually came to the conclusion that the oligarchs would never implement even the most basic reforms voluntarily and that they would have to be forced to change, and he saw both the NFSW and the BCC as the means to that end. But although there were, at the movement's peak, more than 1,300 BCCs on Negros and thousands more throughout the archipelago, they never succeeded in realizing their true potential, in part because the *hacenderos* demonized and attacked them as a tool of the Communist party and the New People's Army. In fact, for many young sugar workers, the BCCs were the last stop on the road to the revolution. Church and NFSW union organizers who found they were unable to effect peaceful change often opted for what they saw as the only alternative. Consequently, they became the most frequent targets of harassment and "salvaging," or summary execution by the police, the military, and the death squads.

Fortich himself was a constant target of right-wing intimidation. He was roundly castigated—most often anonymously—as a "subversive," a "radical," and a "Communist," and was referred to in elite circles as Commander Tony or Ka Tony—short for *kasama* or "comrade," the implication being that he was a member of the NPA. From time to time Fortich's name also appeared on vigilante hit lists. The shady "Masses Against Communism" identified him as one of the "lapdogs of the Communists who are leading our brothers astray here on Negros" and sentenced him to death. In 1985, the bishop's residence in Bacolod was burned to the ground in a suspicious fire, and two years later a group called Christians Against Communism claimed responsibility for throwing a hand grenade into Fortich's residence while he slept. The bishop wasn't hurt; the only casualty was a small brown sparrow. The bishop had the bird stuffed and keeps it in a glass case on his desk. "It's a sparrow without a unit," Fortich jokes, alluding to the NPA assassin teams known as Sparrows.

Fortich said he personally opposed violence and revolution, but he was in close accord with many of the rebels' goals and steadfastly refused to criticize his priests and parishioners who went to the mountains. "You cannot blame young people for going up to the hills because they have found out that here in the valley life is really miserable." Although it would be hard to make a case that Fortich and most of his priests were Communists, it is also true that neither the party nor the NPA on Negros would have been able to succeed to anywhere near the extent that they did had the church been united in its opposition to them. Even priests who were ambivalent about the New People's Army could see when the rebels were offering more tangible and immediate results than the government. If the NPA was willing to provide people a ladder to exit a burning building, or even a bucket of water with which to cool themselves down, neither Fortich nor most of his priests were going to stand in the way. But neither did they stand in the way or speak out when the NPA began killing people indiscriminately.

*   *   *

In 1973, one year after Marcos assumed dictatorial powers, the New People's Army began in earnest the tedious process of building a "mass base" on Negros—educating peasants in the remote, despondent barrios about the movement's goals, convincing them through argument or intimidation to work for the revolution. The new organizers were prepared to dig in for the long haul, aided by some of Fortich's priests and nuns, as well as by middle-class, anti-Marcos sympathizers who gave them food, sheltered them from the police and the military, and helped them to move undetected around the island. This collaboration thrived despite the inherent antipathy between the Vatican's anticommunism and the Communist party's Maoist, and traditionally atheistic, dogma.

NPA organizers were drawn almost entirely from the local population. Most thought of themselves as Catholics, and they deliberately steered wide of confrontation with the church. They were familiar with the party buzzwords—what the leadership inelegantly called Marxism-Leninism-Mao Zedong thought—but when you asked the average NPA rebel to define communism, he'd come up with an explanation that had to do with simple matters of survival.

Deciphering exactly what the party stood for was no easy matter. Initially, the leadership had talked about nationalization of the country's industries and collectivation of farms along a Chinese model, but over time the big thinkers moved to embrace a mixed economy of state and private enterprises with free education, free housing, and free health care. How these services would be financed was anything but self-evident, particularly since everyone anticipated massive elite emigration and capital flight should the party take power.

Like all good Marxists, party leaders loved to analyze "contradictions" but never seemed able to reconcile some of their own: how they would encourage middle-class investment while advocating land redistribution; how to preserve freedom of worship while taxing and confiscating church properties; and how to support "free elections" and create a "coalition government" that would include non-Communists while imposing strict limits on the kinds of political parties allowed to participate.

Common people like Moret De los Santos weren't particularly interested in political and economic theory, though. Recognizing this, the NPA organizers on Negros kept dogma to a minimum and acted like ward heelers or precinct captains, listening to people's problems, explaining their own views, and offering practical solutions where they could. Since the Negros NPA leadership had broad authority to conduct the war as it saw fit and kept the level of violence in the early years of its organizing to a minimum, the rebels earned a generally favorable reputation in the countryside. They were known for maintaining strict discipline, paying their own way, preventing their members from stealing, hitting people, or swearing at them, and for keeping their hands off the local women. People joked that NPA stood for "Nice People Around" or "No Permanent Address," and the rebels were compared to bands of Robin Hoods who stole land from the rich and gave it to the poor. In return, peasants in isolated barrios like Mambagaton gave the rebels a percentage of their crops, let them sleep on the floors of their shacks, and tipped them off to the presence of government troops.

Perhaps most important, residents of rural barrios came to rely on the NPA to maintain a semblance of law and order and to deliver justice, however imperfect, where there had never been any. The NPA was in effect the local police force, judge, jury, and executioner of thieves, rapists, and murderers. If there was one thing the Communists could get just about everyone to agree on, it was that the official system of justice worked exclusively for people with money, and that even then it was a seriously flawed proposition. Manila attorney Alfonso Felix, Jr., who practiced before the country's highest courts for fifty years, confided shortly before his death that he had never once worked on a case where he failed to bribe the judge—as well as the clerks and administrative personnel—to secure a favorable ruling for his client. According to Felix, "Ninety percent of the cases are decided on the basis of money."

Unlike the interminable official court system, NPA justice, "revolutionary justice," was generally swift. The accused was brought before a so-called people's court and asked to defend himself—no outside counsel allowed—against his accusers and their witnesses. The "jury," which often consisted of whoever happened to show up for the "trial," listened to the case and delivered a verdict. Penalties, including death, could be meted out within minutes.

Fair or not, the less the government was able to deliver on its promise of justice, the more readily people relied on the rebels. In a corrupt and largely lawless society, it was not uncommon to hear, even among members of the elite such as Bacolod criminologist Joe Lopez-Vito, words of admiration for the rebel movement. "The NPA drives home the point that they're men of their word," Lopez-Vito explained. "They deliver summary justice, and the government delivers no justice. All the government delivers is promises." In much of rural Negros, the rebels were viewed as the only Filipinos with the strength of their convictions, the only ones willing to make sacrifices and endure hardships for something larger than themselves. For a while it looked as if the Negros rebels were going to build the people's army they needed to overthrow the government.

Last Rites

Some malady is coming upon us. We wait, we wait,
And the saints and martyrs wait, for those who shall be
martyrs and saints.

—T. S. Eliot, *Murder in the Cathedral*

Ernesto Tongson paid for the funeral of Moret De los Santos and his family, and the *tsismis* in Himamaylan was that Tongson's brother Rodolfo was responsible for having both Moret and his good friend Fred Veraguas murdered. Nobody seems to know who tried to kill Rodolfo's alleged hit man, Lito Ruiz, but whoever it was missed and shot Lito's wife instead. Mistakes happen.

People said there was a "good Tongson" and a "bad Tongson," but there were actually quite a few Tongsons, Raymundo Tongson, Sr., having sired twelve children, all of whom went on to raise families of their own. The "bad Tongsons" had a private army, worked with the military against the church and the sugar workers' union, and allegedly operated a death squad in Himamaylan. The "good Tongsons" minded their own business, more or less. Of all Raymundo Tongson's children and grandchildren, it was Rodolfo who seemed to cultivate an especially unsavory reputation. Even Rodolfo's brothers Ernesto and Rojelio didn't get along with him.

Ernesto Tongson paid for the De los Santos family funeral because he and Rojelio had been Moret's most faithful benefactors. Ernesto hired the hearse to move the bodies and paid for the carpenter who hammered together the five coffins and painted them silver. Each had a little window so that mourners could view the face of the deceased—even Cerila's, which was bandaged to cover the wound that had so disfigured her. Ernesto didn't think that paying

for the funeral was any big deal, although the surviving De los
Santoses did. He said he's always giving coffins away, that it's just
part of the old-fashioned paternalism practiced by his family. "My
father was a politician, so even today we still give help to the people.
Anybody who approaches me or my brothers, if they need help—
medicines, a prescription, if they can't afford something—we give
to them." Ernesto said he and his brothers had all helped Moret,
which was true, and Moret's survivors said they were deeply grateful
to the Tongsons. They considered the Tongsons among their best
friends.

Although Ernesto Tongson was Moret's *padrino,* his patron, he
didn't attend his funeral. That might have been misconstrued by his
neighbors as a sign of weakness or even betrayal, a statement of support for the enemy, not that Ernesto considered Moret an enemy.
But some of his friends might, and he could just as well pay his
respects quietly with his money. No one demanded justice for the
De los Santos family, Ernesto said, "because there were rumors that
Moret was in the NPA, and the community is against the NPA"—rumors he said he sometimes believes and other times does not. One
minute Ernesto would say, as if he were stating a fact, that Moret had
been targeted because "the NPAs sometimes stayed in his house";
the next, he would say he personally thought of Moret as "a peace-
loving person" and would never have helped him or his family if
he'd thought he was working for the Communists.

If Ernesto had any differences with Moret, they never surfaced
publicly, but the two men had definitely been at odds when it came
to the local church. Moret was heavily involved with the church at
the time of his death, and the Tongsons had become estranged from
it. Ernesto said he supported demonstrations against the church in
Himamaylan because it was allied with the insurgents.

Ernesto's brother Rojelio, the chief engineer with the highway department, had also employed Moret. Officially, Moret was on the
public payroll as a highway foreman, but his paycheck also covered
work at Rojelio's hacienda. Despite a ten-year relationship, Rojelio
acts as if he knows very little about Moret, and claims he doesn't
know whether Moret had any enemies, whether he was involved in
the NPA, or why exactly anyone might have wanted to kill him. He
is equally blasé about the lack of any investigation into the massacre.
"People are really very passive." The only thing Rojelio seems at all

animated about is his certainty that Moret had nothing to do with the murder of Serafin Gatuslao. He says people in Himamaylan loved Gatuslao. "People there would never try to kill Serafin. He was very close to the Himamaylanons." The same could not be said for Rojelio's brother Rodolfo, however.

It was right around the time Serafin Gatuslao was murdered that people began referring to Rodolfo Tongson as a murderer, and it wasn't long before the *tsismis* was accepted as conventional wisdom, although there was never any hard evidence to prove it, and at least one close associate of Tongson's denied that his boss had ever been involved in compiling hit lists. People did come up with plausible motives to explain why he *might* have wanted to kill certain Himamaylan residents, but no one dared bring a case against him, so the accusations remained hearsay. A close friend of Rodolfo, a planter, said he personally knew of ten murders Tongson had ordered, including the hit on Fred Veraguas on Christmas Eve, 1988, eight months after the De los Santos massacre. "Tongson is just drunk with power," this friend said. "He thinks he can kick anybody around."

It was Rodolfo who the butcher, Willy Villacanas, claimed had offered someone 30,000 pesos to have Willy killed. And Willy also believed Rodolfo was involved in killing Moret. So did Moret's two stepbrothers. One, Auelos Aminoto, said he believed Rodolfo was involved because some of the Scout Rangers who participated in the massacre had had a drinking session at Tongson's home the day of the massacre. Not exactly an indictable offense.

The Commission on Human Rights also came up with Rodolfo's name when it conducted a cursory investigation into the Fred Veraguas murder, but the file on the case has mysteriously disappeared, and officials at the commission's office in Bacolod said they couldn't afford to pursue the inquiry because they had no money to travel back and forth to Himamaylan. (Round-trip bus fare is approximately one dollar.) So Rodolfo's name just lingered like the stench of rotting flesh. But nobody ever seemed able to tie it to a corpse.

Rodolfo's home in Himamaylan is surrounded by a concrete wall capped with menacing shards of glass, long jagged pieces of brown San Miguel beer bottles, and broken windowpanes. The compound is guarded by Tongson's "private army," thirty-five armed "goons," as Negrenses call them, whose principal occupation seems to be casting intimidating looks at anyone who passes by. The group was organized after the NPA invaded Rodolfo's home and relieved him of a small arsenal of weapons, including seven assault rifles and a grenade launcher, more than the average homeowner would normally need for personal security.

A quarter-mile of concrete road runs west from the coastal highway past Rodolfo's home to the edge of the Talaban River, where it stops in a thick heap of emerald green *talaban* shells, small mussels harvested from these waters from which the river and Barrio Talaban take their name. At the river's edge, a dirt road doglegs south toward Tampok, the "mound" or "pile" where the bodies of prisoners from the Himamaylan fort were dumped following an unsuccessful rebellion in 1833. There was supposed to be a bridge at the dogleg, continuing straight across the Talaban River to Punta Talaban about a hundred yards farther west, but although the Tongsons' construction company was awarded a half-million-peso contract to build it, the money vanished and the bridge was never begun. Instead, people continue to rely on a "ferry," a tiny boat carved from a single twelve-foot log, which is balanced with pontoons and operated by a little boy about ten years old. For half a peso, about two cents, he paddles people back and forth across the river, navigating between anchored rafts where fishermen haul up nets using bamboo cantilevers that rise twenty feet above the water like giant praying mantises. In less than five minutes, the pontoon scrapes into the pebbled shore at Punta Talaban, the southern end of a thin tentacle of peninsula that separates the Talaban River from the Gulf of Panay. Fred Veraguas used to live on this picturesque peninsula with its gentle breezes, susurrus coconut palms, and omnipresent fishing nets draped across the bamboo slat fences that run along a single dirt road. The area is inhabited exclusively by fishermen, whose brightly colored *bancas* rest on the beach.

A flock of turkeys gobble about the yard of Rustica Veraguas, a stone's throw from the gentle waters of the gulf. Mrs. Veraguas and her husband, Orlando, occupy a small iron-roofed house with a cement floor. Orlando has warned her not to talk about their son Fred's death, but Rustica ignores him. Without hesitation she tells anyone who will hear her out that Rodolfo Tongson ordered Fred's murder. She says she's absolutely certain of it, that the incident took place on Christmas Eve, eight months after Moret's death. Fred left Our Lady of the Snows Church just as the priest was marrying a local nurse and an Army Scout Ranger, hailed a tricycle going north, and had just reached the Governor Valeriano M. Gatuslao Hospital near Crusher Crossing when two men drove up behind him on a motorcycle and one of them shot him twice in the back, killing him instantly. Mrs. Veraguas says there were numerous witnesses and that the killer was driven away in a red car with tinted windows that was owned by Rodolfo. She says both Fred and Moret were killed because they had been involved in the Basic Christian Community.

Fat Fred, as he was sometimes known, was precisely the sort of person whom powerful people in Himamaylan might see as a troublemaker. Through the BCC, he had successfully organized a cooperative that provided small loans to local fishermen, and like Moret, he was also active in the BCC's Justice and Peace Committee, which handled complaints against the military and planters. Fred was a natural leader, which was enough for some people to think of him as dangerous. Rustica says witnesses identified the gunman who shot her son as Lito Ruiz, a Tongson "goon," but said a case was never brought because none of the witnesses would testify. Mrs. Veraguas said Lito Ruiz was also responsible for murdering the husband of one of her cousins three months before the De los Santos massacre. "Everyone here knows Rodolfo Tongson ordered the killing of Herson Luberas. He was working along the highway when Lito Ruiz came by in his automobile and beckoned, and when Herson approached, Lito shot him down."

Herson Luberas's widow says her husband was fifty-five when he was murdered and that he had been preparing to testify against Rodolfo Tongson in a case involving a multimillion-peso highway contract. "Herson was the star witness. He would have testified that Rodolfo manipulated the bidding. My husband worked for the Tongsons and knew how they resorted to under-the-table deals to get contracts. He knew all of their anomalies, including how they fixed elections" in Himamaylan. Mrs. Luberas said Rodolfo Tongson ordered his hit man, Lito Ruiz, to murder Herson. While she, too, would like to see Tongson indicted, she says the witnesses are all afraid to testify.

Lito Ruiz hated the Communists. He joined the Army Scout

Rangers after his father was murdered by NPA assassins. When Lito
quit the Rangers, Rodolfo Tongson gave him a job in his private
army. A halting, nervous man, Lito Ruiz was twenty-four years old
when Fred Veraguas and Herson Luberas were killed. He himself
went into hiding after a group of men strafed his Himamaylan home
with machine guns, killing his wife. Lito's baby daughter wasn't hurt
in the incident, but a neighbor, a sixty-year-old woman, was shot
through the neck, and Lito himself was hit by three bullets in his left
leg. Lito said he knew exactly who the assailants were but wouldn't
file a case against them because they would kill him if he did.

Lito denied that he had killed anyone—not Fred Veraguas, or
Herson Luberas, or one of Rodolfo's drivers who had threatened to
blow the whistle on his boss. Lito said the accusations were "all
lies—they're trying to destroy me with rumors." He also denied allegations that Rodolfo Tongson was involved in putting together lists
of suspected Communists to be killed in Himamaylan, including
Moret De los Santos and Fred Veraguas. "Mr. Tongson concentrates
on his businesses, his trucking and prawn growing," Lito said of his
former boss. "He's an *hacendero*."

*   *   *

It was not so long ago that a visitor to Bacolod, arriving by steamer
after a twenty-four-hour trip from Manila, might have thought he'd
landed in some quaint banana republic port made up of little more
than palm trees, rust-red roofs, and nearly empty offices in a permanent state of siesta. He could not help but be impressed by the
rattling skeletons of decades-old taxicabs with their corroded floorboards and grimy black seats, or by the lethargic pace, the deaden-
ing heat, and the pervasive sense of neglect. But a few years back, the
capital began to change. The city attracted a McDonald's, installed
its first traffic lights, and built a convention center, and several up-
scale hotels went up to accommodate the investors and associations
that were to be part of an economic boom that never quite material-
ized. Before, most visitors stayed at the Sugarland Hotel, at the end
of the airport runway, or at the Sea Breeze, which used to be near the
sea, until the waterfront was pushed west by a massive landfill project undertaken in expectation of an earlier economic boom that
never happened. The Sea Breeze sits catty-corner from the Plaza del

Seis de Noviembre, which honors the short, successful Negrense revolt against Spain. It's a pretty square, shaded by royal palms and betel-nut trees and bounded by Gatuslao, Rizal, San Juan, and Gonzaga streets.

If the story of a city is etched in its public buildings and monuments, it is hard to say what one is to make of the bronze sprites adorned in underpants in the Bacolod plaza. One explanation has it that the shrouds were welded to the waists of the boyish figures to cover their genitalia and to assuage the bishop and some of the city's scandalized *doñas,* perhaps the same ladies who were responsible for the charming Victorian bandstand that sits on a checkerboard apron at the center of the square. The bandstand is guarded by four concrete lions and is inscribed just below its roof with the names V. Beethoven, W. Mozart, R. W. Wagner, and J. Haydn in black capitals. Each name appears twice on the octagonal structure, and although most residents have never heard of these men, it is the kind of statement some notable undoubtedly thought appropriate for a "cultured" community whose character has always had as much to do with elite pretensions as with the more mundane concerns of a people yet to be exposed to classical music, fine flatware, or porcelain figurines of adorable children.

When the war with the NPA broke out in the countryside, Bacolod became the principal redoubt of the elite as well as the refuge of many of the island's less well-off victims, who built little squatter encampments on public and private land. On the day his family was massacred, Joaquin De los Santos fled to Bacolod and was taken to the Corazon Locsin Montelibano Memorial Hospital, the only provincial facility that could treat his bullet wound and broken collarbone. It was also the only institution on Negros with an international reputation, thanks to its infamous malnutrition ward, where, in the final year of the Marcos dictatorship, nurses tallied 500 infant deaths on a grimy posterboard graph. The Montelibano Hospital, with its dank hallways, peeling paint, and sooted wards lined with gray, rusted, iron cots, dates to the American colonial period and looks like the kind of place where Walt Whitman and Clara Barton might have comforted amputees during the Civil War. Joaquin arrived at the hospital on the wind of rumors that the Scout Rangers wanted to kill him, so Romeo Subaldo, an attorney who worked for the church and had known Moret from the BCC, posted a guard outside Joaquin's room—not that it would have done much good if the Rangers really had wanted to get in. But because Joaquin was afraid to stay there, he was moved as soon as the doctor said he was able to the home of Father Niall O'Brien.

If Joaquin wanted to keep a low profile, O'Brien might have seemed an improbable guardian. The military had identified the priest as one of the island's leading Communist provocateurs and had accused him of everything from carnapping to subversion, murder, and any number of other heinous yet unproven affronts to the good citizens of Negros. The fact that O'Brien was a priest made him less of a target, although the priesthood was no *anting anting.* Father Narciso Pico, a forty-two-year-old advocate of land reform and a vocal opponent of planter-financed vigilantes, was murdered in broad daylight in the town of Pontevedra, about midway between Bacolod and Himamaylan. Unlike Pico, though, O'Brien had the additional advantage of being a white foreigner, which, in this postcolonial culture, also reduced the chances of his being murdered.

O'Brien is a man with a restless sensibility who seems to thrive on a life that constantly fails to live up to the idealized script he has fashioned for it. As a child in Dublin, O'Brien read about the Society of St. Columban, a group of Irish missionaries who had been working in China since 1920, and decided to become a priest. But by the time he was ordained in 1963, Mao Zedong had expelled the Columbans, many of whom relocated to the Philippines, where they built the country's largest foreign missionary society. O'Brien was assigned to Negros and spent the next quarter-century there.

For five years he lived with sugarcane workers just north of Himamaylan on a hacienda owned by the Yulos, one of the island's wealthiest families. He got to know workers' problems as well as anyone and quickly figured out why so many young people were picking up the gun. "If you accept the 'Just War Theory,' then the NPA has all the conditions here on Negros to justify rebellion," O'Brien says. Yet he personally remained an unreconstructed pacifist, and his Bacolod residence and office, directly behind the Sugarland Hotel, is filled with pacifist religious magazines that have eye-glazing titles like *Reality, Reconciliation, Fellowship, Survival, Peace*

News, and *Word.* His personal diaries—written in Gaelic and French to confound the police, should they decide to steal them—are replete with accounts of his efforts to dissuade various victims of military abuses from taking revenge or joining the rebels. And he actively promoted "peace zones," which challenged both the Army and the NPA to take their war somewhere else. The idea was to organize people in a growing multiplicity of small communities who would refuse to have anything to do with armed combatants of any persuasion and to eventually deny them any battlefield at all. It was an idea well ahead of its time, however, and was rejected by both warring parties.

Despite his pacifism, O'Brien's vision for Negros clearly had more in common with that of the rebels than that of the caciques. When Father Luís Jalandoni went underground following Marcos's declaration of martial law, O'Brien took him in. In his book, *Revolution from the Heart,* O'Brien wrote that Jalandoni's decision to join the rebels "probably did more to legitimize the revolution for church people on Negros" than any other single action.

O'Brien was also heavily involved in the BCC and in building cooperatives. Moreover, in what the elite took as a direct affront, he attempted to rescue the liturgy from the oblivion of disembodied spiritualism and its obsessive concern with the afterlife, insisting that the "Word" be applied to daily life on Negros. It was a theology guaranteed to drive the *hacenderos* bananas. O'Brien's reconstructed baptismal sacrament asked the devout to affirm their belief that Christ had come into the world "to bring good news to the poor and to liberate the oppressed," a pronouncement that, if nothing else, convinced elite families to have their children baptized by someone other than O'Brien. Where renunciations once consisted of attacks on the shadowy nemesis Satan, O'Brien rewrote them to condemn such worldly manifestations of the Devil as land-grabbing, militarization, usury, and torture, the very things that had made Sugarlandia such a comfortable place for those at the top—a sort of "safety net" for oligarchs.

O'Brien and other priests, as well as growing numbers of ordinary citizens like Moret De los Santos and Fred Veraguas, threatened the rich above all because they were getting people to speak up for themselves. "Silence of ordinary people," O'Brien wrote in *Revolution from the Heart,* "has been the most decisive political act of the twentieth century."

For O'Brien to claim he was a pacifist and anti-Communist was hard for many of the island's most powerful people to believe. Even those sympathetic to his efforts on behalf of the poor could not help but notice that most of the priests refused to condemn specific acts of violence by the NPA, in a failure of will or moral vision O'Brien acknowledges was a mistake.

In 1983 it was the Negros establishment that, with the help of President Marcos, sought to silence O'Brien once and for all, charging him, two other priests, and six BCC workers with murdering Pablo Sola, the mayor of Kabankalan, the town due south of Himamaylan. Sola's untimely death in a hail of gunfire was silently applauded by a significant segment of the local populace. At the time of his death, the mayor was under indictment in connection with the torture and murder of seven peasants who were allegedly buried alive in a sugarcane field about 150 yards from his home. Sola's legal counsel was another pillar of Negros society, warlord Armando Gustilo of Cadiz, then president of the National Federation of Sugarcane Planters. Gustilo, a tiny man, operated the island's largest private army and was known as the bionic warlord because he had transplanted kidneys, no gall bladder, and eyes that shed a constant, uncontrollable stream of tears. He effectively controlled the military in northern Negros, including the notorious Civilian Home Defense Force, a national paramilitary organization set up to fight the Communists and maintain order in the barrios. The CHDF, which was filled with poorly trained recruits, many of them criminals, was notorious for its abuse of the civilian population. In 1985, Gustilo allegedly ordered the militia to fire on striking sugar workers in the town of Escalante, resulting in the deaths of twenty-one people. One of Marcos's closest friends, Gustilo was given control over a newly created province, Northern Negros, which was carved out especially for him so that, aided by his private army, he could rig the voting to favor the dictator in the 1986 presidential election.

Needless to say, Gustilo was powerful enough to guarantee that there would be no possibility of Mayor Sola being convicted. But in true Negros fashion, Sola was murdered before his case ever came to trial. Although the NPA had claimed responsibility for the killing, and a police investigation had confirmed that the NPA was indeed responsible, charges were nevertheless leveled against O'Brien and the others.

The trial of the Negros Nine, as they were baptized, was one of the more ham-fisted efforts by the island's warlords and the Marcos dictatorship to discredit the Negros church, but it suggested the lengths to which powerful Negrenses would go to silence their enemies. Both sides knew from the outset that the charges were preposterous. O'Brien had been in Manila for the entire month, up to and including the date of Sola's slaying, and most of the other defendants had equally plausible alibis. None of that mattered in the fantasy world in which Marcos and his friends operated. The dictator had by then embarked on a crusade to destroy the activist elements in the church and wasn't about to let the facts get in the way. Eventually the case became such an embarrassment to Marcos internationally that a face-saving agreement was reached to drop the charges —but not before O'Brien had spent four months in jail, the lay workers more than a year. As a condition of the settlement, O'Brien was forced to leave the Philippines; he didn't return until after the 1986 People Power Revolution. In his absence, Marcos's campaign against the church continued.

The Negros Nine proved a useful, if temporary, vehicle for rallying the opposition to Marcos on Negros. The trial was also tremendous publicity for the very Basic Christian Community that the dictator and the oligarchs found so threatening, and it reinforced O'Brien's faith in the power of active nonviolence. As a young man, O'Brien had been schooled in the practical applications of martyrdom. "When I was in seminary, we would read the *Martyrologia* in Latin over breakfast," he said. "There were two hundred priests sitting there, and each day they'd read about people being drawn and quartered, roasted alive, this one with his arms chopped off, beheadings, et cetera. This was served to us every morning with our tea." It was a menu consisting of what the editor of one martyrology described with ghoulish enthusiasm as "persecutions as various and horrible as the mind of man, inspired by the Devil, could invent." Even though O'Brien said he and most of his fellow priests found the daily incantation of horrors "ludicrous," after living on Negros since 1964, he became an expert in exploiting cases of persecution and victimization for his own social agenda. "I find myself recalling a new *Martyrologia,* getting life and strength from all these simple people who have been killed."

The identification with victims and martyrs runs like a dark vein through Filipino culture, constituting one of its recurring themes. Indeed, the country's heroes are almost invariably martyrs. Three priests publicly garroted by the Spaniards in 1872, and Dr. José Rizal, the writer and father of the country, are the great heroes of Philippine nationalism and of the 1898 revolution; the greatest modern-day hero is Ninoy Aquino, whose assassination led to the collapse of the Marcos dictatorship. Ninoy's case is perhaps the archetype of the country's martyr complex. Ninoy himself practically yearned to be assassinated. Following a three-year exile in the United States, he predicted that he would be murdered on his return to the Philippines. (He was actually killed as he walked down the airplane's steps, minutes after arriving in his homeland.) The speech he'd prepared to deliver at the Manila airport contained this sentence: "According to Gandhi, the willing sacrifice of the innocent is the most powerful answer to insolent tyranny that has yet been conceived by God and man." Prescience and a flair for the theatrical dictated that Ninoy wear white, as Rizal had before his firing squad, a clean canvas for the bloody scene he anticipated. His mother, Doña Aurora, forbade the morticians to clean up the body, which was put on public display in its open casket so that none of the horror would be lost on the hundreds of thousands of mourners who came to pay their respects.

Ninoy had called death "the final liberation," and his sacrifice eventually brought down a dictator. Rather than rallying the masses to revolution, though, Filipino martyrs have collectively reinforced the fatalistic notion that worldly liberation is an abstraction, that the only true liberation lies beyond the grave.

Nevertheless, the martyrs continue to be exploited by politicians, the government, the NPA, and particularly by the church. In their struggle with the *hacenderos,* the Negros priests and activists seized on the most horrific brutalities to argue their cause. Time and again, the mutilated bodies of the dead would be raised up as catalysts for mobilization, just as the church over the centuries has resurrected its martyrs as beacons of the faith. "Martyrdom is the final accomplishment of life," wrote the Peruvian Gustavo Gutiérrez, whose *Theology of Liberation* was so influential on Negros. "What brought Jesus to his death, and is bringing his present-day followers to their death, is precisely the coherence of message and commitment. It has traditionally been said that the church is enriched by the blood of the martyrs; the present vitality, amid distress, of the people of God . . . is due in great part to the same experience." As for the living heroes who occasionally rise up among the Filipino people, as Ninoy did in exile and his widow did in 1986, they are, more often than not, swiftly cut down by enemies and friends alike.

In parades, rallies, funeral masses, film, and literature, the dead have been glorified on Negros, and everyone knew that the De los Santoses would be elevated to the local pantheon of martyrs. "The crowning glory for Moret and his family," a church publication proclaimed, came "when the Fourth Scout Ranger soldiers strafed their home, killing him and his wife and three children." Similarly, an obituary for Moret's friend Fred Veraguas called him a "prophet" and martyrdom his "last and most powerful word." The church later produced a poster showing the dead body of Fred and the faces of the De los Santoses, accompanied by the message, "The blood of the martyrs is the seed of Christianism."

It is highly unlikely that Moret and Cerila would ever have thought of themselves as Christian martyrs, as "witnesses," or that they would ever have conceived of following such a path as that chosen by Ninoy Aquino. In April 1252, a Dominican inquisitor, Saint Peter, was lying on the ground dying from multiple stab wounds when he dipped his finger in his blood and wrote his final words in the dirt: *Credo in Deum*, "I believe in God." What Cerila De los Santos wrote with her own blood—MOROY—seemed more an anguished cry for revenge. And Cerila's only surviving son was consumed by thoughts of revenge. In his fantasies, Joaquin saw himself in the Army, searching for the men who killed his parents, brothers, and sister, waiting for his moment. He would have to be patient, Joaquin told himself, enter the Philippine Military Academy, work from inside the beast, slowly and methodically, until he had killed every last one of them. But as the priests prepared to bury the unshriven remains of the De los Santos family, they had a quite different script in mind for Joaquin.

Shortly before the funeral, Father O'Brien asked Joaquin to discuss the massacre for a weekly television show called *The Negros Church in Focus*. The program that eventually aired was a fairly straightforward account of the massacre as told by various eyewitnesses. Joaquin stood before his bullet-riddled house in his basketball jersey, his shoulder bandaged, his arm in a sling, and told his story—how the Rangers came and killed members of his family one by one, how they tried to kill him, and so on. True, the show was not entirely balanced (the military's position was not presented), but it was the only serious attempt to call attention to the event, and it was provocative enough to elicit howls of protest from elite viewers and an angry letter of warning from the church superior in charge of the television station. "It has been observed that your program, 'Negros Church,' has deviated from its original format . . . and has been featuring coverages [sic] of protest rallies/walks, massacres, interviews of victims of atrocities, et cetera. In view of this, we are reminding you to stick to the original format of the program, or we will be constrained to effect its cancellation." Bacolod society might have been willing to tolerate the slaughter of the De los Santoses, but it was not about to have its nose rubbed in it.

Perhaps the most interesting part of the interview with Joaquin was a brief segment that was edited out before the television audience got to see it. In it, Father O'Brien asked Joaquin to describe how it felt to be suddenly orphaned. Without hesitating for an instant, Joaquin replied: "The only thing I can do now is to try to get revenge." Before he could elaborate, the camera recorded a short discussion between O'Brien and Father Brendan O'Connell, who was filming the interview, and then the screen went blank. When the tape resumes, Joaquin is asked again to describe his feelings, but this time he offers a dramatically different and decidedly more "Christian" response, suggesting a miraculous epiphany. "I don't have the capacity for revenge," he now says. "I leave everything in the hands of God, and because of my faith, it seems the Lord has looked after me."

Years later, Joaquin would recall this interview with amusement. "They didn't like what I said." But Joaquin also acknowledged that the priests may have been trying to save his life. "They said they had been thrown in jail for saying things like what I had wanted to say."

O'Brien said Joaquin had been preoccupied with revenge, although, surprisingly, he said the boy never discussed joining the NPA. "I know Joaquin. He lived with me for six months and he couldn't spell NPA," O'Brien said. "He was mesmerized by the Army. Even after the massacre he wanted to join the military. He wanted to be a soldier. Can you imagine? He wanted to kill the killers. I remember one night he went out drinking with a bunch of Army guys and came back saying they'd help him find the killers." O'Brien insists he did not impose his beliefs on Joaquin. But he, Father Gill, and others had long discussions with Joaquin before the funeral. "Revenge is a major cultural theme here," O'Brien said. "I felt we owed it to Joaquin to share our point of view that hate is wrong."

On his visit to the De los Santos house with Joaquin, O'Brien had seen the family's Santo Cristo, the sepulchre with its shattered glass front and the remains of its plaster figurines spilled out on the floor. He said Joaquin's relatives were afraid to remove the failed icons from the house, but O'Brien recovered a brown plaster crucifix that had hung in Moret and Cerila's bedroom. "I remember sitting with Joaquin and holding the crucifix," O'Brien recalled, fondling the seven-inch-long icon with exposed rusty brown wires. "It had been hit by two bullets. I sat there with the crucifix, and I said, 'When the bullets went through your family, they went through the Lord.' I said, 'I feel great anger, and it's all right to feel anger, but hate is a spiritual disease.' And I told him he had to choose. Will you be a disciple of Christ and forgive them for what they did, or a disciple of the military, which has written on its trucks, 'We Never Forgive'?"

Whether Joaquin absorbed O'Brien's message or not, he later attributed his own survival to the fact that his gunshot wound was in the same place on his body as was a gash in the bullet-pocked plaster crucifix.

A church statement announced that there would be a requiem mass for the family four days after the massacre. "The church is urging the people to take the courageous step of both denouncing the evil and also forgiving, in the Spirit which Jesus taught us during this holy season." A thousand people showed up. They pressed into the Snows Church at 2 P.M., dipped their fingers in the white alabaster font at the entrance, passed the Santo Entierro in his glass coffin, and packed the wooden pews. The mourners were peasant farmers, fishermen, sugar workers, and members of the BCC. The National Federation of Sugar Workers and the League of Filipino Students, another alleged front organization, also sent groups of their supporters down from Bacolod. People came in solidarity, out of curiosity, to express their sympathies, or for reassurance, increasingly aware that they were all potential targets. They pushed to the front of the church below the dais, and they milled around the silver coffins, each with a bouquet of wildflowers and a large pink and blue ribbon set on a piece of green fern. People wanted to see the children in their tiny caskets, the bandaged face of Cerila, and the bullethole in Moret's forehead.

The sanctuary was stifling, the air thick with sweat, and women and men were cooling their faces with waves of handkerchiefs, pieces of paper, and little hand-held fans, woven fans, bamboo and plastic fans, paper fans, in every color of the rainbow. Someone had hung a giant poster of the doe-eyed gamine from the *Les Misérables* musical, an incongruous icon of homogenized sorrow, to the right of the huge crucifix that is the focal point of the church.

Vicente Navarra, the recently inducted bishop of southern Negros, presided over the mass wearing a blood-red skullcap, joined by Bishop Fortich and twenty-nine priests in white vestments with gold, embroidered stoles. Also in attendance were seven Army Scout Rangers in civilian dress and a handful of civilian informants who were sent by Captain Melvin Gutierrez. Joaquin De los Santos sat in the sanctuary surrounded by a phalanx of priests and nuns, who feared an attempt to kill him. The portly but youthful-looking Bishop Navarra hadn't fully acclimated himself to the new political environment in which he found himself, and although he would eventually issue a single strong attack on the military and the political elite for their ongoing assaults against members of the Basic Christian Community, he remained a very traditional priest who defined his mission as one of spiritual awakening and healing, divorced from either politics or economics. Navarra's was the voice of the old, immutable church reasserting itself, the church whose rituals Elias Canetti described as "an infinite dilution of lament spread so evenly over the centuries that scarcely anything remains of the suddenness of death and the violence of grief."

Bishop Navarra didn't see his role as one of eulogizing the De los Santoses. What was there to say, anyway? That Cerila was demure, quiet, and reserved, that she brought the children to school, took them to church, worked in the barrio health program? What high point in the lives of the children might constitute an appropriate testimonial? Jun Jun playing with toy cars made from tin cans, or walking in his sleep? Mary Joy—they called her Kulong, or Curly, because of her hair—chasing ducks outside the house? Joenes riding the carabao as he went into the fields with Moret? Navarra couldn't very well explain that the children were all afraid of the winged witches, *aswangs,* that could poke their long tongues through the roof of a hut and suck the life from you while you slept. And Moret—the devout Catholic, defender of the BCC, Communist, murderer of Serafin Gatuslao, and friend or enemy of Moroy, depending on whom you believed—which Moret might Bishop Navarra choose to eulogize?

The bishop said nothing about any of them. Didn't even mention their names. It was almost as if they were immaterial to the greater spiritual mission at hand, as if the only people who mattered were the saints and angels of the Scriptures. Navarra painted a picture of Negros in broad Biblical strokes. He said he didn't know who was responsible for the massacre—which wasn't quite true, because everyone knew it was the Army Rangers, and Navarra had been fully briefed about the incident—but he condemned the killers and those who sent them to kill the De los Santoses, as well as the men who had strafed a home in Candoni a month earlier, killing the wife of a BCC leader and three children. "They have sinned not only against people, but against God—most especially against God," the bishop said. The massacres resulted from "the perversion of man" and the fact that men had strayed from God. Navarra alluded to Cain and Abel and condemned those who are "concerned only with power and are influenced by evil, who refuse to listen to reason anymore." He compared the latest massacres to the slaying of the firstborn in Egypt and to Herod's killing of "the innocents," his attempt to kill the Christ child by ordering the deaths of all of Bethlehem's male children under two years of age.

"This pestilence in our land is the work of agents of darkness, trying to mislead and divide us," the bishop continued in his even, measured tones. He acknowledged the widespread foreboding of his parishioners in southern Negros, including many of those in his audience, and adjured them to ask for God's help. "People are asking me, 'What will be the next place?' It has already happened in

Isabela, in Bacolod, in Candoni. Where next? I cannot really tell you where, but what we must do is pray to God so that He may help us, so that these incidents will be avoided. If we only depend on ourselves, we cannot do anything. We must ask for the intercession of God." The bishop warned the faithful against responding with hatred and vengeance. He told the mourners that God had allowed the killings "so we will be enlightened."

It was nice to believe the deaths had not been entirely pointless. On the other hand, the concept was hard to digest. The church was forever finding meaning no one else could fathom in these atrocities; there had just been so many of these "lessons" lately. Were people supposed to find meaning in all of them, or merely be moved by the cemetery of numbers? What exactly was His plan? Sometimes a world with a God was even more horrifying than a world without one. As the bishop held forth, Joaquin, in his green and white basketball shirt, sobbed into a rag.

A carefully arranged symbolic offertory followed the prelate's remarks. Two cardboard rifles, each three feet high, and a papier-mâché bullet the size of a grown man were brought to the altar, where a priest prayed that the weapons be turned into farm implements. A ten-foot-high crucifix with the names of the De los Santoses nailed to it was paraded down the center aisle. "This cross is being offered to you, O Lord my God, as a symbol of our sufferings and the hardship of our people," a voice said. "Like the man You created with dignity but who has his freedom no more." A blue-gray dove was released from a bamboo cage, flew toward the ceiling, then settled on the crossbeam of the crucifix. Finally, someone turned on a tape recorder and Joaquin listened to his own disembodied voice broadcast over the loudspeakers. The priests had asked him to record his statement so that he wouldn't have to make himself a ready target by standing in front of the crowd. On the tape, Joaquin renounced any desire to seek revenge and said he had no "evil intentions" against those responsible for the massacre, a statement that surprised many in the audience because it was rare that anyone publicly relinquished the right to seek revenge. To hear it from the lone surviving son was astonishing. Most people assumed not only that the survivors of such a horrendous incident would do everything in their power to avenge the deaths but also that it was their obligation. "Father, forgive them, for they know not what they do," the young voice from the loudspeakers intoned. It was Joaquin's final statement to his family, but one he only half believed.

The funeral procession, dotted by hundreds of colorful umbrellas, snaked nearly a mile from Our Lady of the Snows Church, the coffins carried by hand north along Route 1, then onto a narrow road lined with bamboo trees and seven-foot-tall sunflowers. A gray concrete arch marked the entrance to the main cemetery, a low wall of stones running away from it to either side. Two prominent mausoleums stood just inside the cemetery amid an otherwise ordinary jumble of tombstones. The smell of goats, tethered to some of the markers, wafted across the wall. The mausoleum for the family of Francisco Ramos looked like a fanciful, gated house with eight swimming pool–blue steps leading up to it and two tall angels on its roof. The other large mausoleum was the fenced-in grave of Don Serafin Gatuslao—grandfather of the Serafin Gatuslao Moret allegedly had killed—and his wife Julita Monton, which was decorated with another angel and a garland and crucifix painted in the same shade of aquamarine. The remains of the De los Santoses were not carried through the arch but instead were brought along the road that runs parallel to the cemetery's stone wall, to the very back of a nearly empty adjoining lot, a recently created, public paupers' cemetery. There, in the midday heat and shimmering, dizzying air, they were placed beside an already prepared grave just in front of a sugarcane field.

Many of the mourners refused to approach the dark open wound in the ground, afraid that there might be soldiers hiding in the thick sugarcane. Father Gill sprinkled holy water on the coffins as Joaquin trembled and the girl, Juvi, wailed, her sister Jenelyn holding her tight. Then someone said a prayer, the coffin lids were sealed over the glass windows, and five men standing in the wide common grave received each of the coffins of the five De los Santoses. Finally, the dark earth was shoveled over them amid the sobbing of friends and relatives, the sweet voices of people singing, "Our Father, Who art in Heaven, hallowed be Thy name," and the bloodcurdling cries of revenge from members of the League of Filipino Students. "A blood debt will be paid," the students chanted. "The debt will be paid with blood."

Mario and
the Chicken

Mario Chiu is an intense and earnest man with a passion for aphorisms and a convoluted way of making a point. At the same time, he has no particular axe to grind and is willing to entertain arguments that undermine or contradict his own, a quality rare among the island's often didactic cane planters but one that allowed him to become friends with Moret De los Santos. Separated by more than twenty years, the two could not be described as intimates, but they were about as close as the boundaries of Negros society would allow, which is to say that, in Mario's eyes, Moret had succeeded in rising above the indistinguishable anthills of peasants whom rich Negrenses encounter in their comings and goings without a blush of recognition. Mario was able to attach a name to Moret's face, knew where he lived, that he worked for the Tongsons, and that he had a brood of children who played along the Mambagaton Road and in the stream where fierce-looking *halo-halos,* two-foot-long iguanas, come to drink at night. Every time Mario traveled to or from his Hacienda Calance in the foothills of Mambagaton, he would pass by Moret's home, and he and the De los Santoses would wave to one another. If they crossed paths in the market, they greeted one another respectfully. Mario's regard for Moret made him more than a mere acquaintance, and he will sometimes refer to him as "a good friend." Still, he knew little about Moret or Moret about him, and the two were not the kind of friends who would have staked their lives for each other.

When Mario learned about the De los Santos massacre, he was horrified, even more so since he'd suspected that something was amiss the night before, when someone asked to borrow his car so a group of soldiers and planters could conduct a "surveillance" of the De los Santos home. With the news of the massacre, that little piece of undigested intrigue fell into place, and he himself had become an accessory. It was amazing how easy it was to be engaged even when you did your best to remain aloof. Even though he hadn't really known, hadn't been a willing accomplice, hadn't been in on the planning, Mario felt a certain responsibility. He also knew the surviving De los Santoses would be grateful for whatever help he could give them, and he immediately ordered one of his men to deliver a sack of rice to the house. It was, in the greater scheme of things, not much of a gesture, but it was more than most people did, and Jenelyn De los Santos was deeply appreciative. Even today she has only kind words for Mario.

As Mario remembers it, he first met Moret De los Santos when he was driving down the Mambagaton Road one day from Hacienda Calance, not exactly barreling toward the highway, but moving at the normal thirty-odd mile-per-hour clip the road will tolerate before exacting its revenge on a vehicle. He was just about to reach Ernesto Tongson's prawn farm when he caught a fleeting glimpse of an opalescent, green-black chicken that was startled by the oncoming vehicle and, in a fraction of a second, seemed to calculate the best avenue of retreat, began to move away from the road, reconsidered, and then inexplicably, suicidally, darted under the front wheels of Mario's jeep. Mario slammed on his brakes, flattening the bird in a squawk of dust.

Now the local protocol for a road kill obliged Mario to stop, look for the owner of the bird, and attempt to make him whole. But Mario had a busy day ahead of him, and he knew that the ostensibly simple matter of settling on a payment for a chicken held out the potential for an afternoon of complex negotiations. "Hit and run" isn't a normal prescription for drivers, but many Filipinos will tell you that even if you hit a human being, the best thing to do is to beat a hasty retreat, that if you stick around to find out whether you killed someone you run the risk of being torn apart by a mob of outraged relatives. Even if you survive, you might be forced to pay an extravagant recompense to settle the score.

A similar logic applies to farm animals. Take a chicken such as the one Mario Chiu had just pulverized on the Mambagaton Road. Conventional wisdom has it that, despite the fact that thousands of chickens are mangled on the country's roads on any given day of the week, the odds of hitting a normal, run-of-the-barnyard fryer are something on the order of one in a million. The exaggeration makes the point: Despite the fact that garden variety chickens are a common sight on the country's roadways, most of the chickens killed by drivers, or rather by drivers dumb enough to stop, turn out to be prized breeding cocks about to deliver a dozen golden eggs. Thus, a driver who should probably shell out fifty or sixty pesos for a dead bird will more likely end up negotiating over the mama hen and a dozen baby chicks valued in the thousands of pesos. Mario knew all of this, but being the honorable man that he is, he stepped down from the cab of his jeep, where his eyes met those of Moret De los Santos, who was approaching the road from the direction of Tongson's prawn pond.

Mario could see immediately that the bird lying at his feet was not any average piece of poultry but was, in fact, a fighting cock, and he offered profuse apologies, telling Moret he was prepared to pay him whatever he thought the bird was worth. To Mario's surprise, Moret would have nothing to do with the offer, insisting that he'd witnessed the whole incident, that it was clearly an accident, and that Mario shouldn't give it another thought. Since such transparent grace may be a face-saving way of inviting the offending party to press the case for compensation, or a poor man's awkwardness when confronted by someone of means, Mario persisted in trying to get Moret to accept a payment. But Moret held his ground. The two men talked for a few minutes, shook hands, and Mario departed, impressed that someone of Moret's transparently modest means would fail to exploit such an easy windfall to his own advantage.

Moret's friends described him as generous to a fault—a man who would buy drinks at the cockpit and lend money to just about anyone—so one could fairly assume he felt it would be wrong to exploit the situation. Although there was no reason to question Moret's motives in this little matter, it was a fact that he was shrewd, practical, thoroughly conversant with a culture that rarely let magnanimity go unrewarded, and he would have known intuitively that a rich man like Mario Chiu could someday prove a valuable ally. Also, Moret was a gambler, and he could easily have calculated that wagering the value of one dead fighting cock on the assumption of Mario's friendship would be a pretty good investment. It was a simple matter of *utang na loob*. Mario was in his debt.

Mario believes Moret was murdered to scare people involved with the church and the Basic Christian Community. "The De los Santos family was a sacrificial lamb. They had to make an example of someone," he said, remaining deliberately vague about who exactly "they" were but leaving no doubt that local sugar planters were involved. Mario also said some of the killings by the military, the vigilantes, and the right-wing planters were reprisals for terrorist attacks by the NPA and the so-called fronts, suggesting that De los Santos may have been killed to even some score, such as the murder of Serafin "Apin" Gatuslao. "Because there's so much injustice, you take justice into your own hands," he explained—the "you" referring to people like himself and his planter friends. "It's not only the poor who do this; the rich also do it."

In the immediate aftermath of Gatuslao's killing, there had been a lot of private discussion about how his death would be avenged, although no one in Mambagaton recalled hearing any specific mention of Moret. Moret knew Apin; he'd worked for him briefly years before. But no one knew of any feud. Even members of the Gatuslao family said Moret had nothing to do with the killing. Moret's family, close friends, and neighbors all dismissed suggestions that he had ever had links with the NPA. "Moret worked for a living" was the way his neighbor Rudi Garcia summed up the collective wisdom, as if to say that Moret wouldn't have time to waste running around with a bunch of desperate, thieving, Communist misfits.

Even if he was just getting by, Moret had steady work, a job he couldn't afford to put at risk by antagonizing his anti-Communist boss, a house to protect, and a big family to provide for. The De los Santoses were also deeply religious, Moret had informed for the military, and his son was trying to get into the Philippine Military Academy. At least on the surface, the De los Santoses appeared to be improbable recruits to the revolutionary movement. Rudi Garcia, for one, sees the stories tying Moret to the NPA as nothing but an after-the-fact rationalization for the massacre. "Those stories about the NPA only started after Moret was dead."

Nevertheless, the stories linking Moret to the Gatuslao slaying were repeated by the military and took hold in some peoples' minds, and Mario Chiu couldn't dismiss them out of hand for the simple reason that, although he respected Moret, Serafin Gatuslao had been his lifelong friend. Indeed, it would be fair to say that Mario Chiu loved Apin. *Tito* Apin—he called him—Uncle Apin. Mario loved Apin's wife, Panching, and he adored their daughter, Myla Christine, whom everyone called Bambi. Mario had grown up with the Gatuslaos, and *Tito* Apin was like a second father. He was a close friend, a *kumpare,* of Mario's real father, Juan Andama Chiu, who, when he first came to Himamaylan, had befriended Apin and remained loyal to him until the day he died.

Mario remembers the dragonflies that darted around the sugar fields when he was a little boy, how he and Bambi used to catch them, and how they'd hide below the bamboo slats of his father's cottage floor, listening to the click and shuffle of ivory mah-jongg tiles above them as their fathers passed the afternoons gambling and telling stories. From time to time *Tito* Apin or Juan would drop a coin through the slats and laugh as the children scurried after it. Mario says Apin used to cheat when he played mah-jongg, that he liked to provoke people, but only for fun. His friends expected it. Mario talks about Apin's marriage to Panching as if it was something he'd lifted from a romance novel. Panching was "my ideal woman," Mario says. "I saw them together constantly, from morning until evening." Panching, beautiful and intelligent, managed the family business and was able to keep the volatile Apin under control. "Apin always showed his feelings. He was too aggressive. But Panching knew how to cool him down when he got angry."

Mario could see the same qualities in Bambi and fell in love with her. It was easy to imagine being with her, like Panching and Apin, always together, taking care of each other. If you had money on Negros, it could be a good life. But Bambi had other ideas. "I courted her for three years. Then she broke up with me," Mario says, and it's clear from the way he tells the story that she also broke his heart. The day Apin was killed, Mario met her in Bacolod. He remembers that she gave him a kiss. A few weeks later she moved to California.

For all these reasons, Mario couldn't ignore the charge against Moret. He was savvy enough to know how worthless *tsismis* could be, though, and didn't believe everything he heard. If Moret had been involved with the NPA, Mario was inclined to believe that it was probably as "an accessory," that he might have been "used" by the rebels or forced to help them. Mario knew firsthand what that was like, that anyone could be squeezed by the NPA or the military or both. It had happened to him.

Although he was inclined to give De los Santos the benefit of the doubt, Apin Gatuslao was family, and Mario's loyalty to him was bound up with memories of Juan Chiu and matters of inheritance, the years of hard work his father had devoted to his land and to securing the comforts Mario and his mother enjoyed, all of which made it impossible for Mario to say that he fully trusted Moret. As a general rule, when it came to anything that mattered, people tended to be wary of anyone outside their immediate family and circle of closest friends; sometimes even they couldn't be trusted.

Mario had heard that the plot to kill Gatuslao had been hatched in Moret's house, and while the fact that he was killed so close to where Moret lived and worked wasn't exactly evidence, it wasn't nothing, either. When forced to ponder the random pieces of this puzzle, Mario acknowledged that Moret made him a little uneasy, made him think that oftentimes when he'd observed his neighbor, Moret really did seem to be up to something, something Mario couldn't quite put his finger on. "He always had a sour face," Mario recalled, to cite just one example. "I would spot him in church, and he'd always be looking around, sneaking looks at people." On reflection, Mario said Moret probably had some link to the underground. "He wasn't exactly working for the NPA, but for one of the fronts," Mario surmised, although he said it as though it were fact.

"From the vapor of suspicion is evolved the certainty of intended wrong," General Arthur MacArthur wrote about the Negrenses shortly after the Americans wrested the Philippines from Spain in 1899. It wasn't that they were paranoid; rather they harbored an inbred caution and wariness, a conspiratorial sensibility fostered by three centuries of Spanish colonialism. The mistrust, the debilitating doubts and fear manifest in the conflict between the landowners and the military, on the one hand, and the NPA and the landless, on the other, are of ancient vintage. It is a pervasive, socially corrosive phenomenon found at all levels of the society—in the government bureaucracies, among politicians and businessmen, in the cities and barrios, and between such "good friends" as Mario and Moret.

Part
Two

The Gatuslaos

The worst form of oppression is internal colonialism,
and Filipino nationalists never address that. The country
is being plundered by oligarchs.

—F. Sionil José

During most of the three-hundred-year Spanish occupation, the Negros church was like a man stranded on a tiny island,
floating messages in bottles, waiting to be rescued. The priests were
largely cut off from Manila and Spain, and even the island of Panay,
only nineteen miles away and visible from the northwest shore of
Negros, remained a distant neighbor. The isolation was a simple
matter of economics: Negros had a minuscule population and in the
eyes of the Spanish government in Manila was of no economic consequence. The popular wisdom neatly summarized the forlorn friars'
predicament: "The Governor-General is in Manila, the King is in
Spain, and God is in heaven."

Between 1840 and 1850, all that began to change. Almost without
warning, Negros was caught up in a frenzy of exploration and agricultural development, an economic boom that would last for the
next five decades and radically transform the face of this pristine
backwater. Between 1850 and 1893, the population leaped from
30,000 to 320,000, forests were cleared and replaced by farms and
plantations, and roads, schools, prisons, and churches were built.
The reason for all of this growth could be stated in a single word:
sugar.

During the first part of the nineteenth century, sugar represented
an insignificant percentage of the national economy. As recently as
1819, the sale of bird's nests had been a larger source of export in-

come. In 1855, however, the Spanish government in Manila opened the port of Iloilo on nearby Panay Island to foreign commerce, setting off a chain of events that led to the creation of the Negros sugar industry. Settled by Chinese merchants in the fourteenth century and occupied by the Spaniards since the sixteenth, Iloilo had become a thriving commercial center dominated by a Chinese mestizo business class that oversaw production of fine handwoven fabrics of cotton, pineapple fibers, and silk. But with the opening of its port, Iloilo fell victim to the industrial revolution, as cheap, machine-made cotton cloth began pouring in from England. Within a decade, the local economy had collapsed.

The English shipping companies, looking for something to bring home in their empty holds, hit on sugar, which was ideally suited to the soil of Negros. With the foreigners offering credit and a guaranteed market, Panay's Chinese mestizo textile merchants, traders, and investors, along with thousands of peasant farmers, began streaming across the narrow Guimaras Strait to Negros, clearing its rain forest and planting sugar.

Sugar production, boosted by the introduction of the first steam mills, soared from 200 tons in 1850 to 120,000 tons in 1893, by which time sugar exports from Negros accounted for a fifth of the nation's total foreign exchange earnings. Negros had suddenly become the principal engine of the Philippine economy.

But sugar not only created capital, it also created class: a sugar elite that began to usurp the once sacred domain of the church as the political, economic, and spiritual life force of the island. An island the Spanish friars had run like some Sunday school–cum–penal colony was remade according to the rules of the free market and the law of the jungle. Where Catholic dogma had long defined the island's culture and values, both were now tempered by the interests of the new sugar elite. Salvation took a backseat to the accumulation of wealth.

Among the wave of Chinese mestizo immigrants from Panay who arrived in Negros between 1855 and 1860 were Agustin Gatuslao and his sister Agustina, who moved from the town of Guimbal and settled in Murcia, twelve miles from Bacolod. Agustin Gatuslao's descendants describe him as tall, fair-skinned, and handsome—although members of the Negrense elite almost invariably describe their ancestors in those terms, regardless of evidence one way or the other. Not much is actually known about Agustin, and Agustina is nearly as enigmatic. Variously referred to as a catechist, choir girl, and laundrywoman, she was wooed shortly after her arrival by a Basque Spaniard named Miguel Alvarez, who had been living on the eastern side of Negros until 1861, when Moro pirates attacked his village. Then twenty-nine, Alvarez moved to Murcia, where he lost no time pursuing a series of scandalous romances with attractive young women, including Agustina.

Today, Miguel Alvarez is referred to as the "founding father" of Murcia, but he was also the father of at least four children, including Serafin Gatuslao, the grandfather and namesake of Serafin "Apin" Gatuslao. That the first Serafin Gatuslao did not take the surname Alvarez but instead that of his mother was an act of discretion necessitated by the fact that Alvarez also happened to be Murcia's parish priest, *padre* to 2,500 souls at the Immaculate Conception Church. Normally, the church's *Libro de Ilegitimo* would have recorded the names of children born out of wedlock, but since that wouldn't do for the sons of a priest, the boys, Antonio and Serafin, were registered on the day of their baptisms as the children of Agustin Gatuslao and Eusebia Toledano Gatuslao, their uncle and aunt.

Although Alvarez was a member of the austere Order of the Augustinian Recollects, which had been given authority over Negros in 1848, leaders of that order seemed acutely conscious of the fact that the minds of restless young men assigned to remote tropical outposts might stray from Scripture to temptations of the flesh. One such leader, Sinibaldo de Mas, was suspiciously forgiving.

> Though it may appear evil, the offense is most excusable, especially in young and healthy men set down in a torrid climate. Duty continually struggles against nature. The garb of the native women is very seductive and girls, far from being unattainable, regard themselves as lucky to attract the attention of the curate, and their mothers and fathers share that sentiment. What virtue and stoicism does not the friar need to possess! . . . Those that criticize them concerning this point, should think what they would do if they were sent to a town without relatives or friends, or other compatriots with whom to converse.

Another local priest who also seemed to speak from direct experience was equally understanding:

> To send a young man out to what might be termed a desert,
> the only white man in the neighborhood, surrounded by elements of licentiousness, with nobody but the Almighty to look
> to, with the climatic conditions urging him to follow the same
> practices as surround him, it is a miracle if he does not fall. . . .
> He sees the women half-clothed . . . his eyes are opened, and if
> he is not strong, he will fall.

Alas, Father Alvarez apparently fell hard and frequently, and his philandering soon taxed the church's tolerance. By 1871 he had provoked enough *tsismis* that church leaders felt compelled to launch an inquiry. "The priest of Murcia, as it is known to the people, was on intimate terms with a woman," the bishop reported in a letter to his superior. "I exhorted him and admonished him to leave her." It is not known what action if any the church took, but the priest's second son, Serafin, was born four years later, and the people of Murcia apparently forgave Father Alvarez because he lived there another thirty years and, according to one church history, fathered "many many" children by at least two mistresses.

The Gatuslaos have no official, recorded history, but family members insist the elder Serafin Gatuslao, invariably referred to as Don Serafin, fell in love with a pretty but poor Murcia girl, much to the disappointment of Father Alvarez, who wanted his son to marry the daughter of Valeriano Monton, who, with more than three hundred acres recorded in his name, was the largest landowner in Himamaylan. Father Alvarez eventually prevailed on Don Serafin to abandon his flame and move to Himamaylan, where he courted and married Julita Monton.

Don Serafin made his home in Himamaylan shortly before Andrés Bonifacio initiated the first phase of the Philippine revolution against Spain in 1896. But the revolution on the main island of Luzon and the subsequent Philippine-American War barely registered on Negros. Nationalism was an emerging but undeveloped phenomenon among the educated Filipino elite in general, and many Negrenses still felt alienated from the center of power in Manila. They did not see their fate as linked with the cause of a greater

Philippine nation. Indeed, most of the Negros planters sided with Spain against Bonifacio's revolution, and some even helped raise an army of volunteers to defend the island against possible invaders. According to local historian Modesto Sa-Onoy, the tangible profits of sugar far outweighed the more speculative potential of independence from Spain. "While the revolution in Luzon raged, the concerns of the *hacenderos* were the milling of cane, the condition of the roads, the price of sugar, and the unprecedented target of two million piculs [133,000 tons] to be produced in Negros Occidental for crop year 1896–97," Sa-Onoy wrote in his *Negros Occidental History*.

By the time the *hacenderos* actually decided to join the fight, the revolution had been absorbed into the Spanish-American War and Spain had capitulated. Two months after Spain surrendered, as discussions over the terms of peace were under way in Paris, the Negrense revolutionaries finally made their move, ousting the Spaniards in Bacolod with a mostly make-believe army: more than a thousand Negrenses "armed" with "cannons" made of rolled-up bamboo mats mounted on carabao carts and sticks of sugarcane or nipa stalks with knives stuck in their ends to resemble rifles. From a distance, the 125-odd Spaniards defending the capital thought they were threatened by a formidable army and surrendered without firing a shot.

Nearly all the priests were deported, but Father Alvarez was permitted to remain behind on account of his age and failing health. A year later, however, following attacks on Murcia by rebels under the command of *baylans,* the native, animist priests, Alvarez departed for Spain, leaving his far-flung progeny behind. Meanwhile, the Spanish-American War had given way to the Philippine-American War, and the Negrense elite, recognizing the futility of waging war against the Americans, prudently surrendered one week after hostilities commenced and before a single shot was fired on Negros. The elite went back to their sugar plantations, but the *baylans* continued to resist, staging a series of raids on coastal towns and plantations that continued sporadically until 1907.

The most prominent of the *baylan* revolutionaries was a southern Negros farmer and herder known by his followers as Papa Isio, or Isio the Pope. Isio, who claimed he was guided by conversations with Jesus Christ himself, had organized a small army in Himamay-

lan and entered the war against Spain shortly after Bonifacio's uprising. When the existence of Isio's band was betrayed by Don Serafin
Gatuslao's father-in-law, Valeriano Monton, Isio and his men fled to
the mountains, where they raised an army of more than a thousand
men. Isio not only opposed the presence of the Spaniards, and now
the Americans, but represented the first serious challenge to the new
hacienda system. Indeed, he might be considered the island's first
proponent of land reform. A nativist who sought to return Negros to
its condition prior to the arrival of the Spaniards, Isio's agenda called
for the expulsion of the Spaniards and all non-Malay people, an end
to sugar production, and the dismantlement of the haciendas, which
were to be redistributed among the indigenous population. Not surprisingly, most of his ideas were anathema to *hacenderos* like Don
Serafin Gatuslao.

In 1902, Don Serafin, twenty-seven and the *presidente,* or mayor,
of Himamaylan, opened his home to a twenty-three-year-old American constabulary captain, John Roberts White, who had been sent to
Himamaylan to liquidate what he referred to as "outlaw wolves" and
"wild beasts of the nights"—the *baylans.* His principal target was
Papa Isio.

In his memoir, *Bullets and Bolos: Fifteen Years in the Philippine Islands,* White calls Don Serafin "the best friend of the Constabulary
in southern Negros." Gatuslao's contributions to the U.S. military
are not spelled out precisely, but he was unmistakably a boon companion for White, who lovingly recorded his adventures and days of
leisure passed in the planter's company. "Together we went shooting
to near-by rice paddies and ponds and loaded the little brown boys
who were our retrievers with duck, teal, snipe, parrots, cockatoos,
and I know not what other strange tropical birds." White took a
river trip to Don Serafin's hacienda—a feat that would be impossible
today, since the rivers of Himamaylan are no longer navigable—
where servants prepared a roast suckling pig while White sat under
a mango tree and fantasized about "the Filipina girls showing
shapely legs as they paddled in the creek with many-colored skirts
drawn up to their knees."

Don Serafin was the perfect host: well-to-do, literate, and white,
or white enough for the liberal-minded Captain White, at any rate.
Gatuslao was actually a combination Chinese mestizo and Spanish
and thus not quite so fair as the pink-skinned Anglo, but, compared

to the Negritos and *Indios,* as close to a white man as you could be on Negros and still be called Filipino. White's experience in Himamaylan apparently made him rethink some of his own deep-seated racial prejudices and led him to the broad-minded conclusion that Caucasians might actually have successful relationships with "Asiatics": "It is possible, though it may not be easy, for an American to maintain his own racial standard of conduct and living and at the same time be tolerant, understanding, and without arrogance of race toward the Filipinos, or other people of widely different race. It is possible, but it is not easy."

Although White paints a heroic portrait of his efforts to capture the bandit pope, he never succeeded, and Isio was still wreaking havoc on sugar plantations long after the Philippine-American War had ended and White had been assigned off of Negros. Isio didn't surrender until 1907, when, according to one account, he was promised a position in the government, only to be betrayed by the Americans, who instead put him on trial and sentenced him to death. The sentence was later commuted to life in a Manila prison, where he died in 1911.

There are no monuments or memorials to Papa Isio on Negros, but by the time of his death, he had become an icon in his own right, a symbol of the "primitives" and *Indios,* the outlaws of the forest whom the church, the *hacenderos,* and finally the Americans fought to subdue. Although Isio couldn't claim to represent the island's entire underclass, he was the principal native revolutionary leader addressing its concerns, and he articulated better than anyone the underlying evils of the hacienda system. Ironically, although his prescription could not have been more different from that of his archenemy John Roberts White, Isio and the American nonetheless shared the same fundamental analysis of what was wrong with Negros. In his book, White offers a devastating critique of the hacienda system, arguing that inequalities on Negros created enormous instability. "Conditions in Negros approximate more closely those which have brought bloody revolution to Mexico and Central American countries for so many years, for the land has been alienated from the peasants and held in large parcels." White would not be the last American to recognize the problem yet do everything possible to preserve the status quo.

It is the feudal spirit and much of the substance of the hacienda system White described to which the Negrense elite so desperately clings nearly one hundred years later and which Don Serafin Gatuslao's grandson, Serafin "Apin" Gatuslao, gave his life defending.

* * *

Don Serafin Gatuslao and Julita Monton had eleven children, and the six who survived gave them twenty grandchildren. The patriarch's family mansion, a handsome neoclassical home with a grand foyer and imperial staircase, was constructed just south of the Himamaylan town square, and the whole extended family would gather there every year for Christmas and Lent. The house was deliberately destroyed by the family to keep it from falling into the hands of the Japanese when they occupied Himamaylan shortly after the outbreak of World War II, and today only its walls remain, the interior having been overtaken by weeds and banana trees.

Despite their substantial wealth, the Gatuslaos were, by the standards of the Negrense elite, an unpretentious group. Even Don Serafin's most famous son, Valeriano, or Valing, who served as governor for thirteen years, was famous for his common touch. A bit absentminded (he was known to light his cigars and put the still-lit match in his pocket) and maybe a bit cheap (he rode the bus to his office every day and never paid the fare), he was nevertheless one of the island's most popular politicians.

Valing did little of anything for Negros that anyone can remember; his widespread support derived instead from his way with people. Valing's wife, Florinda Delgado, was something else again. Doña Linda, as she was known, was a pillar of Negrense society and was awarded a "Pro Ecclesia et Pontifice" medal from the Pope for her "exemplary Christian life of contributing to the cause of the church." People who knew Doña Linda more intimately than the Pope, however, said generosity was not among her salient virtues. Her niece, Carminia Bascon, described her as "stingy," except when it came to politics, and there she spent a fortune. Doña Linda's priest, the jovial John Doohan, was less reserved. "She was mean as Satan, mean as bedamned, a millionaire who was always complaining that she was broke." Doohan said he personally would never have given her the papal citation but "a boot in the backside," instead.

Don Serafin's second son, Miguel, the father of Serafin "Apin"

Gatuslao, led the resistance against the Japanese in southern Negros during World War II. He and his brother Agustin, the mayor of Himamaylan, were famous for dressing up as bandits and staging a raid on the town hall to steal 20,000 pesos for the resistance. After the war, Miguel was appointed governor, but he was best known for his enthusiastic promotion of the Boy Scouts, and had a reputation for strutting around in his Boy Scout uniform like some commissioned officer in the foreign legion, a practice more than a few people deemed eccentric. Father Doohan was somewhat less charitable, calling Miguel "a wild man of Borneo." "He also had a reputation as something of a prick," the priest confided, "and Apin was a chip off the old block."

The Batman

In the middle of our life's path
I found myself in a dark forest,
where the straight way was lost.
Ah, how hard to describe it,
this savage forest, so dense and rugged,
which even in memory renews my fear!
So bitter is it that death is hardly more.

—Dante, *The Inferno*

Hacienda Benedicto nestles in a half-moon of land in the far northeast corner of Himamaylan, in the foothills of the Negros cordillera, overlooking the coastal plain. Straddling the Pangiplan River, the natural boundary separating Himamaylan and Binalbagan, the five hundred-acre hacienda was established by Miguel Gatuslao and named for his wife's foster father, Florentino Benedicto Gonzalez. It is one of a handful of farms the Gatuslao family carved out of primeval forest in central Negros over the last century.

The closest town is Payao, known throughout the Philippines because of an immensely popular song called "Dandansoy." "Dandansoy, I'm leaving you," it goes. "I'm going home to Payao. But if you miss me, just look for me in Payao." That's it. Not much of a song, it would seem, but it somehow speaks to people just the same. Payao was previously known as Soledad, a Spanish word for a lonely retreat, for solitude and homesickness, and "Dandansoy" seemed to convey all of that: the emptiness and loss one feels in waking from a dream, the impossible passions and longings and sense of something absent, which is what so much of Sugarlandia is about. The town itself is a mere ten minutes by car from Hacienda Benedicto along a dirt road, and the main highway is only ten miles away. It's a lethargic, rundown town that looks as if it might have been built by people trying to make a new start, only to find that they'd re-created what they thought they'd left behind. Payao's houses look like they last saw a coat of paint twenty years ago, and all of them are scarred with the deeply eroded ravines of termites that periodically explode from the walls at night in great white clouds and fly into the moonlight.

Conrado Olano was nineteen years old, in pursuit of adventure, when he arrived in Payao. Born in 1909, Olano is an old toothless man now, although he insists he'll be around a long time, that his grandfather lived to be 146, "maybe 150." Olano came to Payao in 1928 from the town of Capiz on the neighboring island of Panay, west of Negros, just in front of the sunset. He sailed alone across the Guimaras Strait and landed in Himamaylan when the mountains behind the town were covered with a triple-canopy rain forest so thick that sunlight barely reached the ground, a black jungle of hardwoods, many rising 140–150 feet in the sky. The jungle was home to deer, pythons, wild boars, mountain lions, parrots, and bands of monkeys, which would invade the cornfields and fruit trees of inattentive farmers. Crocodiles lurked in the rivers, and tales of fishermen gobbled up by the hungry monsters were commonplace. The crocodiles are now extinct, as are the once plentiful tortoises that were harvested along the coastline for their shells and eggs.

At the time, Negros was under the command of the Philippine Constabulary, there to protect American logging companies like Insular Lumber, which had created a whole new town in the north, Fabrica, a vortex for 139 square miles of forests, which the company was systematically grinding up. The U.S. Commerce Department had catalogued more than a hundred species of hardwoods with exotic names like *akle, bulala, camagon, urung,* and *yakal* and was promoting Negros to timber companies in the States. In Himamaylan, the entire forest was about to become the property of the Gatuslaos.

There was no road in or out of Payao when Olano arrived. Apin Gatuslao would be eight years old before the coastal road would connect Himamaylan to Binalbagan, the town directly to the north. The sugar planters were already operating small railroads on their haciendas, though, using transportable sections of track that could be laid out in the cane fields and moved from one day to the next to keep as close as possible to the men cutting the cane. Conrado Olano set out into a forest still inhabited by the few remaining Negrito people who gave the island its name, and walked east into the mountains toward Payao, where he'd been told some of his cousins might be working for the Constabulary. In Payao, he made the acquaintance of twenty-six-year-old Miguel Gatuslao and Miguel's wife, Expectacion Tantiado, who had just given birth to the boy Serafin, later to be nicknamed Apin. Olano took a job with Miguel, and when Miguel retired, he went to work for Apin. "There was never a better employer than Apin Gatuslao," Olano says.

Miguel Gatuslao and Expectacion Tantiado must have seen something angelic in the first of their six children, although the name Serafin would strike many who knew him as an unfortunate misnomer. Years later, Serafin became widely known as the Batman, a nickname that seemed to better suit his temperament. No one is exactly sure how he got the name. Bob Gatuslao says Apin himself invented it, and there's no question that he enjoyed the air of mystery and notoriety it conveyed. Exequil Hagoriles, a cousin, close aide, and bodyguard, first heard Apin use the name to describe the forests above Himamaylan. Hagoriles, a short man with dark cinnamon skin as shiny as a banana leaf, said, "Apin began referring to the family's logging areas as Batman Country. He'd say, 'That's Batman Country up there,' and the name stuck."

The black silhouette bat logo of comic book origin soon began appearing on Apin's trucks, on farm equipment, and on signs reading WELCOME TO BATMAN COUNTRY, which he erected along the logging roads. The family's little logging port was christened Batman Wharf; when Apin built the cockpit in Himamaylan, it was called Batman Cockpit, and his fighting cocks always fought under the name Batman. Today people refer to just about any area owned by the Gatuslaos as Batman. Shortly before he was murdered, Apin built an armor-plated jeep, his Batmobile, as he called it. He planned to use it during visits to his properties in Himamaylan—insurance against an attack by the NPA. But work on the Batmobile was not quite complete when the rebels made their move.

Exequil Hagoriles can't explain Apin's murder. In his eyes, the Batman was a model employer—kind, generous, ever attendant to his workers' needs. "He would give them rice, and when they got sick, he would pay for their medicines. He was always giving money to the poor." On visits to the hacienda, Hagoriles said, Apin sometimes brought gifts for the workers, such as clothing or rice, and as soon as he arrived he would be surrounded by children. Sometimes he would just relax with his laborers at one of the *sari-saris,* buying them beers, telling stories.

Apin's sister, Janet Remitio, idolized her older brother and said everyone looked up to him. "He was very kind-hearted. I think he was very much beloved by his farmhands." In fact, many of his laborers despised Apin, and some were allegedly involved in killing him. "He had the blood of a horse," Himamaylan residents will tell you half-jokingly, referring to a nasty habit he had of kicking his workers. His bad temper was legendary, and his workers knew that when one of them messed up or made him angry, or if the Batman just went off half-cocked, he might let fly with a foot. They joked about it, but it was also degrading, a source of resentment, and no one thought he should be able to get away with it.

The Batman was a solid, compact, narrow-lipped, no-necked man with a face round and unexpressive as a coconut, long thick sideburns, and an almost full head of thick black hair with little curls that fell across his forehead like the ones on marble busts of Greek poets and philosophers. He dressed informally, in polo shirts and baggy western jeans cinched with a cowboy belt. If the Batman had grown up in the States, he would have been a beer-guzzling, butt-patting "good ole boy," unaffected, loquacious, full of what Filipinos call *palabas*—a first-class showman.

A high-stakes poker player, he made a bundle of money gambling with friends, and he had a special way with the elderly ladies whom he charmed with his gentle wit. "The life of the party," his brother-in-law Rudi Remitio called him. His cousin Carminia Bascon remembered Apin in a similar light. "You could never stay mad at him because he was always joking, always making you laugh."

"Courageous" was a word friends often used to describe him—or at least they did once he was dead. They also saw him as frustrated, angry, and volatile, and while his wife, Panching, helped focus his attentions, the Batman was never completely tamed. "People either loved Serafin or hated him," Panching would say. "He didn't care if you didn't like him."

Although firmly rooted in his class, he was, to his credit, impatient enough to eschew its most fatuous pretentions—the family escutcheons and gratuitous name-dropping. Miguel wanted his son to get a college degree, but Apin was a lousy student and agreed to go to a university in Manila only to make his father happy. He never did find his way to classes, however, but instead cut a deal with the registrar, who guaranteed him passing grades in exchange for an unknown fee. It was a simple scam that, had it not been for one unanticipated glitch, would have given him the degree his father coveted. In the middle of the school year, the registrar died. Shortly after, Apin flunked out.

Bob Gatuslao thought of his older cousin as both outrageous and somewhat inexplicable, a loose cannon whose unpredictable shenanigans were best captured in an incident that took place in April 1980 on Bob's thirty-eighth birthday, when he was an assemblyman representing southern Negros in Marcos's rubber stamp parliament. Birthday parties for Philippine politicians are often lavish affairs with live bands or orchestras, pigs and bulls roasting over open pits, and great quantities of beer. Even low-key politicians like Bob Gatuslao will invite a vast network of friends, family, barrio leaders, selected employees, and anyone else who might be useful at election time. Along with annual town fiestas and cockfights, these birthday celebrations are among the rare occasions when one can witness poor Negrenses socially engaged on the same proximate piece of ground as the rich, even if the former remain scrupulously deferential in considering where to stand or sit, when to take their food and where to eat it, and in boosting the self-important guest of honor at the appropriate moments—applauding when he dances with his wife, for example, or when he makes a few sage remarks welcoming one and all as members of his "family." The rich man, in opening his home—or, to be more precise, his backyard—to almost every segment of the community, intends to convey a common touch, a message of unity, harmony, generosity, and, perhaps most important, respect. Although the message is often as disingenuous as the host himself, it's still good politics and good theater, and everyone seems to have a good time.

Bob and his family were in Bacolod making final preparations for the party when they heard the first radio reports about the M.V. *Don Juan*, a passenger vessel owned and operated by the Negros Navigation Company. The *Don Juan* had collided with an oil tanker in the Tablas Strait, about midway between Manila and Bacolod, and sank with almost a thousand people on board. Among the passengers were members of some of the most prominent families of Negros, including Florinda Gatuslao Alunan (the adopted daughter of Governor Valeriano Gatuslao), her husband José, and four of their children, Gerry, Ginny, Liza, and Mai.

As soon as he got word of the disaster, Bob called off his party. Early in the afternoon of the following day, as the Gatuslao family kept a vigil beside the radio, waiting for new details on the tragedy, Apin burst into the house beaming a broad smile. He had fabulous news, the buoyant Batman announced: He'd just spoken to friends in Batangas City who told him that Florinda, José, and the children were all alive, safe, and unharmed! They'd been rescued and taken to Batangas, where they were awaiting transportation to Manila. It was a miracle!

Naturally, the family was ecstatic. Their prayers had been answered. Visions of the dark, shark-infested maelstrom where less fortunate families had been lost were replaced by limpid tears. The Gatuslaos already knew about some of the victims. A close friend, Consuela Gustilo, wife of Armando, the warlord, was already reported dead, and many of the Gatuslaos' other friends were grieving. Nevertheless, preparations for Bob's birthday party resumed, and the evening celebration was infused with a special sense of joy and relief.

It was only the next day that the Gatuslao family learned the truth. Florinda, José, and the children were all dead, along with three hundred other passengers. (The only member of the family lucky enough to have survived was a daughter, Ann Gatuslao, who was in the United States.) Apin had fabricated the whole story of the family's rescue. "He just wanted us all to have a good time at my birthday party," Bob said, explaining that his cousin didn't like seeing people down in the mouth. "Can you imagine that? It was all a joke. But that's the way he was: You couldn't calculate Apin. It was hard to tell when he was telling the truth."

Apin had a passion for his motorcycles, loved to hunt, and owned a 6-by-6 he'd use to go after deer and wild boar in the mountains. Above all, he loved his guns. Panching called them "his diamonds" and said he would spend hours cleaning and polishing them. "They were a pair, him and his guns. They were things of beauty for Serafin. He would feel naked without his guns." The police blotter in

Himamaylan indicates that the day he was killed, Apin, Panching, and their two bodyguards were armed with an Uzi assault rifle, two rifle grenade launchers, two .45 caliber pistols, one .352 caliber revolver, and a .22 revolver, all of which were confiscated by the rebels. It was Apin's standard arsenal for an outing in Himamaylan. According to Bob Gatuslao, the Batman was wearing an air force general's uniform when he was murdered.

Occasionally, Bob Gatuslao said, Apin got hopelessly drunk and ended up in fistfights. His friend Mario Chiu called him a "binge drinker." "He'd drink for three days, just about anything—*tuba,* beer, Johnny Walker." Mario remembers one evening with Apin at Carlos's Italian Restaurant, near the Bacolod casino. Carlos's is a favorite hangout for the sugar planters—dark, intimate, and ersatz, serving pasta and pizza with processed American cheese. Carlos keeps a collection of Johnny Walker Black Label magnums for his regular customers. The mestizo elite has a fetish about its Black Label, and people will warn you about all the bootleg Black Label supposedly being sold. The *hacendero*'s aesthetic demands that his Black Label bottle never stand upright but rather lie flat, horizontal, so the men can see how the amber liquid clings to the glass. The real stuff has an oily way of attaching itself to the bottle, they say. They also shake the bottle before they pour a drink for reasons that appear purely ritualistic.

A few of Apin's friends called him a playboy, but most said he rarely if ever messed around. That night at Carlos's he happened to be with a girl, and his friends said they also wanted company, so they trundled off to the Sugarland Hotel's disco, Reflections, one of the few reliable pickup places for ladies of the night. As Mario recollects the evening, Apin had had a fair amount to drink and decided it would be fun to stage a competition to see which of the girls had the biggest breasts, immediately assigning himself the job of contest judge. With the encouragement of his buddies, and amid the embarrassed tittering of the hookers and some of the other women he roped into his spectacle, Apin got under way. "He was drunk, and he called all the girls onto the dance floor and had them stand in a row, and he began to feel their breasts," Mario said. Apin was joking with the girls, Mario recalled, teasing them as he walked down the row, fondling each of them and offering a running commentary. "Sometimes he would just lose control."

Apin was sometimes described as the "black sheep" of the family, "an embarrassment," someone who didn't quite fit in, crude and tactless, lacking in *delicadeza,* a sense of propriety. With the exception of Apin, all of the Gatuslaos were married at the family's ancestral home in Himamaylan. Apin had a hard time making commitments, and this was especially true when it came to women. Panching, one of several women who pursued him, was working as a pharmacist at Alice Drug Store, just up the road from Himamaylan, when she caught Apin's eye. She was petite, pretty, college-educated, and Baptist, but the Catholic Apin wasn't especially religious, so that was never an issue. Apin's friends said he could have ended up with any one of the women, but for the fact that Panching was the most persistent. When she finally got him to agree to the marriage on Friday the thirteenth, in March 1959, she insisted that they tie the knot immediately.

Apin's sister Janet and her husband, Rudi Remitio, first got wind of the decision shortly before midnight, while watching a movie at a Bacolod theater. Rudi was advised that there was a family emergency, and when they arrived at the family compound, Apin and Panching were waiting for them. Apin said they wanted to get married immediately, and he asked his sister and brother-in-law for their advice. They told him he'd have to get permission from his father. So, at about one in the morning, they piled into a car and drove to Payao, a good ninety minutes to the south, near the far northwest corner of Himamaylan. Rudi recalled Miguel's surprise when he woke up with the four of them staring at him. "Janet talked to the old man, and he just said, 'If you want to get married, there's nothing I can do about it,' and dropped back to sleep."

Now the problem was finding someone to marry them in the middle of the night. A judge in La Castellana refused because they didn't have the proper license, as did a priest at their next stop in La Carlota. So they drove back to Bacolod and approached the vicar general, Monsignor Fortich, who, twenty years later, would be branded a Communist by Apin's friends. But in 1959, the priest probably didn't know what a Communist was. According to Rudi, the monsignor talked to the two of them, and when he satisfied himself that they were really in love, he agreed to perform the rite. "So

they were married," Rudi said, summing up, then added as an afterthought: "There was never any party for them. They just went to live
on the farm. Of course, they didn't live happily ever after."

*   *   *

The Gatuslaos' land came down to Apin from Don Serafin, Miguel,
and Miguel's wife, Expectacion, who had inherited the land of her
foster father, Florentino Benedicto Gonzalez. In Payao, at Hacienda
Benedicto, Apin built his Shangri-la, a walled compound with two
houses: one for his family with five bedrooms, a second with three
more rooms for guests, a large swimming pool, a garden, and a basketball court. Tepees for scores of fighting cocks were lined up outside the house, although they were more of a business than a
reflection of any real interest on the part of Apin, who preferred raising pigs and rabbits.

Apin also built three warehouses the size of football fields that
could hold more than a hundred million pounds of sugar, managed
1,200 acres of sugarcane, operated two sawmills, and employed
about 500 men to harvest his family's cane. Most of them were part-
time workers, among them as many as 300 itinerants Exequil Hagoriles would recruit from Panay.

Bob Gatuslao remembers Payao and Himamaylan as almost par-
adisiacal places when he and Apin were growing up:

> What I enjoyed most was the rain forest, the clear water in
> the streams. At 4 A.M. the whistle at the lumber mill would
> start the day's work. There was a thick fog in the trees and the
> air was cool. People began to gather, and by 4:30, they'd be off
> in the big trucks. It was really beautiful. In the forest there
> were monkeys and parrots. We used to hunt the wild doves
> and the deer.

The Gatuslaos owned more than 5,000 acres of farmland in
Himamaylan, and a 1935 timber license gave them the right to cut
trees from all of the town's public forests. At the time, that
amounted to approximately forty-four square miles of virgin timber-
land, an amount the family's logging company successfully reduced
to zero over the next three decades. The company operated under

several names, most recently as the Negros Industrial Development Corporation, or NIDCO. But from the time Apin Gatuslao took control, most people just called it the Batman Logging Company.

At its peak, Batman Logging's two sawmills turned out more than 200,000 board feet of lumber per week. Together, the logging business and the family's sugar plantations had a payroll of some 2,000 people, making the Gatuslaos the largest employer in Himamaylan. It was this combination of wealth and workers that made the Gatuslaos one of the most powerful families in southern Negros. Their huge work force translated directly into political clout, for the very simple reason that workers voted for whichever candidate the Gatuslaos told them to vote for. Nearly all of them could also be counted on to deliver the votes of other members of their families, as well. Those who thought about it saw no reason to support an opposition candidate because, practically speaking, it made no difference who they voted for. Negros had been controlled by the sugar elite since the Spaniards left—still is today—and whether a laborer voted for planter "A" or miller "B," neither was going to be looking after the worker's interests.

The Gatuslaos' political power was solidified by their control of the Binalbagan–Isabela Planters' Association, or BIPA, which represented the local sugar growers in negotiations with the sugar mill and made numerous decisions that directly affected the income of local planters. BIPA was run by Miguel Gatuslao, Apin's father, and before him, until he slipped in his bathroom and killed himself, by Governor "Valing" Gatuslao. The last Gatuslao to run the association was Apin, who held the presidency at the time he was murdered.

Since there was only one association in the district, if you controlled it, you controlled the politics. "If you controlled the association," Bob Gatuslao explained, "you could do favors for the planters; you do favors, they deliver votes." The BIPA president could decide, for instance, how much of a planter's sugarcane would be placed on the *vagones,* the mill's cane railcars, and when that cane would be processed. Since the sucrose content of sugarcane declines rapidly after it is cut, a grower wants his cane milled as expeditiously as possible. The planters' association also had a representative in the mill's chemical laboratory, which calculated the sucrose content of each load of cane. There the BIPA representative could steal from

one planter by undercounting his sucrose content and simply assign
a larger amount to a friend.

One planter, Franklin Fuentebella, said Apin abused his position
at BIPA, that he rewarded his political cronies by moving their cane
into the mill without delay while pushing others to the back of the
line. In addition, Apin controlled a multimillion-peso BIPA slush
fund that was supposed to provide scholarships to young students
and financial aid to workers. In better times, the fund served a clear
political purpose; for each favor granted, a debt was incurred. But
the slush fund was also a constant temptation, and Fuentebella
and others claimed Apin was "misappropriating funds," siphoning
money for his personal use. Fuentebella and other planters who dis-
approved of the way Apin was running the BIPA decided to form
their own breakaway association and took a third of the BIPA's
membership with them.

Needless to say, growers who benefited from the Gatuslaos' lar-
gesse at the BIPA were prepared to repay their debts. Sometimes
that meant getting out the vote for the Gatuslaos themselves, other
times for the candidates they favored. The family's clout in southern
Negros also allowed it to play politics at the provincial and national
level. They were aligned during the 1970s and 1980s with Marcos
and his closest crony, Roberto Benedicto, a law school classmate and
fraternity brother to whom the dictator had given an all but absolute
monopoly over the sugar industry.

Although Apin Gatuslao never ran for office, he did see himself
as a kingmaker, and he appreciated that politics greased his family's
business and vice versa. BIPA was a tool for controlling political offices—mayor, town council, and the local congressional seat—which
in turn controlled public contracts, the police, and the courts. Even
the Army worked through Apin when it set up operations in Himamaylan. The Gatuslaos provided a kind of one-stop shopping. That
didn't always make them popular.

Families like the Gatuslaos looked to politics as a means of protecting their investments, as a source of wealth, and as a matter of
prestige. Their enemies and rivals spread rumors that the family
hoped to use its power to take control of southern Negros and said
Apin was attempting to become a "warlord" in the south just as his
friend Armando Gustilo had in the north. The rumors were not
completely unfounded. The Gatuslaos and the Gustilos fantasized

about dividing Negros Occidental in two, and the Gatuslaos talked about moving the capital back to Himamaylan, where it had been until 1848, an idea most people found a bit loony, inasmuch as the town has neither a port nor telephone service and, aside from the coastal highway passing through it, only a few short stretches of paved roads.

Public office in the Philippines is most often a license for stealing from the public, and although there were no particular accusations of corruption against the Gatuslaos, Himamaylan residents frequently complained that public money seemed to disappear. The Gatuslao family's actual contributions to the town, most agree, constitute a very short list. There was the church—no small matter—but residents seem generally unimpressed by the many buildings bearing the family's name and bitter about the backwardness of the place. They've been complaining for decades about the poor quality of the drinking water, that even at the Gatuslao Hospital the water isn't drinkable, and they resent the absence of telephone service, particularly when towns immediately to the north and south have been wired for years.

Following the 1986 revolution, a new mayor, Ernesto R. Rodriguez, Jr., appointed by President Corazon Aquino, said he discovered that the Gatuslaos had never paid a single peso in taxes to the municipality. His successor, Daisy Silverio, said the Gatuslaos' lumber company owed the municipality millions of pesos in back taxes. Rodriguez also said the Gatuslaos had numerous ghost employees on their payroll and employed dozens of people who simply did no work. He said he fired twenty-five of them as soon as he took office. "When one family runs a town, it goes to pot," Rodriguez said. "Himamaylan was stagnated. It was the town that God and the Gatuslaos forgot."

*   *   *

A short history written in 1983 and released by Mayor José Gatuslao describes Himamaylan in a way that would be unrecognizable to anyone who has visited there recently. It says, for example, that the town is graced by a "first-class rain forest" and that forested areas "protect the lowland from floods and erosion during the heavy rains and also maintain the atmospheric moisture of the municipal-

ity. These forest areas are properly protected from illegal destruction." In fact, by 1983, Batman Logging and the other timber companies in southern Negros had clear-cut nearly all of the area's
mahogany, teak, and other hardwoods. Bob Gatuslao's recollection
is that most of the trees had been cut and that the family company
had all but suspended operations by 1981. He disputes suggestions,
however, that Batman Logging was responsible for the fact that the
mountains of Himamaylan are completely barren. "It was not the
logger who destroyed the forest. At the time, we had a twenty-five-
year lease on it. So why would we destroy it?" He insists that the
family replanted areas it had cut but that "the forest was lost" because of reckless logging by *kaingeros,* poor slash-and-burn farmers
who cut down trees and planted food crops.

In reality, the twenty-five-year lease was an incentive to "cut and
get out." The Gatuslaos cleared the forest from Himamaylan for the
same reason other politicians, military officers, and entrepreneurs
throughout the archipelago did: because there were enormous short-
term profits to be made, and there was no one to stop them.

Negrense loggers merely followed in the footsteps of the Americans who had "harvested" the archipelago's forests for more than
half a century. The Gatuslaos had a legal right to cut timber, and
their wealth and political power allowed them to go about their business with impunity. Nothing demonstrated this more baldly than
Typhoon Nitang, which slammed into Negros in September 1984,
dumping a torrent of rain onto the mountains. The *Visayan Daily
Star* reported that more than 7,000 homes were destroyed and more
than 100 people killed as a flash flood thundered from the mountains, carrying gigantic logs through populated areas. The Bureau of
Forest Development blamed the disaster on Batman Logging but
took no action against it. Imelda Marcos visited the area and com-
miserated with the victims' families, but there was no official investigation of the damages, the Gatuslaos were never asked to
compensate any of the victims, and no one expected them to.

What the Gatuslaos did to Himamaylan has been duplicated in
thousands of municipalities throughout the Philippines. When the
Americans seized the country from Spain, the archipelago boasted
some of the richest fisheries in the world, thousands of miles of
coral-reefed shorelines, and thousands of square miles of virgin forest. "The wood of the Philippines can supply the furniture of the

world for a century to come," U.S. Senator Alfred J. Beveridge crowed in January 1900. The American companies responsible for most of the destruction on Negros until World War II were cheered on by the U.S. Commerce Department, which praised the high quality of Philippine hardwoods exported to American manufacturers on the West Coast. "It is said that the manufacture of caskets consumes the largest quantity used by any single industry," the U.S. agency reported.

A 1925 Commerce Department report estimated that there were more than 72,000 square miles of virgin forest in the country, an area about the size of North Dakota. The resources seemed limitless. By the time Apin Gatuslao was murdered in 1987, 85 percent of the country's virgin forest was gone, 95 percent on Negros.

The destruction of the country's forests foreshadowed a deluge of environmental degradation: flooding, massive erosion and soil depletion, a loss in water retention, and a diminished source of water for irrigation. These problems in turn brought siltation of coastal estuaries and coral reefs, destruction of spawning grounds for fish, and a dramatic reduction in fish populations. Since there were few trees to burn for fuel, people began to tear up mangrove swamps along the coast, eliminating other spawning areas. When it became more difficult to catch fish with the customary nets and traps, fishermen began using dynamite to blast them from the coral reefs, one-shot harvests ensuring that those areas would never again produce fish.

The only burgeoning natural resource was the population, which, with the church opposed to any form of family planning, offset any gains in gross national product. Declining resources and opportunities in turn encouraged massive migration into already overcrowded urban areas and the export of some of the nation's most talented people. The largest source of foreign exchange today is dollars sent home by more than 2 million Filipinos working abroad: as nurses, doctors, and artists in the United States; as musicians, accountants, and managers in Singapore, Kuala Lumpur, and Jakarta; as construction workers in Kuwait, Saudi Arabia, and Israel; as maids throughout Asia and Europe; and as "cultural artists" and prostitutes in the bars and nightclubs of Tokyo and Hong Kong.

In recent years, the Philippines has become almost synonymous with natural calamities of biblical dimensions, and Filipinos are regularly reminded of their vulnerability. In 1990, a massive earthquake leveled much of the mountain resort city of Baguio, killing 1,700 people. The quake was followed by torrential rains, which, because of deforestation, caused massive mudslides. In 1991, Mount Pinatubo erupted, killing more than 800 and leaving more than a million homeless, with 300 square miles of farmland and two dozen towns buried under a blanket of ash. The same year, a flash flood caused by massive deforestation killed more than 7,000 people in the town of Ormoc.

On Negros, profits from the ravaged forests supported the monocrop sugar economy and financed investment in Manila and abroad. There has been almost no significant investment in industry or manufacturing on Negros, and any statistical gains from growth in sugar have been overwhelmed by the relentless increases in population. Removal of the forests opened up more areas for agriculture—stunted forests of sugarcane—but it also made land previously farmed by poor farmers and squatters more accessible, and therefore more desirable, to wealthy landgrabbers, who had the courts and guns to "legalize" their claims. Many small farmers thrown off their land took their grievances to the NPA.

Like many of his friends, Apin Gatuslao moved to expand his land holdings in previously remote or forested areas. With more land under the plow, he also found he had a greater need for the water in the Pangiplan River. Water and especially land are recurring themes on Negros. Indeed, in the end, they are everything: the source of the island's wealth, the reason for its insurgency, the explanation for Apin's murder.

Land

I chop your feet, I drink your blood. What am I?
Sugarcane.

—Old Visayan riddle

Shortly before the Bolshevik Revolution in 1917, the Virgin Mary appeared to three illiterate shepherd girls in Fatima, Portugal, to give them advance notice of some of the most extraordinary events of the twentieth century, which were about to unfold in Russia. The selected audience for this divine annunciation was perhaps as mysterious as the messenger and the message itself—the news that Russia would spread its, at the time, inchoate "errors" throughout the world, that it would persecute the church, wage wars, take over many countries, and eventually be converted to the Christian faith. As a result of this miracle, Our Lady of Fatima has been closely associated with anticommunism and in recent years has become a popular devotion of the Negrense elite. Like the blood of lambs smeared on the doorposts of the Egyptian Jews to save their firstborn from the wrath of God, pictures of the Madonna are posted at the gates to many of Bacolod's fanciest homes—a public statement of the occupants' anti-Communist political faith and, equally important, their displeasure with the allegedly Communist-infiltrated Catholic church of Negros.

Our Lady's reputation was greatly enhanced on May 13, 1981, the anniversary of her first appearance in Fatima, when a Turkish assassin shot Pope John Paul II in St. Peter's Square in Rome. The Pope attributes his miraculous survival to the intervention of the Virgin, and ten years after the assassination attempt he paid a visit to Fatima, bringing with him the bullet that had been extracted from his body. The lead projectile was subsequently set alongside the 313 pearls and 2,679 precious stones of a solid gold crown used on special occasions to festoon an image of Our Lady of Fatima.

Devotions to the Virgin are nearly as popular in the Philippines as those honoring the Santo Niño. Former President Aquino, a devout Marian, keeps numerous images of the Holy Mother in her Manila office, and a huge cement grotto, dedicated to Our Lady of Lourdes, stands a short walk from her family's private sugar mill. It was the Pope's special devotion to Our Lady of Fatima and his strong anti-Communist credentials that were particularly appealing to the Negrense elite. With Communists trying to seize control of Negros and priests spouting "liberation theology," it was comforting to have this tenaciously anti-Communist Pope, who had adjured priests to stay out of politics and explicitly rejected the increasingly popular portrayal of Christ as a revolutionary or political figure, the "subversive from Nazareth." Thus, when the Holy See announced that the Pope would pay a brief visit to Bacolod in 1981, the Negrense elite prepared to roll out the red carpet.

Imelda Marcos, then the first lady and self-proclaimed "mother" of her country, made frequent public displays of her religious convictions: crawling down the aisle of a church on her knees while praying her rosary—a string of diamonds—and erecting a gaudy temple to the Santo Niño near her hometown. Thrilled at the opportunity to greet the Pope on his visit to the only Catholic country in Asia, Mrs. Marcos flew one step ahead of him on her private jet, popping up like a stripper from a birthday cake to greet and be photographed with His Holiness at every stop as he traveled throughout the archipelago.

In Bacolod, more than a half-million people who turned out to see the Pope were first compelled to endure an address from the first lady, who informed the multitude that "Negros is not an island of fear, but an island of love." The Pope had a more somber message for the Negrenses. His address, "To the People of the Sugar Plantations," was delivered in English, which most of his audience couldn't understand, but the basic message quickly got through to people like Moret De los Santos and hundreds of thousands of other poor Negrenses like him who stood in the crowd.

The Pope spoke about land and justice and seemed to condemn the very foundations of elite Negrense society. "Injustice reigns when, within the same society, some groups hold most of the wealth and power, while large strata of the population cannot decently provide for the livelihood of their families, even through long hours of back-breaking labor in factories or in the fields. Injustice reigns when the laws of economic growth and ever greater profit determine social relations, leaving in poverty and destitution those who have only the work of their hands to offer." In their specially designated souvenir seats in front of the dais, the oligarchs squirmed. The Pope continued. "Being aware of such situations, the church will not hesitate to take up the cause of the poor, and to become the voice of those who are not listened to when they speak up, not to demand charity, but to ask for justice. . . . Because the land is a gift of God for the benefit of all, it is not admissible to use this gift in such a manner that the benefits it produces serve only a limited number of people, while the others—the vast majority—are excluded from the benefits which the land yields." The Pope mentioned the words "justice" and "injustice" eighteen times in his brief remarks, speaking directly to landlords like Serafin Gatuslao. "The landowners and the planters should therefore not let themselves be guided in the first place by the economic laws of growth and gain, nor by the demands of competition or the selfish accumulation of goods, but by the demands of justice and by the moral imperative of contributing to a decent standard of living and to working conditions which make it possible for the workers and for the rural society to live a life that is truly human and to see all their fundamental rights respected."

It was a devastating indictment. Short of a call to surrender to the NPA, it is difficult to imagine a speech that could have been less well received by the oligarchs. Ironically, the great anti-Communist Pope never mentioned the issue of communism. Yet he had cast his lot with the island's poor and seemed to be calling on planters to share their wealth and power and to endorse land reform, the idea they most despised.

The Negrense elite was beyond shame or guilt, however, and there was to be no spiritual awakening in Bacolod as a result of the Holy Father's visit. To the oligarchs, the Pope's agenda sounded frighteningly similar to the Communist party's calls for "land and justice." Rather than attack the Pope directly, most landowners simply dismissed his remarks, explaining that they looked to the church for spiritual, not political, guidance. They suggested that the Pope— who, after all, had never actually spent any time traveling around

Negros—had somehow been conned by Bacolod Bishop Fortich and other alleged friends of the Communists. The planters were not entirely off base; Bishop Fortich and some of his priests had in fact advised the Vatican that Negros was the scene of some of the most deplorable living conditions in the Philippines. Nonetheless, the validity of the Pope's remarks was difficult to challenge.

As the NPA grew in the early 1980s, members of the gentry began feeling as if they'd awakened in a foreign country, surrounded by madmen with guns, by aliens speaking the impenetrable mumbo jumbo of comrades Mao and Stalin. Rebel leaders accused planters, millers, businessmen, and government officials of crimes they'd never heard of, attacked them as members of the "landlord-comprador elite," whatever that was, as collaborators with foreign "monopoly capitalists," as "bourgeois populists," "pro-imperialist liberals," Trotskyites, and agents of the Central Intelligence Agency. The rhetoric alone could be daunting.

"The counterrevolutionary Rightists are hitching a ride on the wagon of the imperialist ideological and political offensive," Communist party founder José Maria Sison declared in one of his lengthy and turbid sermons on the state of the revolution. The comfortable elite hadn't a clue what Sison was talking about. It's not even certain that Sison did. And it's a safe bet his rank and file couldn't penetrate Sison's solipsism. For the elite, the only thing that came through was that their Sugarlandia was being torn apart. Armed revolutionaries, some of them the children of the oligarchs' own friends and laborers, were living like savages in the forests, engaging in wanton destruction. Why, even the girls, whom everyone referred to as amazons, some from proper Catholic schools, were running with the men through the mountains, killing planters, burning their fields and farm equipment, trying to steal their land, their homes, their birthright. The rich didn't need Mao's Red Book to know that the island was being overrun by Communists.

Five years after the Pope's visit, Ferdinand Marcos was living in exile in Honolulu, Corazon Aquino was president, Negros was more impoverished than ever, the NPA was killing sugar growers, and the latter were probably less interested in making any concession on the land question than at any time since the Japanese occupation during World War II. A large number of Negros planters had come to see the ouster of the dictator as a necessity, and now that he was finally gone, they weren't about to allow the NPA, the church—or a democratic government—to deny them the economic opportunity they felt was their due.

No doubt, the planters, traders, and millers who constituted the island's unofficial aristocracy managed to live far better than anyone else on the island, but the truth was that under Marcos many of them had suffered considerable financial losses. They weren't walking around in rags like their workers, and their children weren't hungry, but 75 percent of the growers were so deeply in debt that the banks actually could have foreclosed on their farms. All of them were used to dealing in the volatile sugar market, had seen prices rise and plummet wildly in the course of a single year, and had accepted that good years would be followed by lean. Between 1974 and 1978, however, Marcos completely monopolized sugar trading, placing it in the hands of crony Roberto Benedicto, who was, after the dictator himself, probably the greatest kleptomaniac in Philippine history.

A native Negrense, Benedicto owned or controlled 106 sugar farms, 85 corporations, 17 radio stations, 16 television stations, the Manila Casino, a Holiday Inn, and a major piece of the national oil company. Known as the Sugar Czar, he dictated the price planters were paid for every pound of sugar and controlled a vertical monopoly that eventually extended from planting to trading to transport and milling. For good measure, Marcos appointed Benedicto chairman of Republic Planters Bank, which became the planters' principal lending agency. Benedicto's monopoly effectively allowed him to steal tens of millions of dollars from his neighbors on Negros, paying them a third or a fourth of the price he received when he resold their sugar.

Benedicto also controlled the operations of Marcos's political party in the Western Visayas. On Negros, his closest political allies were the Gustilos in the north, the Montelibanos in Bacolod, and the Gatuslaos in the south. So when Benedicto asked Bob Gatuslao and his cousin, Tony, to run for the National Assembly, the two were more than happy to accommodate him. Both were elected. Benedicto was the best kind of friend a family like the Gatuslaos could have hoped for, but as with Marcos, Benedicto's increasing greed eventually alienated even his most faithful followers.

In 1974, as prices of sugar on the world market rose steadily with no apparent end in sight, Benedicto began hoarding, speculating that the price would continue to rise. The Gatuslaos' warehouses and every other storage facility on Negros overflowed, and sugar was "banked" everywhere—on tennis and basketball courts, in swimming pools, churches, schools, and along roadways. Then Benedicto's gamble went bust. Sugar prices reached a historic peak of sixty-seven cents a pound and then began to plummet, hitting seven cents in 1978, rising to twenty-three in 1979, and falling to four in 1984. Losses ran into the hundreds of millions of dollars. Some of the *hacenderos* were able to ride out the storm by borrowing, but for many others, and even more so for their workers, the situation was catastrophic.

As head of Philex, the government sugar-trading bureau, Benedicto began paying planters less than it cost to grow sugar. The planters responded by taking their land out of cultivation. As a result, between 1975 and 1985, production dropped by 50 percent. Thousands of people were thrown out of work. According to one study, the average sugar worker's income declined by a third between 1975 and 1981. The normal three-month dead season, when hundreds of thousands of sugar workers are unemployed, now extended to six months. Hunger and malnutrition set in on a massive scale. In 1975, one study reported that four out of five households of sugar workers lived below the subsistence level and that nearly all of those families had lost at least one child to malnutrition-related illnesses, especially pneumonia and gastroenteritis. Nearly a third had lost two or more. By 1978, 78 percent of the infants in and around Bacolod were malnourished, and by 1985, UNICEF put the figure islandwide at 82 percent. The only ones who benefited from all this were Benedicto, Marcos, and the NPA.

When sugar prices began to recover in the early 1980s, Benedicto failed to pass the benefits on to the growers. By the time parliamentary elections were held in 1984, Benedicto had become the single most detested individual on Negros. Even wealthy families like the Gustilos and Gatuslaos turned on him, helping to defeat Benedicto's entire slate of candidates. The same elite families were turning on Marcos as well.

When Marcos finally fled, the heavily indebted planters at last saw an opportunity to recover their losses, and none of them were in any mood to begin discussions about land reform. They insisted that their own land holdings were dwindling anyway through "natural land reform," the division of estates into smaller and smaller parcels as a result of inheritance.

Suddenly they were faced with a new government, which had nationalized the banks, and a president operating without a constitution whose "revolutionary powers" would have allowed her to implement an agrarian reform program by decree, with the stroke of a pen. Some of Aquino's advisers were telling her she should, and most of the planters feared she would.

During her presidential campaign, Aquino had told the planters: "Do not look at agrarian reform as taking of your lands, but as an opportunity for the wider partnership of all our people toward progress and peace." It is difficult to convey precisely how outrageous this ostensibly idealistic preachment sounded to landowners. It was bad enough that Marcos had cheated them out of their profits; now it looked as if they had to deal with someone who was prepared to remove the very source of those profits. In their eyes, Aquino was another shill for the Communists. On her first visit to Negros as president, she did nothing to reassure the planters, boldly telling them, "The sugar industry is finished."

Aquino had campaigned on a platform of "genuine" land reform. "Land to the tiller"—the same terminology used by the Communists —"must become a reality, instead of an empty slogan," she said, making the case for land redistribution. Aquino told voters: "I shall ask no greater sacrifices than I myself am prepared to make." It was this statement, more than any other, that convinced both rich and poor alike that Aquino was serious. After all, she was not only the widow of the country's most revered martyr, but one of the country's wealthiest landowners. If she were willing to sacrifice her land, the *hacenderos* figured they were in deep trouble.

Aquino's family, the Cojuangcos, owned the largest and most lavish sugar plantation in the Philippines, the 16,000-acre Hacienda Luisita in Tarlac Province, two hours north of Manila. During the harvest, Luisita employs more than 8,000 people, and it is so vast that ninety miles of railroad are laid out on the hacienda to get the cane to the family's private sugar mill, the Central Azucarera de Tarlac. A 180-man security force is on call twenty-four hours a day to protect the family, their five mansions ranged around a swimming pool, an eighteen-hole golf course, and the stables for thirty-five racehorses. Aquino's brother, Congressman José "Peping" Cojuangco, breeds fifteen to twenty yearlings annually, which he sells for $300,000 to $400,000 apiece. He is also one of the country's foremost breeders of fighting cocks, and a thousand knee-high wood tepees for the birds occupy acre upon acre around the family's homes.

In her campaign, Aquino left the unmistakable impression that she was prepared to give this all up, insisting that Luisita would not be exempted from land reform. "I will be the first to admit that my pronouncements on agrarian reform would sound hollow if I cannot get Luisita to come under the CARP [Comprehensive Agrarian Reform Program]." She even promised that Luisita would be sold to its tenants. Although the landlords panicked when Aquino talked about land reform, she had also said she would ask for no sacrifices greater than those she herself was "prepared to make." The reality was that she and her family were not prepared to sacrifice much of anything.

Hacienda Luisita is a monument to elite aspirations, and the idea that Aquino's family would ever part with a single square inch of it was never more than fantasy. If the sugar industry was really "finished," as she had claimed, then so were the Aquino–Cojuangcos. Once elected, Aquino began to equivocate. "It is not so much a matter of distributing land," she said less than a month after taking office, "but of enabling people to share profits. By sharing out the land, you only create more problems because sugar cultivation, for instance, is definitely uneconomic if carried out in small plots."

People thirsting for the kind of radical reform the Pope's remarks had implied were barely represented in Aquino's government, and the handful who supported even modest changes in the pattern of landownership were either silenced or hounded from office as Communists. Rather than implement a land redistribution program by decree, as many reformists recommended, the president procrastinated on the issue throughout her first year in office and was compelled to act only after her military fired on a group of peasants— killing eighteen and wounding more than a hundred—who had marched on the presidential palace to demand land reform.

Six months later, she came up with a land bill but promptly

dumped it into the lap of a new democratically elected Congress dominated overwhelmingly by landed interests. She might as well have appointed a crack addict to run her drug treatment program.

*　　*　　*

If there is a case to be made for land reform anywhere in the Philippines, Negros is the place that is almost invariably cited. Fully 70 percent of the island's population is impoverished; half of it makes a living off the land, but 80 percent is landless. All of the sugar land is held by 2 percent of the people, and half of the arable land is held by a mere 5 percent of the sugar planters.

It is nearly impossible to find a Negros *hacendero* who believes that the people who have been planting, weeding, and growing his sugar for generations would have a clue as to how to farm it. "It's like saying the guy who installs the wheels at General Motors is capable of running the company," is how Danilo "Nil" Gamboa, a founder of the secessionist Negros Independence Movement, explained it. "I have friends who have gone broke on a hundred hectares. You give a guy five hectares [twelve acres] and it boggles the mind how he's going to make it work. I don't think it's good for the country to give people land who don't know how to farm it." Moret's employer, Ernesto Tongson, was of a similar mind, insisting that peasants given land could never make a go of it without capital, trucks, and so on. "You need at least twenty hectares [50 acres] to make a profit. In fact, you really need fifty [125 acres]. You can't make money on three, four, or five." On an island where a third of the schoolchildren were underweight and suffering moderate to severe malnutrition in 1990, though, Tongson misses the point. Even if you can't make money on twelve acres—a statement many agronomists would dispute—people can grow enough food for their survival, and Moret, who grew his family's total annual rice needs on the two and a half acres Tongson provided him, was living proof of the error in his patron's thinking.

Nil Gamboa and most planters say they are neither unaware of nor unsympathetic to the plight of their workers, but there's nothing they can do. "We'd be the first to want to see the upliftment of the rural people, but there isn't enough land. If you give a man one hectare, he'll plant food. And then what will you and I eat?" It is an extreme formulation of the problem, but it articulates one of the wilder and more perverse articles of faith among the elite: not everyone can eat. Planters like Gamboa don't see the land primarily as a source of food—as do the church, the NPA, and various peasant organizations—but rather as a way of life. The problem is that no one has yet found a middle ground between the worldview of the gentry and that of their workers.

Not knowing exactly what "land reform" would mean, the landowners assumed the worst: that the government was going to steal their land and turn it over to ignorant peasants. In fact, there isn't enough land on Negros to make everyone a member of the elite, and the planters noted correctly that rice and corn lands distributed to peasants by Marcos in a limited land reform program quickly reverted to their original owners. Poor farmers lacked the technical expertise, money, and financing they needed to make their farms viable, and when they went broke, they sold it back to the big *hacenderos*. The paucity of land on Negros, combined with the failure of reform under Marcos, was evidence enough for most planters that land reform could never work.

The NPA had been screaming about land for years, and on haciendas where it successfully intimidated landowners, it had managed to improve wages and working conditions, control usury, and secure "farm lots" where peasants could grow food. The NPA pressed landlords to give sharecroppers a higher percentage of the proceeds and encouraged peasants to secretly withhold (that is, steal) a portion of the landlord's crop. The Communist party claimed it had seized and distributed 12,000 acres on Negros, and planters assumed it would bust up farms islandwide if it took power.

Some planters, like Moret's boss, Ernesto Tongson, had given laborers "farm lots" for growing food, but they rarely gave workers legal title to those lands. Although some of these planters talked as if they supported land reform, they were paralyzed when it came to actually doing something about it. The most salient case was that of Eduardo Locsin, a prominent *hacendero* who said he favored reform and had been labeled a "traitor to our class" by the Negros Anti-Communism Crusade, an amorphous group that leftists insisted was part of a CIA plot. The group, whose members are generally assumed to be planters, called for Locsin's assassination in one of its typically understated handbills headlined: "Kill for Democracy! Kill for Peace! Kill All the Communists!"

But Locsin is hardly a Communist. Although he established a charitable foundation to help prepare the poor for eventual land-ownership, after pursuing his upliftment programs for thirty years he remained convinced that workers were not ready to own land and would need further tutelage from the elite before they could be entrusted with their own property. Whereas most planters categorically rejected any accommodation on the land issue, Locsin proffered circumlocutory arguments for land reform that ultimately demonstrated its unworkability.

"Our fear is that people will become materialistic, which is not according to God's plan. So we believe economic development first requires the development of man. The hacienda system has deprived these people of their personhood." Put another way, Locsin would prefer to suffer with the current distribution of wealth—a hacienda system that has allowed people like himself to live very comfortably—than to risk seeing the poor further dehumanized by becoming rich and materialistic like his fellow planters.

"To change the system will take one or two generations," Locsin says with self-assurance. Meanwhile, he is content to tend the hundreds of orchids that fill the backyard of his Bacolod home, gorgeous lavender, white, yellow, and copper blooms that seem to live on nothing but air.

Negros Governor Daniel "Bitay" Lacson, Jr., was another patrician reformer. Appointed by Aquino, he and the president had a great deal in common. Like Mrs. Aquino, Lacson was born to great wealth, was a sugar planter (as well as president of the Negros Navigation Company), and had never before held any political office. On Negros, he was seen as a progressive in a sea of reactionaries and reprobates. Often described as "Aquino's favorite governor," Lacson, like the president, was full of good intentions but rarely bothered with the gritty details of government; he viewed politics as an avocation beneath his station and repeatedly offered "sincerity"—a vague and highly valued measure of character in the Philippines—in place of substance.

Whereas Aquino was seen as the Virgin Mary ready to deliver the nation to its savior, Lacson was one of the new, urbane, technocratic wise men, the embodiment of the mature, modern pragmatism that was supposedly taking hold among younger planters and businessmen committed to change and to improving the lives of the poor. A darling of the U.S. embassy in Manila, Lacson was given its Ninoy Aquino Award (named after the president's late husband) for unspecified accomplishments on Negros. Lacson saw himself as a "visionary," a term friends often used to describe him, a man who cast out ideas like seeds, sat back, and waited for them to germinate in the rich volcanic soil.

His actual achievements were somewhat more modest. He *did* run a corruption-free government. He was one of the first planters to invest in prawn farming, which subsequently became a lucrative enterprise for many of the island's *hacenderos*. He helped spawn several small backyard enterprises, such as orchid cultivation and handicraft manufacturing, which generated a small number of low-wage jobs. And he was also perceptive enough to recognize that Negros was in deep trouble.

Lacson identified Negros's extremely inefficient sugar economy as the root cause of its underdevelopment. Fully 90 percent of the population was dependent on sugar for its survival. Lacson knew that tens of thousands of people were completely unemployed for at least three months each year, many for six, and he recognized that there was a direct causal chain from sugar to hunger and malnutrition to insurgency and communism. He also believed that the concentration of land in too few hands, as well as the environmental destruction and land degradation that had reduced small farmers' yields, further fueled the rebel cause. Unlike most politicians, Lacson seemed willing to take on the land issue, and he proposed a plan that, at least in the abstract, seemed to address the concerns of both the planters and, to a limited degree, the landless sugar workers. The plan, known as "sixty-thirty-ten," would have allowed the heavily indebted planters to keep 60 percent of their land and to finance their debts to the banks with the remainder. Thirty percent of their land would then be turned over to cooperatives and planted with crops other than sugar in order to diversify the island's agrarian economy, and the remaining 10 percent would be used by sugar workers to grow their own food.

"Basically, the proposal calls for the planter to cede his land to his creditor bank," Lacson said, operating on the dubious assumption that banks could, and therefore would, exercise their rights of foreclosure on the heavily indebted planters. But the bankers knew what everyone else knew as well—that if they foreclosed, there would be no one to buy the land, and the Negros economy, on which they too depended, would fall to pieces. Put another way, there was simply no money to finance Lacson's plan. The island's laborers hadn't the means to buy property. Foreign governments might have put up some money to purchase land had sixty-thirty-ten been enacted before the glow of the People Power Revolution had worn off, but the initial international enthusiasm for Aquino rapidly evaporated following repeated encounters with her paralytic bureaucracy. Since there was no support for the plan in the federal legislature, Lacson's idea never had a chance.

Surprisingly, some planters on Negros were initially supportive of sixty-thirty-ten, but only because they thought Aquino was planning to expropriate their lands without any compensation. When it became clear that Aquino's land reform proposal was a paper tiger, the same planters withdrew their support for Lacson's plan as though it were something dreamed up by the NPA. Lacson, like Aquino, didn't like confrontation and quietly shelved his land plan for Negros, advising Aquino to do the same at the national level. "It's not doable," he said. "It simply creates expectations the government can't deliver on." Lacson surrendered so completely to the planters that when he ran for election in 1988, the oligarchs didn't bother to field a challenger. He was elected with 95 percent of the vote.

The *hacenderos* also fought the land reform battle in Manila. Negros Occidental contributed six representatives to the landlord-dominated House of Representatives, each from one of the island's preeminent sugar families. The final, loophole-riddled land reform bill, drafted and railroaded through Congress by Peping Cojuangco, Aquino's brother, included a provision allowing the president's family and other large landlords to offer workers corporate stock in their haciendas rather than land. Instead of owning farms, Aquino's workers became investors in Hacienda Luisita: nonvoting, minority shareholders in a family corporation. Their stock was practically worthless. But "land reform" had become law.

It was a classic Philippine solution: If you couldn't deliver the real product, offer a make-believe version instead. The new law did set limits on the amount of land an individual could own, but the Congress postponed the effective date of most provisions in the law so that even the most dim-witted *hacendero* would have time to divide his properties among members of his family or into dozens, sometimes hundreds, of separate dummy corporations, each with holdings too small to warrant government-imposed redistribution. Meanwhile, the NPA's land confiscation agenda proceeded in the countryside.

Asked how he would address the poverty on Negros, one of President Aquino's most trusted senior generals, a man actively involved in the counterinsurgency effort, threw up his hands. "For the life of me, I can't see a solution except to kill all the oligarchs," he said. "It can't go on forever. There's just repression, repression, repression. It's a struggle between the rich and the poor, and the rich have all the guns. The military, unfortunately, has to be with the government. We can't side with the NPA." All sides to the war on Negros increasingly saw the conflict as an all-or-nothing matter. The oligarchs, feeling more and more under siege, threw all their energies into military solutions.

Boys with Guns

"Don Miguel, let me ask you this: Just what is the purpose of cockfighting?"
"It has no purpose. That's what makes it a perfect
thing. . . . The perfection of it consists in running mad
without any necessity whatever."

—Alejandro Roces,
"Portrait of a Poet, Cocker, and Lover"

One tree at a time, the Gatuslaos removed the Himamaylan forest, and before anyone knew it, the forest was a memory.
Once it covered the mountainside, black as night, and then it was
gone. Replaced by sugarcane. Nobody recalled seeing it disappear,
only a few would swear it had ever even been there, and nobody
pointed a finger of blame. Grandparents and great-grandparents recalled that the morning air had been cooler, fresher, sweeter before.

The growth of the New People's Army had been nearly as imper-
ceptible. One day there were a few men with guns, then there were
a thousand troops, among them a considerable number of so-called
amazons. The rebels infiltrated a few remote barrios, then moved
hamlet by hamlet toward the population centers. Himamaylan became a crossroads for NPA traffic moving north and south.

Even before the NPA came into its own, though, rural Negros
had lost its attraction for people of means. Tired of its monotonous
repetitions, they began moving out, mostly to Bacolod, where there
were better schools for the children, movies, restaurants, a big cockpit, shopping, and an airport to take them to Manila, only an hour
away. Apin Gatuslao and his friends kept homes in the countryside,
repositories of nostalgia, but even those attachments faded over
time. The haciendas, the great family homesteads of their youth, became abstractions, little more than trust funds, milking cows that
paid quarterly dividends.

"The footprint of the planter is the best fertilizer," the *hacenderos* continued to tell one another. The principle remains sound: If a planter doesn't manage his hacienda personally, he usually can't expect to turn a profit. But it had all become a conceit: None of these planters had any dirt stuck to their soft leather shoes or beneath their manicured nails, and as the insurgency grew, fewer and fewer of them dared set foot on their haciendas for fear of being shot. Most handed day-to-day control to *encargados,* overseers who took the heat from the NPA while the absentee landlords kept in touch by two-way radio—"remote control," as they liked to say. They had become superfluous.

As for their laborers, those "children" they cared so much about? They were left to the *encargados,* who were less sentimental than the *hacenderos* about their wards. Some planters detached themselves even further from the haciendas, leasing them to investors who assigned their own *encargados.* The workers were orphaned.

The most comprehensive examples of the modern, cost-effective farm management methods were pioneered by Eduardo Cojuangco, one of Ferdinand Marcos's wealthiest cronies, who ran unsuccessfully for the presidency in 1992. Known as Danding and the Boss, the stoop-shouldered Cojuangco, an estranged first cousin of Corazon Cojuangco Aquino, is a godfather who speaks in a mobster's monotone, looks after his faithful followers, and is renowned for ruthlessly crushing his opponents. Under Marcos he controlled the notorious coconut monopoly, which stole millions of dollars from small farmers, and he was linked to an attempt to assassinate Emmanuel Pelaez, the monopoly's leading opponent and subsequently Aquino's ambassador to the United States. A one-time member of Cojuangco's huge private army on Luzon told a congressional committee in Washington that he and his men, under orders from the Boss, murdered political opponents of Marcos and rigged elections. Cojuangco was also tied to an aborted coup against Aquino. He denies any involvement in the attempted assassination of Pelaez, the alleged murders of political opponents, and the coup.

On Negros, Cojuangco's violence assumed a more businesslike countenance. Before purchasing his properties in Himamaylan and other towns, he demanded the eviction of all resident workers and their families, thereby eliminating the last, untidy vestiges of paternal obligation from the hacienda system. Instead of costly workers with their mewling requests for food, better housing, loans for medicines, funerals, and so on, Cojuangco's plantations were depopulated and then relied on day laborers, who were paid piecemeal or the minimum wage and nothing more. Land that was once used by workers to grow food or for housing was converted to sugarcane. Next to Cojuangco, other Negros planters began to look like philanthropists. The NPA made Cojuangco its number one target and issued orders that he was to be shot on sight.

Cojuangco had attempted to change the rules of the game overnight, but the much-vaunted paternal hacienda system was changing on its own, and as it did, hacienda workers began to realize that as limited and degrading as it had been, the alternative—no work at all—was worse. By the mid-1980s, with most of the *hacenderos* deeply in debt and the workers unemployed and hungry, the only ones who seemed to be thriving were the NPAs.

* * *

The NPA arrived in Payao in 1979, and by 1983 they were parading around the town plaza with their rifles in broad daylight, harassing upstanding citizens like Apin Gatuslao, running what was tantamount to a protection racket. Hacienda Benedicto was no longer safe. Like most of his friends, Apin gave in to the extortion demands, hoping the rebels would leave him alone, then learned that once they had him in their grasp, they wouldn't let go. Apin's "taxes" went from 5,000 pesos a month to 10,000 and eventually to 60,000, which was when he decided to fight back. Himamaylan Mayor Daisy Silverio, a close friend, said Apin couldn't afford to pay the NPA any more. "His last word was, 'Instead of giving you more taxes, I'm going to buy more guns.' " The NPA retaliated, burning his fields and destroying his farm equipment and logging machinery.

In itself, Apin's refusal to pay taxes probably would not have led to his murder, but Gerson Balitor, a priest close to Apin, says the NPA had a lengthy brief against the planter. The most egregious of his "errors" was the decision to forge a close working relationship with the military and with Marcos's notorious Civilian Home Defense Force, a huge 70,000-man militia that was technically under military control but often operated more like a government-sponsored terrorist organization. Apin's brother-in-law, Rudi Remitio, said Apin provided housing as well as materiel and financial support to the military. "If they needed a liaison with other government agencies, Serafin would provide it." His friend Ernesto Tongson said Apin's hacienda became an armed camp. "Serafin was targeted because he was helping the Army. The Army had a battalion at Hacienda Benedicto. That was the main reason he was shot."

Most planters tried to remain anonymous, and distanced themselves as much as possible from the war, but anyone with sizable interests in the countryside supported the armed forces in one way or another, and some—like Apin and Ernesto's brother Rodolfo— were active and enthusiastic collaborators. Both men employed government-trained paramilitary forces, which they supplemented with their own private armies. Apin's was known as the Batman Army, and he gained a reputation as the leading "warlord" in southern Negros. Thomas McHale, an American who was an official at the Binalbagan sugar mill, described Gatuslao as a man who "lived by the gun" and recalled how Apin had visited him in his office one day, slammed his pistol down on McHale's desk, and offered to help him eliminate "troublemakers" from the sugar workers' union. "When he took over the planters' association, he came into our office and said, 'Just give us some financial support and we'll take care of these people.' He always came in with his .45 on his hip. He was a tough son-of-a-bitch, a typical strong-arm man. I told him we'd take care of any problems ourselves."

When Father Balitor was assigned to southern Negros and became the spiritual advisor to residents of the remote reaches of Kabankalan, Binalbagan, and Himamaylan, he saw planter armies and government troops forcing peasants off their farmland and taking it over. "Apin was involved in land-grabbing way back in '68 or '69. At night people would come to my nipa hut and ask for advice. They said they had cleared the area for their little farms and that men with bulldozers and guns drove them away. There was a lot of land-grabbing going on at that time." Balitor said it was easy for people like Gatuslao to gain title to the land because the peasant farmers often had only the thinnest of legal claims, and even when their claims were valid, they couldn't afford the payoffs or the lawyers needed to make a case in court.

Father Balitor continued hearing complaints about Apin a decade later when the priest moved to Payao: "The workers were afraid of him. People whispered to me about delayed wages, even the full-time employees living on his hacienda. If it hadn't been for their loyalty, they would have transferred to other haciendas. Some of them felt *utang na loob,* but they also thought he would eventually pay them."

Balitor said workers in the logging concessions weren't paid for months at a time. "They'd go and talk to Apin, but they'd get no results. Even the NPAs tried to convince Apin to give the people justice. But he said he couldn't meet their demands. So the people in the mountains began stealing vital parts from his bulldozers" to incapacitate them. Balitor said the problem escalated until, during the last year of the Marcos dictatorship, Apin asked the military to deal with the dispute. "Rather than address the problems, the military bombed the area and forced people to evacuate."

Another priest assigned to Payao, Victor Dumalaos, said he was also aware of land-grabbing by Apin:

> One time he wanted to build a road in the mountains to transport his lumber, so he tried to bulldoze the land of the small farmers up there, and they organized themselves and formed a human barricade. The next day he sent in an Army platoon. He used the army of the government to push people off their land. You could see the soldiers bulldozing the land, destroying the crops. He promised to pay those whose land he took for the road, but he only ended up giving them some rice. I tried to convince him to change the crooked style he used at the hacienda. Some months, he would pay them, then they'd have to wait four or five months, and he'd give them a rice ration instead of their salary. I told Apin, "Why not give the laborers their salary directly every month?" I told him, "There is going to come a time when the roots of your cane will grow up into the air, and the tips will grow into the ground."

Father Dumalaos said Apin even cheated the church out of thousands of pesos in rent payments on a property he leased from the diocese.

The workers shared their grievances with the priests, but they also went to the NPA. They complained about their unpaid wages, about the land-grabbing, and about water—the water in the Pangiplan River, which Apin controlled. As the upstream farmer, he had a legal right to take as much of the water as he needed, but that didn't mean his neighbors had to be happy about it. At times Apin's water demands grew so great that the downstream rice farmers weren't getting any. Their biggest fear was that Apin would try to put them out of business, to make their farms so unprofitable that they'd be forced to sell out to him. When they could get away with it, the small farmers would sneak onto Hacienda Benedicto at night, open the floodgates, and divert the water from Apin's fields to their own. Apin knew how seriously people took the matter of water. He'd been warned about it repeatedly by the NPA and by his friends. His neighbor, Manuel "Dondon" Villafranca, had gotten into a similar tiff over water at his Hacienda Tungo, and one of his men had been shot and killed as a result. But Apin wasn't known as a great conciliator.

*　*　*

Mario Chiu was nearly as knowledgeable about Apin's problems with the New People's Army as he was about his own. During the years immediately preceding Apin's death, the two men discussed the insurgency almost daily. Mario knew about the water, the landgrabbing, and the way Apin treated his workers. Apin wasn't alone in refusing to pay the three-dollar-a-day minimum wage; hardly any of the *hacenderos* bothered. There was no need to. Nobody had ever enforced the law, and no one was about to start anytime soon. Mario said Apin was worse than most, however, paying only half the minimum wage, and Mario said he had raised the issue with Apin's wife. "I told Panching it wasn't right what they were doing. I'm not a religious person, but it just wasn't right." Apin was stubborn, though. Once he'd laid out his course, there was no turning him back. It was a matter of pride.

It was the same with the NPA: Once he decided to fight them, he couldn't back down. Friends at the planters' association said Apin never let on that he was afraid of the NPA. Maybe he wasn't. But Mario could see that Apin's private war with the rebels was escalating out of control. Mario's father, Juan Chiu, had been dead a decade already when Apin was killed. If he'd been around, Mario is convinced, his father would have talked some sense into the Gatuslaos and saved Apin's life. "Apin wouldn't have been in that big mess. Panching would have listened to my father. They both had Chinese blood. My father could have reasoned with her as a Chinese." Mario said his father would have convinced Apin to cut a deal with the rebels and said he himself had tried unsuccessfully to reason with Apin. "I knew some of the NPAs from Mambagaton, and I told Apin I'd be an intermediary with them if he wanted. I offered to resolve the dispute."

That was before Mario began having his own problems with the NPA. Like Apin, he initially thought he could do business with the rebels, but slowly he learned that the game could be far more complicated than it appeared. "At first, all the NPAs wanted was a kilo of rice, some cigarettes, small amounts of money." Later, a group of rebels stopped him near his hacienda in Mambagaton and questioned him about the way he treated his employees. Mario started giving the rebels food and clothing.

Mario acknowledges that he was hardly a model employer. "I also have dirt on my face," he said, explaining that, although he wasn't paying the minimum wage, he was not cheating people as much as Apin. He said he gave his workers benefits such as rice that were "better than what the law required." During the sugar crisis, however, Mario, like everyone else, cut back on wages. "We told our people we'd pay them less than the minimum but would support them during the lean months when there's no work." To get them through the dead season, Mario advanced them rice and offered loans.

Mario said he hated to do it, but he was also forced to reduce his workers' food allowances when they were unproductive. "Sometimes it breaks my heart if I have to cut back on the rice ration because I know that it's not only the father who won't eat, but his whole family." Mario said he worries about the inequality on Negros and the malnutrition. "Twenty or thirty years from now, if this situation continues, we're going to have a nation of retarded people," he lamented. Like others in the elite, though, Mario sees no obvious solutions.

Mario's problems with the NPA grew progressively worse over the years. It seemed the rebels never let up. One day he was attending a town fiesta when a member of the NPA pointed a pistol at him and demanded that he turn over his guns. Another time the NPA ransacked his house. Then they stole a truck. Finally, they tried to kill him, ambushing him and his driver. Mario wasn't hurt, but his driver was shot in the shoulder and the back. Mario sped to Bacolod at 100 kilometers per hour singing Christmas carols the whole way, trying to keep his driver from passing out. That incident convinced him it was time to settle with the NPA, and over the next few years he paid them 150,000 pesos in "revolutionary taxes" and another 150,000 in extortion to retrieve the trucks, tractors, and carabaos they had stolen. He lost hundreds of thousands more to thefts of equipment and rice. All told, he has put his losses at more than a million pesos. In retrospect, he suggested, he never should have played their game. "If you let people eat from your palm, they will eat your elbow," he says.

Mario blames the Americans for some of the problems on Negros because they trained the armed forces to conduct deadly counterinsurgency operations. He blames the leftist National Federation of Sugar Workers, which the planters do their best to keep off their haciendas because they see it as an incipient, infectious disease, the recruiting office of the NPA. "If you have no wounds, you will have no germs," explains Mario. He also blames the church for teaching people that the rich are the enemy. "The church coddles the NPA. This whole war was instigated by the priests. They said, 'Look, your boss is driving a jeep, and look at you.' It became a sin to be rich. In this country, if you're rich, you're a criminal and an exploiter."

Like Apin, Mario became convinced that the church financed the rebels. Although he won't say exactly what his own role was, he acknowledges that the planters, the military, and the vigilantes in Himamaylan were all involved in the threats, intimidation, and killing of church workers. "What you sow, you reap," he says in their defense.

Whatever Mario himself did, it wasn't enough for some of the more bellicose *hacenderos,* who saw Mario and his friends as no better than collaborators with the Communists. "We were seen as enemies of the Ballesteros brothers because we paid taxes to the NPA," he said, referring to two anti-Communist planters murdered by the rebels. All the planters recognized that it was suicidal to pay taxes to the Communists—the money was used to buy bullets to shoot people like themselves, after all, not to mention the police and the military—but most paid up anyway, because they saw the NPA's extortion as cheap insurance. The unstated planter ethic assumes that it's always better if the rebels burn your neighbor's house and fields than your own. The NPA leadership knew Filipino psychology well enough to conclude that most planters would betray their friends to save their own necks. It was every man for himself, one aspect of what Filipinos self-deprecatingly call their "crab mentality" —each crab in the basket clawing at the others, climbing over one another, trying to get on top. In the end, all but a few are cooked.

The payments to the NPA were, however, also an obvious vote of no confidence in the armed forces, which many *hacenderos* believed could not be relied on to defend them. Like the rebels, military leaders throughout the country extorted money from the rich, who had no choice but to pay these "insurance" premiums. It was a game of double indemnity. But the military and police were also sabotaging their own counterinsurgency efforts. A soldier could sell his M-16 rifle for about 20,000 pesos, claim it was lost or stolen, and purchase a new one for 8,000, pocketing the difference. Most often, these "hot" weapons were sold to planters. But the NPA could also buy them and just about anything else it wanted from the military.

In fact, the NPA bought nearly all of its ammunition from the armed forces for about five pesos per round. Silvino Gallardo, known as Ka Macao when he headed the Negros NPA, said the transactions were routine. "A dealer would come by with a military escort and sell us as much as we wanted. There was no charge for delivery." He laughed. "They'd also try to sell us machine guns, but we preferred to buy just the bullets. We get our weapons at a better price." The "better price"—free—often meant that the owner of a weapon—a soldier or policeman—paid with his life. Military commanders, recognizing that their men could barely survive on a government stipend, excused them for stealing and selling thousands of rounds of ammunition to the rebels. "The need of the moment is stronger than the abstraction of a bullet coming back to you sometime," one officer explained. "The average soldier thinks, 'If I don't sell, someone else will.' "

Mario discovered that the games in which he and his planter friends were caught up had multiple variations. One year, despite his regular tax payments to the NPA, he began receiving threatening letters demanding 1,000 pesos for each hectare of cane fields he owned. If he didn't pay, the letters said, his crops would all be burned. That meant coming up with more than 400,000 pesos. Mario decided he'd had enough of the NPA, refused to pay, and the next thing he knew, sixty hectares of sugarcane went up in smoke. Only later did he find out that what he assumed were extortion demands from the NPA had actually come from the military. The Army pretended to be NPAs and burned Mario's fields to get him to support the Army, which was fighting the NPA precisely because the rebels were burning the planters' fields. "The idea was to scare me so I'd go to them [the Army] for protection." It required a special mentality to come up with this stuff.

When Mario considered the fates of people like Moret De los Santos and Apin Gatuslao, or when he examined his own encounters with the military and the rebels, the absurdity of the drama became apparent. Mario initially resisted pressure from the military as he'd done with the NPA. He was convinced the armed forces were, as he put it, "totally corrupt," and was reluctant to allow soldiers onto his hacienda because he feared their presence would invite attacks by the NPA, as had happened to Apin. In addition to the detachment based at Hacienda Benedicto, at least eleven haciendas in Himamaylan alone supported military units, and there were more than a hundred islandwide. Yet despite the proliferation of detachments, the planters still had problems with the rebels. Eventually, his own repeated run-ins with the NPA persuaded Mario that he had no choice but to opt for what he saw as the lesser evil. "I said I would stop dealing with the NPA if the military would agree to arm me."

Mario gave up thinking about solutions to the problems of Negros, invited an Army detachment to his Mambagaton hacienda, and erected a cyclone fence around his home. He estimated that he paid the armed forces about 100,000 pesos a year for their services. As always, he was philosophical about his predicament, insisting there was no alternative. "Where there's sugar, there are ants," he said with a shrug.

*   *   *

Following Corazon Aquino's election, the military's top brass, their tongues set free, took to blaming the insurgency on the economy, arguing that the war couldn't be won on the battlefield because the NPA was largely a political and economic problem for the civilian government to handle. Everyone knew, however, that there were insufficient resources for the fledgling civilian administration to address the country's basic social problems and thereby stop the war. So the military simultaneously pressed for more and more men and weapons, all the while disclaiming responsibility for its failure to produce a victory over the Communists. There was nothing fundamentally wrong with the notion that the way to put an end to insurgency was to address the underlying causes of peoples' unhappiness, but the argument was more than a bit disingenuous coming from members of the armed forces, many of whom were working overtime to undermine or topple the civilian government.

Negrense landlords voiced the same economic arguments while assiduously evading payment of taxes that might have permitted the government to begin addressing the myriad problems of poverty. Since they were unwilling to buy off the island's malcontents through land reform, government programs, or major private-sector investments, the oligarchs' only recourse lay with the military and its surrogates.

Responsibility for combatting the insurgency on Negros fell to the two largest branches of the armed forces of the Philippines, the Army and the Philippine Constabulary, or national police. The mastermind of the Negros counterinsurgency effort was the Constabulary's regional commander, Colonel Miguel Coronel, proclaimed by President Aquino one of the "Outstanding Young Men of the Philippines." For Coronel, democracy and liberty were abstractions, useful for propaganda purposes—as in "the armed forces are defending democracy against communism"—but with little practical bearing on either his mission or the everyday realities of Negros. Coronel's philosophy is laid out in his 768-page tome, *Pro-Democracy People's War*, published in 1991, which details the strategy he tested on Negros for defeating the Communists. Coronel writes:

> Liberty is the most attractive and desirable feature of democracy. However, it happens to be also its most disadvantageous vulnerability. This is due to the trade-off relationship between freedom and security. It means that the more freedom you give to the people, the less secure or more vulnerable is the security of the state to would-be power grabbers; while if

you give no freedom to the people, then the security of the
state is most enhanced.

Coronel's preference for the state, which is to say, the rich, was
transparent. He paid lipservice to the supremacy of civilian government, but his book is a manual for its cooptation by the military.
Like most military men, Coronel was interested in getting as
many men and weapons as possible under his command, and he inflated the strength of his enemy accordingly. While he acknowledged
that the NPA on Negros had only about 1,000 firearms, he estimated
the NPA's "mass base" at the end of 1986 as more than 100,000, suggesting that the island was inundated by Communists and that the
military was vastly outnumbered. Coronel warned his superiors that
the NPA had already demonstrated its capacity to paralyze Bacolod
through its terror tactics and that it "could easily mobilize 50,000 to
80,000" men to "converge on the city."
Even conceding a huge element of hype in Coronel's analysis,
there was no question that he'd inherited a serious problem. During
the last two years under Marcos, the size of the NPA on Negros had
doubled, and companies of seventy or more NPAs, most of them the
sons and daughters of sugar workers, were engaging the Philippine
Army in combat. The rebels had routed one entire company of Army
Scout Rangers, had accumulated a sizable cache of weapons, and
were publicly predicting a full-blown civil war within three to five
years. In a raid on the Visayan Maritime Academy in Bacolod, the
rebels had walked off with more than 400 machine guns, grenade
launchers, and mortars, enough weapons to arm an entire NPA battalion. NPA Sparrow units were entrenched in Bacolod, where
killings of police were becoming an increasingly common occurrence. In the countryside, it was possible to walk for days through
NPA-controlled areas unchallenged by the military. Coronel managed to have Negros designated a top-priority counterinsurgency
province, and the military began pouring in men and materiel.
Within three years of Aquino's 1986 inauguration, something on the
order of 5,000 members of the Philippine Constabulary and Army,
plus an estimated 2,000–3,000 paramilitary forces, were operating
there. The Philippine Air Force was conducting bombing raids
against mountain villages, creating more than 30,000 refugees. According to the vice-governor, an additional 3,000 paramilitaries were

employed in the so-called private armies or personal security forces financed by politicians, planters, and warlords. And five sizable vigilante groups were doing their part for "peace and order" with the blessing of the military, which called them "civilian volunteer organizations" in deference to queasy liberals and foreign human rights organizations.

Coronel's calculus was brilliantly successful in beefing up his forces even as the political environment in the Philippines was shifting dramatically in his favor. The election of Corazon Aquino had called into question the very raison d'être of the Communist party and the New People's Army. The party's strategic analysis traced all of the country's problems back to "the U.S.-Marcos dictatorship," with the paramount emphasis always on the United States and the dreaded Central Intelligence Agency. Marcos, according to party doctrine, was merely a puppet of the United States and the CIA, which had been the real enemy before the dictator and remained so after his demise. After all, party loyalists argued quite accurately, the United States had robbed the country of its sovereignty following the Spanish-American War; waged a ruthless war against Philippine independence; deliberately stifled domestic economic growth; plundered the country's natural resources; suppressed an agrarian peasant revolt in the 1950s; assiduously defended the country's wealthy oligarchs; and rigged national elections. During the 1980s, the United States had poured hundreds of millions of dollars in military aid into the Philippines to prop up Marcos and preserve U.S. access to its military bases in the islands, and members of the Philippine armed forces regularly received combat, intelligence, and psychological warfare training in the United States. Following a notorious, rigged election in 1981, which Marcos won with 86 percent of the vote, President Reagan and Nancy Reagan warmly congratulated the dictator, and Vice President Bush waxed exuberant in his toast at the dictator's inauguration. "We love your adherence to democratic principle and to the democratic processes," Bush gushed.

For ordinary Filipinos, it defied common sense that the world's leading champion of democracy would continue to support a tyrant most people held responsible for the destruction of the national

economy and the death of Ninoy Aquino. In spite of the difficult historical relationship, Filipinos generally held the United States and
Americans in high regard. Indeed, for every Filipino who resented
the Americans, there were twenty with relatives in the United States,
and hundreds lined up patiently outside the U.S. embassy seeking
emigration visas. Rural Negrenses didn't blame Americans when
U.S.-made helicopters, mortars, and machine guns provided as foreign aid were used in operations that drove them from their homes;
they blamed their own government. When leftists and nationalists
accused the CIA of running the war on Negros, the typical cane
worker scratched his head in bewilderment.

Filipinos are said to be exceedingly forgiving and to have unusu-
ally short memories. Once Marcos had fallen and the United States
had endorsed Aquino, the legacy of U.S. support for Marcos seemed
to vanish in the mist of ancient history. And few Filipinos were
willing to buy the Communist party's argument that what it now
called the "U.S.–Aquino regime" was really no different from the
dictatorship.

The elections that doomed the dictator had been a rout for
the Communists. In December 1985, as Filipinos were flocking to
Aquino's cause, the party newspaper, *Ang Bayan,* had labeled the
upcoming February balloting announced by Marcos a "swindle" and
a "circus of the reactionaries" and had urged a nationwide boycott. After years of fraudulent elections under Marcos, though, the
boycott decision proved a complete misreading of the national
mood and the proletarian masses the party leadership professed to
represent.

The Communists knew Marcos well enough to accurately predict
that he would fix the vote count. They also recognized that the problems the country faced would not be solved by removing one man.
What they failed to appreciate was how desperately Filipinos wanted
change, any change; they underestimated the potency of Ninoy
Aquino's martyrdom in the figure of his widow, as well as the risks
ordinary people were willing to take to effect Ninoy's "impossible
dream" of bringing the dictator down. Ultimately, they refused to
recognize that next to Marcos and the vulgar Imelda, a simple, soft-
spoken housewife like Cory Aquino would have extraordinary appeal, regardless of what she actually stood for.

Following their brief revolution against Spain in 1898, Negrenses had held the first democratic elections for a legislative assembly any-where in Asia. Under the American colonizers, elections in the Phil-ippines had become a firmly rooted tradition that gave people some sense of shaping their own destiny, or at least a belief that they were entitled to real democracy, even if it remained an abstraction. Like the church's holy days and the barrio fiestas, elections were also enormously popular social events enjoyed by the *tao* without regard for the higher purposes of either church or state. Ordinary citizens voted even though they knew their ballots made no difference.

The Communist party had no patience for such joyful indul-gences and stood by dumbfounded as Filipinos threw themselves into the biggest fiesta anyone had witnessed in decades. If the Peo-ple Power Revolution of 1986 was a purely vicarious experience for most Filipinos, it was also a source of tremendous pride for a nation lacking a strong identity. It produced a sense that Filipinos could succeed and that there was an alternative to the bloodshed of a war that had already gone on for sixteen years at a cost of some 40,000 lives. By denigrating this accomplishment, the Communists dissoci-ated themselves from the greatest collective experience of Filipino nationalism since the country gained its independence at the end of World War II. Many Filipinos viewed People Power as the dawning of a new age, and the Communists had elected to be absent at its creation.

With its legitimacy seriously undermined, the party could lay no claim to a role in the new, popularly elected government. It was also confronted by a military reinvigorated and, at least temporarily, le-gitimized on account of its key role in staging the coup that finally brought down Marcos and allowed Aquino to take office. The Com-munists correctly predicted that Aquino would fail to make revolu-tionary economic changes, that she would be incapable of seeing beyond the narrow interests of her class, that she would squander her impressive mandate, and that the military would continue to abuse people. But the party's prescience counted for naught with the *tao*.

Already badly damaged, the Communist party's credibility suf-fered still more when several of its top leaders—including the founder of the New People's Army—concluded that the war no longer made sense and resigned. This, in turn, triggered a major internal debate at the highest levels of the movement between those who favored accommodation with supposedly progressive democratic forces aboveground and those who advocated an escalation of the guerrilla war. Also, the party was divided over its participation in peace talks held with members of Aquino's government during the first year of her presidency. The negotiations themselves did little to bolster the movement's image as its leaders stumbled to make their complex political and economic agenda comprehensible to the average Filipino.

Then, less than a month after the peace talks collapsed, as Colonel Coronel was pulling together his forces on Negros, the party blundered again, boycotting a nationwide referendum on a new constitution, which was supported by a three-to-one majority of voters and was widely construed as a popular endorsement of Aquino's presidency. The Communists objected that the document failed to address the land issue and a handful of other concerns, which was absolutely true but irrelevant to the great mass of Filipinos, who delighted in their new constitution and year-old government regardless of the imperfections.

There was, however, even more bad news for the Communists, news that was only beginning to become known to the public, problems that had been percolating within the NPA in places like Negros for years. These problems would prove a great boon to Colonel Coronel.

Back in 1983, in the wake of Ninoy Aquino's assassination, thousands of young people had flocked to join the NPA, bringing with them a handful of military spies and saboteurs called deep penetration agents. Known as zombies among the rebels, they provided intelligence to the armed forces, incited conflicts within the movement, and perpetrated criminal acts designed to discredit the NPA. Nobody inside the NPA knew exactly how serious the problem was, but some reports put the number of zombies nationwide in the hundreds. Furthermore, the NPA leadership on the island of Mindanao acknowledged that zombies had worked their way into top positions in its command structure. Seized by paranoia, NPA leaders in Mindanao undertook frantic efforts to "purge" the movement, and by 1985 reports of mass killings there began circulating in the Manila media. By the time the purges were called off, hundreds of rebels were reportedly dead, and the rest were wondering whether they would be next.

On Negros, the first indication of a zombie problem surfaced one day after the murder of Serafin Gatuslao, when a top NPA propaganda officer defected from the movement and released a stinging videotaped indictment of what he called its "indefensible acts of terror." The defector said he knew of suspected informers who had been tortured and executed based on nothing more than flimsy allegations.

In retrospect, it seems likely that the zombies would not have become a serious problem on Negros if the NPA's leadership hadn't abandoned the very tactics that had worked to the movement's advantage. Battlefield successes during the last years of Marcos's regime convinced these leaders that the rebels could take on much larger concentrations of government forces, when in reality the NPAs were badly outgunned and Coronel's massive reinforcements were shifting the balance of power even more heavily against them. As the war escalated, the NPA recruited new men and women whose sole responsibilities were to fight. At the same time, it abandoned much of the tedious political and educational work that had been critical to building its mass base. Discipline deteriorated and, in some units, broke down completely. Armed NPAs began entering peasants' homes without permission, demanding food or a place to sleep. They interfered with religious ceremonies, meted out arbitrary punishments, stole property, and committed sexual assaults.

At the same time, Coronel's strategy was taking a toll on NPA finances. The rebels still relied heavily on taxes they levied on the sugar mills, hacenderos, and other "class enemies," but the military was convincing a growing number of planters like Apin Gatuslao and Mario Chiu that they could risk bucking NPA extortion demands. Planter resistance, in turn, led the rebels to shift the burden of taxation to smaller farmers and peasants, alienating the very people whose support they needed most. Villagers would be asked to choose: pulo ukon polo, ten pesos or the barrel of the gun. Desperate for money, the rebels took to robbing bus drivers and truckers delivering beer and soft drinks.

Support among rural peasants, already demoralized by the government killings, bombings, and evacuations, quickly plummeted. Common people who may once have been sympathetic to the movement's broad goals, or tolerant of having the "Nice People Around," were finding they no longer wanted anything to do with the increasingly violent revolutionaries. In barrios and even within families, loyalties to the government and the NPA became divided, resulting in instances of what locals referred to as "clan warfare." NPA units that adhered to strict standards of discipline and shunned the growing violence were nonetheless tainted by the lawlessness of their comrades. As the movement lost its focus, defections grew, and as its militant leadership ordered more and more encounters, it suffered a growing number of casualties. Repeated combat defeats fomented suspicions of betrayal and zombie paranoia, which eventually led to "cleansing" operations—the liquidation of suspected spies. More than sixty rebels were reportedly liquidated in central Negros alone.

*   *   *

The words of Marx, Lenin, and Mao are like *anting antings* for anti-Communists in the armed forces, as if by quoting their enemies they somehow imbibe their powers and sap their strength. Colonel Coronel's strategy for defeating the NPA was invariably explained with Mao Zedong's parable about fish swimming in water—the fish in this case being the rebels, the water being the rural populace in which the NPA was able to move about freely. When the fish are taken from the water, they die and victory is achieved. A major problem for the Philippine military, however, was the one the Americans encountered in Vietnam: They couldn't figure out who the "fish" were until they started shooting. To be on the safe side, Filipinos, like the Americans in Vietnam, erred on the side of overkill and assumed that anyone was an enemy until proven otherwise.

Alas, Coronel's enemies list was rather extensive. It included unions, student and human rights groups, organizations of sugar workers and fishermen, and dozens of other "fronts" such as the Basic Christian Community, which together represented the overwhelming majority of rural Negrenses. Although Coronel knew that the average, unarmed rural peasant was in no position to resist the NPA, he nonetheless set out to demonstrate how miserable life could be for "collaborators," making entire communities pay the price for the infractions of any one of their members. Draining the water from the fish often meant driving farmers from their homes and fields or forcing them into new settlements called "enclaves" or "hamlets," which were controlled by the military or paramilitary forces.

Meanwhile, the planters hunkered down in the enclave of Bacolod, surrounded by a squawk of radio static and phalanxes of armed bodyguards. By the time Aquino took office, the elite were desperate enough to support just about anyone who might return Negros to a semblance of its former "normal" existence, and they agreed to underwrite a large part of the campaign against the "Communist grand design and deception," as Coronel characterized the insurgency. Planters and other businessmen acceded to a proposal by Coronel to create a Sugar Development Fund, taxing themselves a few centavos on every pound of sugar they produced. In one year, the fund raised 50 million pesos, which, in addition to providing the Constabulary with vehicles, fuel, radios, and other equipment, was used to arm, feed, and clothe paramilitary troops hired to defend the plantations. "They're not the best kind of troops," acknowledged planter Nil Gamboa, who, as a Philippine Marine colonel received sniper training at Fort Benning, Georgia. "They're poorly trained and unmotivated. But they're a stopgap. We'd have been overrun if we didn't use them."

Ironically, the various troops and vigilantes Coronel collected to defeat the insurgency might just as well have joined the rebels, for all the good their alliance with the military would bring them. Certainly most of the vigilantes had more in common with the NPA than with the planters; typically, they were poor, uneducated, and often desperate. But on Negros, there was never any shortage of men prepared to do whatever was required to earn a few pesos, and being a mercenary was better than nothing.

President Aquino couldn't seem to make up her mind about the vigilantes. She had campaigned against abuses by paramilitary groups, but one year after taking office, she publicly endorsed Alsa Masa (Masses Arise), the largest vigilante group in the country. Six months later, she decided she was opposed to vigilantism, but by then more than two hundred militia had sprung up nationwide. Aquino eventually issued an executive order outlawing vigilante groups and di-

rected her armed forces chief of staff to disband them. Simultaneously, however, she announced the creation of Civilian Volunteer
Organizations, which, in practice, amounted to the same thing.

Laws were frequently passed in Manila that might just as well
have been issued from Mars for all they mattered, and the news that
vigilantes were illegal never seemed to make its way to Negros. If
it did, the military simply ignored it. The island was home to
"Greenans," who wore green headbands; "Pulahans," or "Reds,"
who identified themselves with red headbands; "Putihans," or
"Whites," members of a group called "Power Spirit," as well as Alsa
Masa. Most people simply referred to the lot of them as *fanaticos,* a
term that seemed to carry none of the pejorative connotations one
might expect. The *fanaticos* cast their lot with the military neither
out of ideology nor out of any sense of debt or obligation, but because they had been ambushed or extorted by the NPA, needed
work, had been directed to join by their employers, or saw an opportunity to exact revenge against personal enemies. Some of the
vigilantes were "surrenderees," captured NPAs who, as the military
patois would have it, had "returned to the fold of the law." Others
were "fake surrenderees," simple farmers and laborers the military
had commandeered into vigilante units.

When it came to vigilantes, murderers, lunatics, and other assorted
misfits, Himamaylan was a living Madame Tussaud's, so it was no
surprise that Governor Daniel Lacson began hearing horror stories
from there as soon as he took office.

The mild-mannered and well-meaning Lacson implored citizens
of rural Negros who had complaints against the military, the vigilantes, or the religious nuts to file cases in court. Most Negrenses
found this idea laughable, given that bringing a case against the military, the police, or their assorted mercenaries only invited retalia-
tion. Like President Aquino, Governor Lacson endorsed vigilantes
while trusting—contrary to empirical evidence—that men of good-
will reasoning together could impede the cycle of murder and revenge exacerbated by these very groups. But one incident involving
a vigilante by the name of Regino "Ehen" Marcelino briefly roused
Lacson to action.

Marcelino, a World War II veteran, headed one of the Marcos-era

Civilian Home Defense Forces, which continued to operate on Negros with the tacit support of local military commanders, despite Aquino's having officially abolished them. When Marcelino's CHDF vigilantes burned twenty-one Himamaylan houses and murdered several of their inhabitants, Lacson resolved to get to the bottom of the matter. He ordered an investigation and dispatched a top aide, Roberto "Toto" Pineda, to the town.

Conrado Anday, a member of Marcelino's group, would later testify that Marcelino instructed him and several of his colleagues to murder Pineda and his guide, Roberto Bajos, and to incinerate their bodies because they were working for the NPA. Anday said the killers relieved the victims of their clothing, wristwatches, a camera, and a tape recorder, all of which were turned over to Marcelino. He also said that one of his colleagues removed an eye and an ear from Bajos, as souvenirs, before the body was burned. Bajos's bloodstained red cap, which now had two bulletholes in it, was hung on a nail in Marcelino's house. Anday said he carried out the order because he was afraid of Marcelino.

Since his close aide had been murdered, one might have expected Governor Lacson to have had a personal interest in addressing the vigilante problem in Himamaylan, and the governor *did* order another investigation of the incident. But he never demanded that the military either control or eliminate the vigilantes because he, like Aquino, was afraid of the military and had concluded that it was beyond his power to control. Even though he continued to suggest that peasants file complaints against the military and vigilantes in the courts, he himself—with considerably greater political power, financial resources, and class status—wasn't about to tackle these forces in the courts or in any other forum. Instead, he washed his hands of any responsibility for the war and its impact on the civilian population and concentrated on less unsavory matters, such as his never-realized plan to turn Negros into an economic titan—a "mini-Taiwan," as he was fond of calling it.

Paradise Lost

This world presses in on us from every side; it scatters
fistfuls of our dust across the land and takes bits and
pieces of us as if to water the earth with our blood.
What did we do? Why have our souls rotted away?

—Juan Rulfo, *Pedro Páramo*

Apin Gatuslao had spent enough time with his friends
in the armed forces to know he couldn't really trust them. It was one
thing to use the military and paramilitary to guard his farms and
equipment, and another to use them for his own personal security
and that of his wife and children. For this, Apin turned to blood
relations: cousin Exequil Hagoriles and nephews Roy and Clinton
Giconcillo. Roy and Clinton, the youngest of eight children born to
the pastor of the United Church of Christ in Escalante, at the north
end of the island, were low-key but highly trained and reliable bodyguards. They did have one major liability, however, a liability Apin
apparently mistook for an asset. Both had been faithful employees of
Armando Gustilo, the "bionic warlord," and Apin probably reasoned
that anyone who had proved himself to his friend Gustilo would be
both professional and trustworthy. What Apin didn't realize was that
the Giconcillos had been marked for assassination by the NPA.

Roy Giconcillo, twenty-nine, was the first to sign on with Apin.
Later, he brought along his younger brother, Clinton, twenty-five.
After that, the three men were rarely apart. For Clinton, this constant companionship became a nagging problem because Joy, his
lover and the mother of their son, Milton, wasn't happy with the fact
that Clinton was making very little money working for his cheap-
skate uncle, whom everyone knew the NPA could blow away at any
moment. Joy knew that good old Uncle Apin had been receiving
death threats from the NPA for about three years, and she worried

that if, God forbid, Clinton and Roy were both killed, she and Milton would be left penniless. Clinton listened to her arguments and was convinced it was time to quit. On what was to have been his last day of work, he drove by Apin's house in Bacolod to return a .45 pistol, thank his uncle, and say his good-byes. But Roy suggested that the three men spend the day together one last time, for old time's sake, that they take a trip south to Himamaylan and Payao.

Although Apin's name had appeared on a widely circulated NPA hit list, Mario Chiu said that his friend didn't seem concerned, that Apin "ate death threats for breakfast." But his priest in Payao, Gerson Balitor, had no doubt that Apin was afraid the NPA was going to kill him. "Sometimes when he'd go to the hacienda, a whole military convoy would go ahead of him to clear the area." Apin's friends and family urged him repeatedly to leave Himamaylan, but he didn't trust anyone else to run the business. It was only recently that he had succumbed to the pressures and made plans to spend some time with his children in the States. He was scheduled to leave in two weeks.

The morning of the day he died, Apin stopped by his office at the planters' association and spoke briefly with Araceli Valenciano, his secretary for the past twenty years. She also said she knew Apin was an NPA target but insisted he never let on that he feared for his life. Apin talked with her about her salary, acknowledged that she wasn't being paid enough, and promised to give her a substantial raise. Although she didn't know exactly how much money he was talking about, Araceli felt reassured that Apin was going to take care of her. Apin's cousin, Junior Monton, had had a similar conversation about money, and the two were supposed to discuss the matter again that same afternoon.

Apin was having drinks with friends at radio station KYKW in Binalbagan when he got a call on his radio from Panching telling him lunch was ready at the prawn farm in Himamaylan. A group of thirty NPA rebels watched in silence as Apin's yellow Toyota Land Cruiser rumbled up the Mambagaton Road and turned into the farm, about a half-mile from the home of Moret De los Santos. The rebels had been there since the night before, when they had dug into the drainage ditches that run alongside the road, just in front of some of the Gatuslaos' cane fields. Their instructions were to let Apin's vehicle pass in front of them unharmed as it headed east through the cane fields. They were to make sure there were no children with him and that he wasn't being followed by Army troops. It was only when Apin retraced his route, now with Panching seated beside him and his bodyguards in the back, that the rebels opened fire. Dozens of M-16 rounds pierced the vehicle's thin metal skin and shattered its windows.

Panching's first thought when she heard all the explosions was, "My God, this must be New Year's." As she threw herself onto the floor and curled her tiny frame beneath the Toyota's air conditioner, she heard someone shout the word "surrender" and thought she heard Serafin say something to her. "I whispered to him not to make a sound, but it was his last. I saw that he had a bullet wound in his head. I knew he was gone."

Apin and Roy Giconcillo were killed almost immediately. Roy took a single bullet through his right shoulder, another through his right eye, and a line of bullet holes ran across his back and opened up his chest. His body was so badly mangled that his coffin was sealed for the funeral. Clinton's autopsy showed that bullets had fractured his hands and legs. Nevertheless, he had managed to un-hinge the back door of the van and to fire a single rocket-propelled grenade before receiving a fatal gunshot behind his ear. His sister Katherine said she was told that the rocket grenade killed "at least" eleven of the NPA rebels, but there is no evidence that any rebels were killed in the encounter.

Within seconds, the rebels were swarming onto the roof and hood of the Land Cruiser, firing straight down into the passenger compartment. Panching, who was armed with a handgun, fell out of the jeep onto the road. A bullet passed through her chest just below her left armpit, barely missing her heart. She pleaded with the NPAs to spare her life. "Please don't shoot me," she said. "Have pity on my children; I still have children." Before they left, one of the NPAs fired a single shot at the center of Apin's forehead and a final shot through one of his feet. Another rebel apologized to Panching. "I'm sorry, ma'am" was all he said. The whole incident took less than five minutes. The NPAs retreated north and west toward Calance.

Army Scout Rangers arrived at the scene of the killings within minutes, but they were too late. With the exception of Panching, everybody was dead. A handwritten report on file at the Himamay-lan police station described extensive damage to the Land Cruiser and said that 28,000 pesos in cash, an undetermined amount in U.S.

dollars, and some jewelry were stolen, along with a small arsenal of rifles, grenade launchers, and pistols.

Father Eamon Gill drove to the scene of the shooting from Our Lady of the Snows Church and performed last rites for Apin and the Giconcillo brothers. It no longer mattered whether Apin considered Gill a "Red." Panching was taken to the Himamaylan hospital, and Papa Johnny Silos drove her north to Bacolod, where her wounds were treated at the provincial hospital.

Mario Chiu paid a visit to his friend Tito Apin in the Bacolod morgue and made a mental note of his wounds. Apin had lost two fingers; he had a gunshot wound in his chin, a bullet hole below one of his eyes, a wound in his arm, and a dark powder-burned hole in the center of his forehead. Oh yes, and the gunshot wound in his right foot. Mario said that the shot to the foot was rumored to have been a deliberate payback for all the people Apin had kicked.

Father Balitor recalled noticing that Apin's workers didn't seem upset by his death. "When Apin was killed, I felt I had lost a friend. But I could also see that the people were rejoicing. They weren't sorry he was dead. They felt a sense of relief. They were happy."

Eventually, friends in the armed forces reported to the family that most of the NPAs involved in the attack had been liquidated. It was unlikely, however, that the military had more than a glimmer of an idea which NPAs were involved or, for that matter, any interest in finding out.

After Clinton was killed, Joy, his common-law wife, who was desperate for work, took a job as a maid in Saudi Arabia. When she returned, she used her savings to build a new house in Escalante on the site of the home in which she and Clinton had once lived together. Directly in front of Joy's house and a lush stand of graceful bamboo is the grave of Roy and Clinton, marked with a thick concrete slab. A plaque at the site reads:

WE HAVE FOUGHT A GOOD FIGHT. WE HAVE FINISHED OUR COURSE.

WE HAVE KEPT THE FAITH.

IN MEMORY OF OUR TWO LOVED ONES WHO FOUGHT BRAVELY

EVEN TO THE END FOR THEIR BELOVED
UNCLE SERAFIN GATUSLAO AND AUNTI ESPERANZA UY GATUSLAO.
A LOVING MEMORY CAN NEVER BE FORGOTTEN BY THOSE
WHO SAW THE INCIDENT AND HEARD.

The Gatuslaos had a shorter memory for the two men. They paid for the funeral, but neither Joy nor any of the Giconcillos was offered a single peso of assistance by the Gatuslaos once the men were buried.

Funeral services for Apin were held at the Redemptorist church in Bacolod, a somewhat ironic choice given the fact that many of the elite had boycotted the church. In addition, the local office of Task Force Detainees, the country's principal human rights group and one of the most prominent of the alleged Communist fronts, is located on the church grounds. Panching would later confide that Apin had become very "bitter against the church" in his later years, and that she held the church responsible for her husband's death. "I felt the church stoked the fire; they instigated. You would go to church, and a priest would tell the people, 'You are nothing but a carabao, a beast of burden, and these lands belong to you.' I would say they were brainwashing people."

Although no one in the church ever stood up to publicly condemn Apin's murder, ten priests officiated at his funeral. Panching had her husband's body cremated, and she buried half of the ashes in a marble tomb that is part of an open-air family mausoleum at the Bacolod Memorial Park. Apin's tomb sits beside two others on a beige marble floor beneath a glass canopy that is supported by four pillars covered with white porcelain tiles. Four palm trees, one dead, stand in front of the structure. Behind the three tombs on a wall, a relief shows Christ with his hand outstretched, as if in benediction, toward a plaque inscribed in gold to Serafin Gatuslao: "Greater love no man hath than this, that he lay down his life for his friends (John 15:18)." Apin probably would have liked the inscription Panching had chosen for him.

Apin's murder provoked an extremely short-lived public response. In the final analysis, what was said was actually less interesting than how little was said. People had a tendency to distance themselves from victims of the NPA, as if they might be contagious. *Visayan Daily Star* editor Ninfa Leonardia normally lavished her attentions on the social calendar of Bacolod's upper crust, their travels abroad, and the latest adventures of expatriate Negrenses in Los Angeles, but Apin's murder moved her to dash off a few words in his memory. "That was terrible news we had yesterday about Apin and Panching Gatuslao being ambushed right in Himamaylan," she wrote in a brief editorial. "We condole with the Gatuslaos, to whom this tragic incident must be a horrible shock."

Like many people, Leonardia thought of Himamaylan as a sleepy, innocuous town, a signpost on the way to Kabankalan and the dusty, untraveled south, and she seemed almost surprised to learn that something was amiss. The new mayor of Himamaylan was calling it "the killing fields," she marveled. "What is happening to that once peaceful place?" But you had only to read the ongoing litany of carnage in the *Star* to have a pretty good idea what was happening all over Negros. In the month preceding Apin's killing, the NPA had attacked two police stations in Bacolod and one in Manapla. There had been a massacre of six members of Himamaylan's Basic Christian Community, the same BCC to which Moret De los Santos belonged. In the far south, the Army had bombed the town of Santa Catalina, which triggered the evacuation of a thousand people, and just outside of Bacolod, Julio "July" Ballesteros, a prominent sugar planter, had been murdered. Julio and his brother, Ike, had resisted efforts by the National Federation of Sugar Workers to unionize their cane cutters. Mario Chiu remembers that after Julio was killed, Ike said he was going to "go tooth for tooth with the NPA" and that Ike and several other planters actually went out hunting rebels. "He was very aggressive. Just like Apin," Mario says. "When the NPA got Ike, they tortured him to death."

It took some doing to remain oblivious of all of this, especially for the publisher of what was then the island's only newspaper. If Leonardia was naive, though, the comments of her right-wing columnist, Primo Esleyer, were downright obtuse. "Apin Gatuslao was a civilian. He was a planter and not a combatant. Why should he be ambushed? And why was the killing so brutal? These and very many more [questions], the NPA leadership must answer." Esleyer seemed to believe there was something ungentlemanly about Apin's killing, as if the guerrillas adhered to some protocol or had changed the rules of engagement without consulting the captain of the other team. Coming from Esleyer, who was rumored to be a member of one of the Bacolod death squads, the comments seemed nothing if not disingenuous.

Only columnist and historian Modesto Sa-Onoy came close to an appreciation of the situation in his protest against the Batman's death. "How can one explain who, indeed, is the enemy?" he wrote in the *Star*. "Unless, of course, the terrorists have declared war upon us all." In fact, that was precisely what many among the elite had come to believe.

It took several weeks before the Communist party circulated a flyer claiming credit for the attack on Apin. The perfunctory statement said that Gatuslao had been killed because of his "whole-hearted" cooperation with the military, because he allowed the soldiers to use Hacienda Benedicto as a staging area for their operations, because he had used the military "for his own ends," because the soldiers based at Benedicto continuously abused residents of the area, and because Apin's logging operations had denuded the forests and placed people in danger from landslides during the annual monsoon rains.

The head of the NPA explained that Apin had a private army of "Batman soldiers" who wore the Batman emblem on their uniforms and guarded his properties and that small farmers in the area had complained to the rebels that Apin had diverted the course of the Pangiplan River onto his own land, denying them access to water. He further claimed that the movement had pictures of a rebel sympathizer who had been tortured at Hacienda Benedicto. "He was lying in an open grave with his sandals on his chest. They pulled out his fingernails before they killed him."

Three months after Apin's funeral, Panching left Bacolod. Dondon Villafranca drove her to the airport, believing that she was moving to Manila. But Panching had no intention of staying in Manila for long, and to the surprise of her friends, she and her daughter, Myla Christine, left almost immediately to join her sons, Miguel Florentino and Serafin, Jr., in the United States. Panching brought with her the remainder of Apin's ashes.

Beside Apin's tomb at the Bacolod Memorial Park are the tombs of his father, Miguel, and his brother, Miguel, Jr., known as Mike.

Within the Gatuslao family there had always been tension, jealousies, over how Apin and Panching were running the family business. Rudi Remitio and some of the others referred to Apin and Panching as the "conjugal dictator," an expression frequently applied to Marcos and Imelda. "Panching was holding the checkbook, and she and Apin signed the checks, so for all intents and purposes, they were the owners [of the family corporation], even though they really weren't," Rudi said. Following Apin's death, there was an internal struggle over control of the family's assets, which led Apin's sister, Janet Remitio, and their brother, Mike, the manager of a Bacolod bank, to have a falling out with another sister, Sylvia. Sylvia and her husband, Perfecto "Jun" Estrada, a former Constabulary sergeant, felt they had been cut out of their fair share of the family fortune.

Late one night, two years after Apin's death, the guards at the Gatuslao family compound in Bacolod admitted three men who proceeded directly to the swimming pool bathhouse, where they spent the night. At 8:45 the following morning, the men, wearing hoods over their heads, entered the den of Mike's house. Mike ran for a bathroom and locked the door, but came out, apparently because he was afraid the intruders would hurt Janet. He was told to lie flat on his stomach and was immediately shot dead. The *Star* carried a picture of Mike lying facedown in a pool of blood. A story in the paper said he was shot in the back of the head and that the bullet exited through his face. Janet threw herself under a desk, but one of the gunmen ordered her to come out and then fired two shots at her. One shot hit her in the arm; the other entered her back at the right shoulder. The gunmen fled in Mike's white Ford Lancer.

Rudi described one of the hit men as "a gun for hire, an ex-Army man" and said "he'd killed several other people." A police investigator also said the killers were "professionals and likely to be hired guns." But both Rudi and Janet are deliberately vague about many of the details of the attack, including the names of the assailants. Janet, who has fully recovered from her wounds, prefers not to talk about the incident. "You know, this matter is best not discussed," she said. "It's best we forget all about it. It involves members of the family."

Rudi acknowledged that the killers were well known to the guards and were thoroughly familiar with the compound. Other members of the Gatuslao family—and just about anyone in Bacolod

—will tell you that the hit men were hired by Estrada and Sylvia, who fled to Dallas shortly after the killing and were last reported to be living in Los Angeles. No one was ever charged in the killing. Mike Gatuslao was fifty-four years old when he died. He left his wife, a ten-year-old daughter, and a two-year-old son.

As usual, the *Star* had little to say about the murder. Publisher Ninfa Leonardia wrote: "I know I will feel badly for a long time over the cruel and untimely death of Mike."

*   *   *

At Hacienda Benedicto, the old man Conrado Olano, barefoot and dressed in patched and repatched shorts, tends to his cow and his vegetable garden. He says he misses Apin. Olano and twelve of the hacienda's employees received small plots of land from the family; the other employees received nothing. Most members of the Gatuslao family haven't returned to Payao for years. There's nothing left for them there. After Apin's death, Army troops occupied his house and guest house, swam in his swimming pool, and played on his basketball court. No one maintained the buildings, though, and when the Army moved out, people swarmed over the houses like vultures, picking them apart, ripping out the toilets and windows and fixtures. They also tore up the cane railroad tracks that ran to the Biscom sugar mill and sold them for scrap. Dondon Villafranca intervened and agreed to purchase what remained of the buildings from the family. He dismantled the structures and sold off anything of value that was left.

The remains of the Gatuslao residence in Payao can be found at the end of a dirt road lined with scraggly, unattended palm trees just before the Pangiplan River. A cinder-block wall that once surrounded the compound has practically fallen down, and what stands is perforated by several large holes. Tall sugarcane grows where Apin's house and the guest house once stood. The swimming pool, its walls crumbling in, is a fetid pond. The only thing left of the sawmill and warehouses are broad slabs of concrete floor, now littered with debris. Apin's cousin, Exequil Hagoriles, says another family property, Hacienda Bi-ao in Binalbagan, was also abandoned and occupied by squatters, who were later "deeded" parcels by the NPA. Hagoriles, surveying the remains of Apin's Shangri-la, shook his head. "This was a very beautiful place before," he said.

Part
Three

Silence

The faraway bulls have the longest horns.

—Popular saying

When a prominent landowner like Apin Gatuslao was murdered by the NPA, Negrenses tended to conclude that the target had it coming, that he'd done something to deserve it. Indeed, there was a widespread if tenuous faith that victims—all victims— were guilty of something, an assumption that had the poisonous con- sequence of allowing people to excuse the death of Apin Gatuslao or Moret De los Santos or just about anyone. The dead, particularly those dead of political murders, were ostracized.

If it was unfair to assume the victim's guilt, it was not altogether illogical to Negrenses like Joe Lopez-Vito, dean of the College of Criminology at the University of Negros. "When you talk about the insurgency, you need to look at the totality. A landowner has to deal not only with the NPA, but with the paramilitary groups, the mili- tary, the police, the local government. So a guy like Gatuslao could have offended any one of them." The precise nature of the dece- dent's presumed crime wasn't important. It was easy to assume that the killing was a way to settle some score having a long and excruci- ating history that would only give you a headache to try to wrestle with, and you weren't likely to figure it out anyway. This was often the case with the cops. When a cop was killed by an NPA Sparrow, or hit man, most people figured he'd gotten a little too greedy, had shaken down a few too many people a little too often or for a little too much money. Certainly there was a kind of sympathy for the victim and his family, but there was also a simultaneous loss of sympathy that constituted a perverse form of betrayal. The fact was that people rarely rose to defend the dead.

Apin's death, like that of other planters who had been killed by the NPA, was threatening to members of the elite, but it was also consoling. On the one hand, the murder was further evidence that they were targets; on the other, it was as if a safety valve had been opened, a blood offering made to placate the great volcano Kanlaon and buy a period of peace for everyone else. Apin himself was both pitied and disdained. There was also something pathetic about his death. It had been so unnecessary. After all, he had been wealthy enough to have avoided this fiasco if he'd only been a little less rigid. Plenty of other planters were having problems with the NPA—death threats, thefts, burned homes and sugarcane fields—but they'd managed, made their compromises, paid someone to deal with the rebels, protected themselves. Apin's death, his friends believed, only proved how foolhardy it was to take on the NPA, proved that they'd been right to take cover, to let someone else fight their fight. "Negros," said Frank Fernandez, a former priest who became one of the island's top Communist party officials, "is a cockpit where two birds battle to the death like gladiators, and those shouting from the sidelines are the only ones who profit." Apin Gatuslao had demonstrated the price to be paid for failing to keep the proper distance. His mistake was that he wanted to be in the pit when he could have been in the bleachers cheering on a winner. He was outrageous, theatrical; his lack of restraint had been almost un-Filipino. He was dead, his friends reassured themselves, because he'd been asking for it.

The Batman's death at fifty-nine had a haunting inevitability about it, as if he'd invited the NPA to kill him; otherwise, why would he have chosen to stay his course, knowing what his loss would mean for Panching and the children? That disturbed some of his friends because it made them wonder, for a few seconds anyway, whether they might not also be inviting death, setting themselves up in some way they might only become aware of when it was already too late. Despite the deals they'd cut, the rules of engagement weren't etched in stone; it was the random and intangible elements of their war that made it so unnerving. A fragrance rose from the monsoon or a freshly plowed field, conjured up something familiar but distant, a memory or perhaps a premonition. Was it a taste of youth, or maybe something sinister, like Papa Isio off in the forest, threatening to drag them down, back into the past? They couldn't be sure.

Apin had had numerous warnings. Rudi said the NPAs often taunted Apin, interrupting his two-way radio communications to tell him they were going to cut off his balls. "Serafin could be very impetuous. He would hurl back challenges to them over the radio; he would tell them to meet him any place, any time, 'and we'll shoot it out.' " Negros often inspires comparisons to the Wild West, but a duel at twenty paces was not the NPA's style. By the time the Communists decided to liquidate Gatuslao, he had already been tried and convicted in absentia. Only the details of the execution remained to be resolved.

Apin was different, no question about it, the planters thought. But when his friends examined the simple bullet-riddled silhouette of the Batman, they could also recognize something of themselves. The particulars of the NPA brief were almost boilerplate, complaints that could have been leveled against dozens of wealthy Negrenses. Apin was by no means the worst landlord on Negros or the wealthiest or the most belligerent. What was so frightening was that beneath the outlandish persona and all the *palabas,* Apin was really quite typical, so ordinary.

In the lobby of Himamaylan's People's Hall, a bronze plaque credits Congressman Agustin Gatuslao with obtaining funds for construction of the building and lists the names of other distinguished officials at the time—Governor Valeriano Gatuslao, Mayor José Gatuslao, and Vice-Mayor Raymundo Tongson. Tacked to a bulletin board just to the left of the entrance is a large poster with a color photograph of a man wading through a room littered with corpses, holding a severed head by its black hair as if it were nothing more than a bowling ball. This poster was "Exhibit A" in the military's propaganda campaign against the New People's Army. It was taken in the immediate aftermath of what is known as the Digos Massacre, in which NPA rebels slaughtered thirty-seven people, including thirty-one women and children, in Digos, on the southern island of Mindanao. Two of the dead were beheaded by the NPA. The Digos massacre photos were distributed widely by the military, along with copies of the movie *The Killing Fields,* depicting the Khmer Rouge genocide, to convince people that the NPA was equally diabolical. There is no photograph of the De los Santos massacre on the lobby bulletin board at the Himamaylan People's Hall. That story was a little too close to home.

The response of official Negros to the De los Santos massacre had been simply silence. Not a calculated, premeditated silence contrived in secret deliberations, or a conspiratorial silence linked to some broad political or criminal agenda, but rather a spontaneous, reflexive silence, disinterested and dispassionate.

No one was particularly surprised by this reaction. Public officials on Negros never condemned atrocities by the military; more often than not, they didn't even comment on assaults against their own friends and allies, Serafin Gatuslao being only one of the more obvious cases in point. If any of the province's elected representatives suspected or believed, as some in the military were suggesting, that the De los Santos massacre was punitive—a response to suspicions linking Moret to the murder of Apin—they kept their peace about it, at least in public.

Negros governor Daniel Lacson, cool and smooth as a tall thin glass of green mango juice, never said a word about the De los Santos massacre. At the time of the killings, he was preparing to leave for a month-long visit to the United States, highlighted by a speech he would deliver at Harvard University. Audiences in the United States would prove far more receptive than those at home to his "progressive" ideas about land reform and employment for displaced sugar workers. There would be no way for them to know that these were the fantasies of a figurehead and that Lacson himself no longer took his own ideas seriously. Educated Filipinos are forever flagellating themselves for seeking recognition and approval from their former colonizer, the "great white father" in Washington. Lacson, however, would find it extremely gratifying to have the Americans applaud his wisdom, idealism, and clear-headed pragmatism.

No other elected official saw fit to address the massacre either— no congressman, councilman, or mayor, including Himamaylan's own Mayor Providencia Silverio. Mayor Daisy, as she's known, held office in the People's Hall, overlooking the plaza and the bust of national hero José Rizal, who had been executed for his eloquent condemnation of an earlier regime's atrocities. A one-way mirror separated Mayor Daisy's dark second-floor office from a waiting room for visitors, allowing her to scrutinize callers while sitting behind an old, paper-strewn wooden desk. It would have demonstrated an unseemly lack of *delicadeza,* propriety, to directly refuse to meet with one of her constituents; but if she didn't like the looks of someone, she could simply tell an aide she was too busy and ask the visitors if they wouldn't mind returning another day—when she might also make herself unavailable. Mayor Daisy, the daughter of a popular judge, is a hefty woman who covers her puffy face with a thick mask of skin lightener, a popular affectation of upper-crust Filipinas who, since the colonial era, have done their best to distinguish themselves from the unwashed masses.

Mayor Daisy and her husband own several large sugar plantations in Himamaylan and Hinigaran, as well as some rice land and coconut farms, but she insists that she's never paid taxes to the NPA and that her crops have never been burned. "God forbid! So far, thank God, I've had no problem with my property, even though there have been so many burnings of cane." She said local planters had recently suffered individual losses of 25–150 acres due to arson. How her properties had escaped was a mystery, particularly since she boasted that, because of her willing cooperation with the military, she'd "always been number one" on the NPA's hit lists, along with Governor Lacson. She says the growers have no alternative but to support the government troops. "If we don't cooperate with the military, how will we get peace and order?"

A small number of middle- and upper-class Filipinos had always supported the radical left and the NPA's campaign against the Marcos dictatorship. During the 1980s, as the effects of Marcos's stranglehold on the economy were felt in the pocketbooks of the bourgeoisie, more members of the elite began forging new alliances of convenience with the left. In the anti-Marcos furor that exploded with the assassination of Ninoy Aquino in 1983 and the subsequent implosion of the economy, many of these elite Filipinos became convinced that they and the rebels were fighting for the same cause. On Negros, sugar planters made their trucks available to transport thousands of anti-Marcos demonstrators to protests in Bacolod, and they provided food, clothing, and small amounts of money to the rebel movement. Even Mayor Daisy insists that she was once a supporter of the NPA. "I believed in their ideology, the upliftment of the poor," she said.

After Marcos fled, people like Daisy awoke from their dreamworld to find that it wasn't only the dictator the rebels were after but the property of Sugarlandia's elite. "Before, their purpose was good," Mayor Daisy complained about the NPA, "but now they resort to killings and confiscations [of land]." With that, her previously expressed concern for the "upliftment of the poor" had somehow lost its urgency. Daisy and other planters quickly found an ally in the soldiers who had earlier defended the dictator. The planters' silence when it came to military atrocities was an implicit part of the contract. Thus, when the military launched Operation Thunderbolt, which drove 35,000 peasants from their homes in the Negros mountains, Daisy defended it. She supported the establishment of a dozen military detachments on Himamaylan haciendas, and she praised the Greenans, the local 700-man vigilante group, despite their transgressions of human rights. "Of course, there was one incident where they cut off the head of, I think he was an NPA," she acknowledged, then added by way of explanation, "but that was during an encounter."

When it came to Melvin Gutierrez and his Scout Rangers, the mayor said she was aware that they had a reputation for thuggery in Himamaylan. "I know what I'm going to say is heresy, but once they suspected people, they would kill them," she explained, drawing a beefy finger across her neck. "This was the complaint of our people. The people want the military in its place. And the NPAs have benefited from the atrocities of the military." Nevertheless, the mayor stood by the Rangers during their stay in Himamaylan.

Although Mayor Daisy acknowledged that she had no evidence that Moret De los Santos had been involved with the NPA, she said she assumed he was because of his work with the Basic Christian Community, which, she said, cooperated with the NPA. "The BCC deals with the other side, according to our surrenderees," she said, referring to rebels who had turned themselves in to the military. "They said they were used by the NPA as tools to organize people." As for the massacre of the De los Santoses, she said, "The sentiment of the people was to sympathize with the family—because of the

children, not the father." Nevertheless, public officials like Mayor
Daisy kept their sympathies to themselves.

For a politician like Silverio, it would have been unthinkable to
condemn the De los Santos massacre or to condole with the survivors, and she made no effort to visit the site of the slaughter, although it was no more than twenty minutes from her office. For her
even to have raised a question about the incident would have been
viewed as a betrayal of her class, as well as of the military. Three
years after the massacre, the mayor couldn't recall how many members of the De los Santos family had been killed. "The wife, the husband. I don't know how many children. Two? I don't know. One of
them escaped and has already vanished. I haven't heard about the
De los Santos family since then. The family is not here anymore." In
fact, several family members were still in town, and the ten-year-old,
Juvi, was attending the school at Our Lady of the Snows Church, a
two-minute walk from the People's Hall.

Mayor Daisy's distrust of the BCC and its membership extended
more broadly to the local clergy itself, which, she said, had incited
the poor against landowners like herself. "Most of these priests criticize the rich in their sermons. Their sermons are very far from the
Gospel." The mayor said she personally had become so thoroughly
disgusted with the church that she actually considered changing her
religion. "Many Catholics have converted to different religions—
Protestant, *Iglesia ni Cristo,* to Mormons, I don't know. If I wasn't so
deeply Catholic, I would have changed a long time ago." Then,
pointing a finger to the ceiling, she added, "A lot of people now say
the best religion is RSD, *recto sa Dios* [straight to God]," explaining
that they no longer felt a need for any church as intermediary.

Mayor Daisy said she never demanded an investigation of the De
los Santos killings because it wasn't her job but was rather the responsibility of the police chief. She also allowed, however, that she
hadn't gone to the funeral mass, an act of omission that sent an unmistakable message that the new democratic government and its top
elected official wouldn't lift a finger to protect citizens from the military. The mayor acknowledged that she was afraid to attend the
funeral, hastily adding that she did not want that fact to be made
public. Then, as she discussed her fears, she seemed to recall that
there had actually been a scheduling conflict that prevented her
from attending the funeral. "I was invited by the priests to attend

the mass, but I think we also had a seminar that day." The mayor noted, "People came to the funeral from all over Negros, many priests and nuns," suggesting that their presence somehow excused her absence.

Even if the mayor couldn't attend the funeral, she and other prominent citizens could have condemned the murders. Why they said nothing, the mayor suggested, should have been self-evident. Silverio said,

> I think the number one reason is that there is fear of both sides. If you stand up and side with the one group, your life will be in danger. If you side with the other group, again your life will be in danger. If you side with the military, you're afraid of the NPA. If you side with the NPA, you're afraid of the military. So they keep silent about it. That is why we cannot solve the problem of killings, because people are afraid. And they're also afraid to testify. That is the problem for us nowadays. And those people who are not afraid just don't want to be bothered.

Democracies don't function particularly well where elected officials like Mayor Silverio are afraid to condemn the killing of little children. But fear was omnipresent, an invisible yet tangible malignancy, inhibiting the growth of Aquino's nascent democracy. For politicians like Mayor Silverio, Governor Lacson, and any number of other local and national leaders, fear colored every calculation. It clouded their perceptions and led them to back away until they were no longer real players in the whirlwind of public life but passive observers of forces beyond their control, forces they implicitly condoned and perpetuated by their silence. The more distant they became from the world, the less they understood it, the more frightening it became.

The complexity and intractability of Negros's problems was, however, also a refuge for these politicians. They pointed out how people were bombarded with *tsismis,* claims, counterclaims, and propaganda, how when someone like Moret De los Santos was killed, the military screamed "Communist," and the other side cried "massacre." So who were ordinary citizens to believe? In Franz Kafka's *The Trial,* Josef K.'s lawyer tells him, "You know perfectly well that various opinions accumulate around a case until a state of impenetrability is reached." That's how it was on Negros. K.'s lawyer doesn't try to sort through the conflicting opinions but concludes there's nothing he can do to prevent the execution of his client. For the politicians on Negros, uncertainty was both an excuse for doing nothing and a source of solace, as comforting as the mudhole to the carabao.

Gerry

The real war will never get in the books.

                    —Walt Whitman, "Specimen Days"

Father O'Brien had a theory about the Scout Rangers, nothing he could prove exactly, more like a loose collection of facts and rumors that, leavened with a dose of theology, might dispel some of the uncertainties surrounding the De los Santos massacre and the subsequent death of Scout Ranger Gerry De los Santos. The priest wasn't saying the theory could be proved, but he acknowledged that he hoped it would. He had heard some of the stories about Gerry's death two weeks after the De los Santos massacre—that he was killed in an ambush, that he was murdered by Captain Gutierrez, that he had committed suicide. But how he died wasn't nearly as important to the priest's interpretation of events as why he died.

O'Brien speculated that some of the Rangers who attended the mass for the De los Santoses might have been so moved by it that they decided to break their silence, to stand up and protest the massacre. He'd heard that as many as three Scout Rangers had complained to Gutierrez about the massacre and that they might have been murdered as a result. That members of the Army had objected to an action against civilians was unprecedented, O'Brien believed, and the possibility excited him no end:

> This just doesn't happen in the Philippines, in the military. Normally they close ranks. If several Rangers had actually been that affected, or if it's true, for example, that Gerry De los Santos actually committed suicide, that is a stunning and

unbelievable and extraordinary thing. It would be a barometer
of the level of feeling of the group who had gone out there and
found that they had killed children; and, if the funeral mass
had more of an effect, so that two or three of them protested
and were killed in revenge, it would be all the more reason for
all the other Rangers to close ranks. It would also be a unique
happening. I've never heard of a soldier repenting, or saying,
"We did wrong, we have killed little children, we have killed a
good man." But isn't that what Judas said? "I have betrayed
a just man."

Finding events in life to recapitulate Scripture is an exercise with
endless possibilities and one men of the cloth pursue with undeni-
able relish. It is also easy to get carried away. Dante put Judas at the
very bottom of the frozen lake of Hell, condemned to have his body
torn apart eternally by the rakelike teeth of Satan; maybe the souls of
the Rangers were similarly wracked by guilt. If one is intent on re-
playing the Gospel on a contemporary stage, Gerry might very well
make a suitable Judas in this Holy Week *pasyon*. He was, after all,
one of the twelve Rangers involved in the massacre, one of the twelve
disciples of Gutierrez; and there was speculation that it was Gerry
who had fingered Moret De los Santos (whom some were now trying
to portray as the Redeemer) and that he had led the Rangers to
Moret's home. "The one I kiss will be the man," Judas said, and like
Judas, who hanged himself, Gerry, according to some, took his own
life. Still, it was hard to cast Gerry as the villain in this drama and
equally plausible to suggest that he was entirely innocent, a victim of
his misguided loyalty and faith in the institution of the Army.

O'Brien was inclined to give Gerry the benefit of the doubt, to
believe he had at least redeemed himself by confessing his sins, not
to a priest, but by standing up to the evil Gutierrez. Biblical parallels
could certainly be found for this version of events as well. On the
day Gerry died, the lectionary assigned the story of Saul receiving
the light from heaven on the road to Damascus. As with Saul, hadn't
the scales fallen from Gerry's eyes? Then again, maybe Gerry's world
—like that of the De los Santoses—had simply imploded; maybe
everything had been rearranged on the day of the massacre so that
he was observing it from an unfamiliar and frightening vantage in
which the war and his career and anticommunism and his religious
faith no longer made any sense. It was possible that Gerry simply

stopped seeing himself as a soldier, patriot, and father, and began seeing himself as a murderer. Unlike Saul, however, Gerry could see no way out.

Gerry had been fighting Communists all over the country for the past seven years, and this wasn't the first massacre he'd been involved in. Four months earlier he'd been with Gutierrez at Double Yarding when a woman and three children were killed. Maybe he'd had enough. If he was thinking of exposing the De los Santos incident, it didn't take much imagination to see why Gutierrez or some of the other Rangers might have wanted to stop him. Some of them saw him as unpredictable. On one operation, Gerry and his colleagues were ambushed by NPAs, and Gerry was ordered to fire his rifle grenades. His commanding officer said Gerry couldn't fire because he was so nervous that the weapon was actually shaking in his hands. Maybe Gerry had also frozen up in Mambagaton at the De los Santos house. Maybe he was singled out because he was the only one who hadn't fired a shot during the massacre, the only one who could afford to talk, who might make a claim of innocence. One could argue that Gerry was not to be trusted.

From the benign to the insidious to the ridiculous, any number of scenarios could explain Gerry's death and the massacre. That there might actually be no rational explanation or, contrary to Bishop Navarra's suggestion, no moral to the story, that God had not contrived a lesson for his sheep, was the one possibility no one seemed inclined to consider. The list of "maybes" and "what ifs" surrounding Gerry's death was a lengthy one, and it marched off toward the horizon, away from Negros, to the outer reaches of the archipelago, to wherever the Rangers had been dispersed to get away from the truth.

*   *   *

A death certificate on file at the Himamaylan People's Hall states that twenty-five-year-old Sergeant Gerardo G. De los Santos died at 7:15 P.M., on April 22, 1988, two weeks after the De los Santos massacre, and that the body was delivered to the Gatuslao Hospital by a Sergeant Cipriano Montajes. The cause of death was listed as "irreversible shock" from a "massive hemorrhage" resulting from a single bullet that entered the abdomen and severed the abdominal aorta. The document gives the name of Gerry's wife, Pelma, and

an address—the town of Hinanungan, on the island of Leyte—
and is signed by Dr. Jude Fernandez, the hospital's senior resident
physician.

Dr. Fernandez, a slight, thin man with fair skin and "educated"
English, lives a half-mile from the Gatuslao Hospital, along a dirt
road just past the junkyard. Fernandez had no recollection of the
case of Gerry De los Santos—at the time of Gerry's death, he said,
he was examining a lot of dead soldiers—and a death certificate he'd
signed didn't jar his memory. Looking at the document, Fernandez
said Gerry could have survived up to fifteen minutes, and concluded
that he was probably dead by the time he reached the hospital. In
fact, the place the Rangers identified as the site of the ambush was
less than fifteen minutes from the hospital, but it wouldn't have
made any difference, since neither Fernandez nor anyone else at the
Gatuslao Hospital was equipped to deal with Gerry's wound. The
closest vascular surgeon was ninety minutes north in Bacolod.

Fernandez speculated that he had probably performed an autopsy on the body because the military generally required one in
order to process survivor benefits. He insisted, however, that there
would be no way to tell from the autopsy whether Gerry had been
murdered or had committed suicide. Gerry's autopsy was kept at the
hospital in a blue, soot-covered ledger, a musty folio filled with reports from 1988 made out in Fernandez's nearly illegible chicken
scratchings. The final moments in the soldier's life were described in
an opaque crossword puzzle of medical jargon: "Gunshot wound
abdomen; peripheral burns, right paramedian above umbilicus penetrating abdominal cavity, lacerated wound left lower lumbar; slug
embedded below the laceration at subcutaneous tissue, hemoperi-
torenum," etc. Absent even an elementary knowledge of anatomy,
the only bit of potentially illuminating information was a notation
that there were powder burns on the body, indicating that the gun
that killed Gerry had been fired at close range.

An American forensic pathologist who examined hundreds of gunshot wounds during the Vietnam War pronounced Gerry's autopsy
one of the shoddiest examples of the art he'd ever seen, lacking the
basic "anatomic landmarks" that would ordinarily delineate the
exact path of the bullet. Fernandez's report notes a gunshot wound
of about two to three millimeters, with "peripheral burns approxi-

mately four millimeters in diameter," and further indicates that the
bullet fractured lumbar number 3 and the coccyx, the small bone at
the base of the spinal column. "My guess is, the bullet went in on a
level trajectory or downward at a slight angle," the pathologist said.
"The autopsy indicates that they recovered a slug, but they don't say
what kind. If it was an M-16 [the standard Ranger weapon], there
would be a copper jacket, if not with the slug, then somewhere inside the body. But an M-16 is designed to pass through things, and
there's no exit wound indicated." In other words, it could have been
an M-16, but it could have also been a handgun or any number of
other weapons. The brief description of the powder wound also provided few clues. According to the pathologist:

> With a handgun, you would get that at six inches. With an
> M-16, you could be three to four feet away and get the same
> pattern. The report suggests the weapon was fired at very close
> range because as you get farther away, the powder spreads out.
> But the report doesn't describe any sooting. The powder tat-
> too indicates an almost contact wound, but with an M-16 you
> would get a lot of gun smoke, which causes sooting, smoke
> which impregnates the skin. If you're very close, you get soot-
> ing inside the wound track.

The autopsy made no mention of any discoloration within the
body, and the entry wound was small, so it was difficult to say what
caliber weapon had been used. "If I had to guess, I'd say the gun was
fired at less than an inch. My guess is, it was a suicide." Considering
the number of uncertainties, "guess" seemed an apt description. The
pathologist didn't seem at all surprised that Gerry might have chosen to shoot himself in the stomach, insisting that suicides shoot
themselves "everywhere," depending on whether they want to succeed, or to avoid disfiguring their faces, or for any number of other
reasons that emerge from the private logic of despair. The bottom
line was that Gerry was shot at close range, either by himself or
someone else. Not much of a lead.

The military in southern Negros normally brought the bodies of
its dead to the Funeraria del Sur in Binalbagan, eight miles north

of Himamaylan. Michaela Sol de Villa, the *funeraria*'s proprietress, is
a slight, excitable, and exhaustingly voluble mestiza with corkscrews
of gray in her reddish brown hair.

Michaela didn't recall the name Gerry De los Santos until she located it in a small brown paperback journal that recorded the particulars of every funeral package she'd sold over the past five years,
whereupon she realized she'd never been paid the 6,500-peso fee for
her services. Then the details of the incident began to revive in her
brain like desert flowers following a flash flood.

I remember this case. You know, I was confined in a hospital in Bacolod for five days after this! I had to go out in the
middle of the night looking for a welder because they needed
the casket sealed quickly so it could be shipped. You know, the
embalming fluids are a health hazard. They affect the heart. I
couldn't refuse the service because the body was already here,
and it would deteriorate. But I have all these costs—the chem-
icals for embalming, the labor—and they didn't pay me! I was
up all night working on this, and after we disposed of the
cadaver, they had to take me to the hospital. The military
has money for this kind of thing, but they don't pay their
accounts!

Michaela suggested that it was difficult to turn military men away,
since they invariably arrived at her premises heavily armed. "I've had
five dead soldiers here, and the bills are all unpaid. Now if they bring
me another body, I'll reject it! You know, if I had some other kind of
business, I wouldn't do this anymore."

Michaela had little to add about the death of Gerry De los Santos,
but her journal contained a small penciled-in note indicating the
name of the man who delivered Gerry's body to her: a First Lieutenant Alan Arrojado. Arrojado was second-in-command to Captain
Gutierrez until three days before Gerry's death, when Gutierrez was
unexpectedly reassigned to Manila and Arrojado took his place as
Fourth Scout Ranger Company commander. Since then, the company had been disbanded, and Arrojado and all of the other men
had been reassigned off of Negros. According to at least some of the
tsismis, it was Arrojado who killed Gerry.

Gerry De los Santos's body spent only one night at the Funeraria del Sur. In the morning it was taken to Bacolod, placed on a C-130 transport plane, and shipped to Fort Bonifacio, the Philippine Army headquarters in Manila. From Manila, it was supposed to travel on a commercial Philippine Airlines flight to the city of Tacloban on Leyte Island, then be taken by military escort to the home of Gerry's wife, Pelma, in Hinanungan, on the southeast coast. A military honor guard went to Hinanungan to wait for the body with Pelma, who had prepared a tomb for Gerry's interment. But Gerry's body never arrived.

*   *   *

The Maharlika Highway is named after a guerrilla organization that Ferdinand Marcos claimed he led into some of the most heroic exploits of World War II. Marcos insisted he'd been the most highly decorated guerrilla fighter in World War II, recipient of, among other awards, the Congressional Medal of Honor. The U.S. Army described Marcos's war claims as "fraudulent," and records in the U.S. National Archives suggest that Marcos didn't head a guerrilla unit during the war but was actually involved with a gang of "hoodlums" who were collaborating with the Japanese. Nevertheless, the Maharlika myth endured. With the name (sometimes translated as "big phallus") pasted on everything from the government broadcasting company to the ceremonial hall at the presidential palace, the legend has been deeply embedded in the Filipino consciousness. Indeed, Marcos reportedly considered renaming the country Maharlika.

Not surprisingly, the Maharlika Highway begins in Ferdinand Marcos's hometown of Laoag, at the northwest tip of the island of Luzon. The road then loops across the island's northern coast, travels south through Manila, and winds its way through a total of twenty-one provinces on four of the country's major islands. When the road finally stops at Zamboanga City, Mindanao, near the southwestern tip of the archipelago, it has traversed a thousand miles and hundreds of cities and towns.

Traveling on this frequently deteriorated, two-lane ribbon of roadway can be slow-going, but it remains one of the best means of penetrating the Philippine heartland—the towns and barrios that exist apart from the often perverse caricature of the country fostered by people like the Marcoses, the politicians, and other snake-oil salesmen in Manila. Occasionally one stumbles onto a rare oasis containing vestiges of the mythical province Filipinos harbor in hazy memory or nostalgia, places unaffected by the convulsions of modern history.

Basud is a town like that, a tranquil nothing of a dot on the map. Basud—the name means "sand"—doesn't invite tourists or other visitors and has no bars or restaurants or entertainment. Anyone who wants that can try Daet, the capital of Camarines Norte, ten minutes to the north, although they won't find much excitement there, either. Basud is set back a quarter-mile or so from the Maharlika Highway on a flat plain of farmland; it consists of nothing more than a couple of hundred diminutive weather-blackened, wood houses with little gardens that front on a grid of narrow dirt roads lined with neat white-painted stones. What is extraordinary about the place is not just its cleanliness and orderliness, its overall ambience of serenity and self-respect, although those qualities are unusual enough. Rather it's the ancient arboretum of fruit and flowering trees and bushes and vines that holds Basud in a cool, dark, mysterious embrace and makes it feel as if it's been there forever, as if the people who first stumbled on it had preserved it all intact, inserting their cottagelike dwellings into the lush vegetation, careful not to disturb a single leaf.

Gerry De los Santos grew up in Basud, in one of those little two-room houses, and his body rests in the ground there, in the Moroso [Sorrow] Cemetery at the edge of town. Although Gerry was supposed to be buried in Pelma's hometown, in Leyte, the body was intercepted by his parents. Gerry's father, Roberto De los Santos, sent a telegram to Fort Bonifacio in Manila, stating that the family wanted the remains brought to Basud. He signed the telegram with Pelma's name, although she knew nothing about it. Roberto then traveled to Fort Bonifacio, where he met with Captain Gutierrez and Lieutenant Arrojado, who approved his request. Roberto also tried to have Gerry's pension benefits taken from Pelma and assigned to him and his wife, but Arrojado, who knew Pelma personally, refused, explaining that since Gerry had no named beneficiary, the pension automatically went to his wife.

Gerry's mother, Rufina, keeps a handful of photo albums of her son. They show Gerry in Leyte, drinking with his Ranger friends, rappeling across a stream, and standing in front of a jeep, a big crucifix around his neck. In one photo, Gerry, wearing a holstered pistol across his chest, stands with Pelma and their son, Gerry, Jr. The little albums also hold photos of Gerry's funeral. One shows him lying in his coffin, smooth-faced, with his black symmetrical hair. Another shows his mother, dressed in black and crying as she embraces the coffin. Two men in olive army fatigues are shown beside Gerry's coffin, which is draped with a Philippine flag and pink ribbons inscribed with hand-painted messages. "Blessed are the Dead who died in the Lord's Service," one of them reads. Rufina says her son was a "hero" because "he died in the service of the Filipino people." At the funeral, the Scout Rangers gave him a twenty-one-gun salute.

Red roses grow at the entrance to the Moroso Cemetery, which rises up from a rice paddy, an austere, windowless village of cement and marble sepulchers stacked tightly but almost randomly in geometric piles, like the scattered pieces of one of those Chinese woodblock puzzles that are easy to take apart and nearly impossible to put back together. Gerry's white-painted cement tomb, its only adornment a small crucifix, is sandwiched in a row of similar tombs overgrown with thorns and weeds. A small, gray marble square is inscribed, somewhat imprecisely, as follows: RIP SGT. GERARDO G. DE LOS SANTOS. IN MEMORY OF HIS WIFE, CHILDREN, PARENTS, SISTERS, AND RELATIVES.

*   *   *

To get to Leyte from Basud, you must either drive two hundred miles, or about seven hours, back to Manila and fly to Leyte's capital, Tacloban, or else spend a full day driving south on the Maharlika Highway, cross the San Bernardino Strait by ferry, drive through the island of Samar, and across the graceful and slightly notorious two-kilometer President Marcos Bridge, which spans the San Juanico Strait just north of Tacloban.

During construction of the span, a project of Leyte's best-known native daughter, Imelda Marcos, a rumor spread that the first lady had grown snake scales all over her body and, in a desperate effort to cure this ailment, was sacrificing children from the bridge. Since many Filipinos viewed Mrs. Marcos as something of a dragon lady anyway, the possibility that she had developed certain reptilian features seemed plausible enough. Given her husband's well-established disregard for human life, the idea that the Marcoses, the "Molochs" of Malacañang, the presidential palace, were demanding to be fed little children could not be lightly dismissed. The rumor was further reinforced by reports of a sudden spate of child kidnappings, and people quite naturally assumed that the hapless victims were being sacrificed from the President Marcos Bridge. This set off a nationwide panic, with parents guarding their children at home until they became convinced that Imelda's scales had disappeared or at least that the danger had passed.

Leyte is best known to Americans for the Battle of Leyte Gulf and for General Douglas MacArthur, who landed there with Allied troops to reclaim the Philippines from Japan. On the east coast there is a town called MacArthur, and at Red Beach in Palo, a clunky, stolid monument depicts the general in sunglasses wading ashore on October 20, 1944, fulfilling his famous vow—"I shall return"— spoken as he fled the country following the Japanese occupation. MacArthur remains something of a folk hero, particularly among older Filipinos, a complex "liberator" who returned to reclaim America's colony, where an estimated one million people had died under the Japanese. Although the battle of Leyte Gulf is considered the greatest naval engagement in history, the invasion of the Philippines was opposed by the U.S. Navy, and many historians say it was superfluous to the defeat of Japan. In the subsequent battle to liberate Manila, an estimated hundred thousand Filipinos died.

Leyte rarely receives much mention in the Philippine press, except when there's a particularly fierce encounter between the NPA and the military, or when there's some natural calamity, like the flash flood in Ormoc in November 1991, in which thousands of people drowned in the span of a few minutes. Imelda's overblown ego is enshrined in numerous Leyte monuments, the most garish of which is the Santo Niño Shrine in Tacloban, a bizarre fusion of the sacred and profane immortalizing the former first lady alongside the country's patron saint. The centerpiece of the shrine is the little pink and mauve chapel just inside the main entrance, where the Christ child stands in a circle of smoke-colored mirrors and flashing electric lights. The Santo Niño Shrine is above all a testimonial to the cult of Imelda, "the Rose of Tacloban," who is celebrated in thirteen small bedrooms that open onto the chapel, each decorated with a diorama sunk into the wall and filled with colorfully painted plaster figurines portraying some milestone in the first lady's career.

———

From Tacloban, the hundred-mile trip south to Pelma De los Santos's home in Hinanungan takes about five hours by car. The Maharlika Highway traverses coconut and banana plantations, curving
back and forth as it squeezes through haystack-shaped hills, one behind the other. Typhoons have washed away huge chunks of roadway which periodically appear upended at the base of a landslide.
Other stretches are littered for miles with mud and rocks.

In Leyte's mountain villages, strands of fibrous abaca, a banana-
like plant—also known as Manila hemp—dry like shiny white cur-
tains on clotheslines. In some barrios, little gardens are irrigated by
an ingenious system of pipes made from thick bamboo trunks split
lengthwise and laid out like aqueducts carrying water from mountain streams. Logging companies have left Leyte's mountains nearly
naked, as they have on Negros, although one occasionally sees men
with hand-hewn planks of coconut lumber, practically the only trees
that remain.

Just south of MacArthur, the road divides where a direct coastal
route to Hinanungan has been washed away. The other leg heads
due south, then east and north, tripling the length of the journey.
The highway divides again at Sogod, where white cliffs drop precip-
itously to a spectacular bay that shimmers at sunset like a big copper
kettle. The final stretch of what seems an endless journey begins at
St. Bernard, where the road east enters a dark tunnel of palm trees
lit by thousands of fireflies dancing to the orchestrations of bats,
crickets, cicadas, and other invisible creatures of the night. From
time to time, slow-moving processions of women holding candles
and three-foot-high blue and white statues of the Virgin Mary—Our
Lady of Perpetual Help—appear dreamlike from the road and just
as quickly disappear.

Pelma De los Santos, a midwife, was born in Hinanungan in the
house of her father, the same house in which she married Gerry De
los Santos when she was twenty-eight years old. Gerry, three years
her junior, and a company of Scout Rangers had been sent to the
town with instructions to drive out the NPA. Pelma's dark living
room is lit by a single gas-wick torch crafted from an empty brown
medicine bottle and barely illuminates the green tile floor, a few

hardwood chairs, and a shelf displaying a souvenir plate that reads:
IN GOD WE TRUST.

Pelma's youthful face is framed in an early 1960s flip, secured by
a black and white headband. Deeply religious—she prays every
evening at a nearby church—Pelma says she has never believed the
explanations of her husband's death given by the military. "The
Army doesn't want to bring out the whole truth; the only people
who know are those of us in the family." She says the military told
her officially that Gerry was killed in an ambush but that some of his
colleagues later told her a completely different story. "What I really
believe is that one of his colleagues shot him. I just don't know
who." Five years after her husband's death, Pelma is unemotive,
melancholic, her voice almost a monotone when she discusses him.
She says she prayed for Gerry every day when he was away and never
imagined that he might be killed. The news of his death came to her
in faint gray ink on newsprint paper, a blunt, bureaucratic telegram,
unmitigated by condolence. There had been a five-minute encounter
between government troops and "CTs" (Communist terrorists), the
telegram reported in English, which Pelma understands but barely
speaks. It went on to say that Army troops recovered three revolvers,
six spent shell casings, and various subversive documents, information one would hardly expect to be of any interest, to say nothing of
consolation, to a woman about to learn she'd just been widowed. At
the bottom of the telegram is stated, almost as an afterthought:
"Government side—one KIA [killed in action] Corporal De los Santos. . . . Cadaver brought to Funeraria del Sur, Binalbagan, Negros
Occidental, for proper dispo [sic]." The dispatch was signed by
First Lieutenant Alan R. Arrojado.

A week after she received that telegram, Pelma was visited by
twelve members of Gerry's Scout Ranger unit, who announced that
they would be bringing his body to her from Tacloban. The team
was led by Sergeant Cipriano Montajes, the man who had taken
Gerry to the hospital and one of the more eccentric members of
Gerry's group. Friends said Montajes neither bathed nor washed his
clothes, fearing it might dilute the power of his *anting anting*. The
Rangers confirmed the story told Pelma in the telegram. They said
Gerry's group was returning to camp from a routine patrol when it
was ambushed by NPA rebels. Pelma could remember only a few of
the names of the Rangers who visited her—in particular, Expedito
Eroles and Melanio Vinluan, both of whom had served with Gerry

in Hinanungan. The two were also with Gerry at the De los Santos massacre, and both disappeared a few months after visiting Pelma. Curiously, one of the Rangers also showed Pelma an Army newsletter that contained an item about the massacre because he thought she might know some members of the De los Santos family. She didn't. Nor did she know whether Gerry's death might somehow be related to the massacre.

Pelma was wary of the explanation provided in the telegram, convinced that the Rangers who visited her had been lying, so she decided to pay a visit to Negros to learn the truth. There she was given another version of her husband's death. "When I spoke to Lieutenant Arrojado and to Gerry's friends, they told me that Gerry shot himself. Naturally, I was very surprised. I really can't believe he killed himself. I asked them why he would have done that, but they said they didn't know." Two days before he died, Gerry De los Santos wrote his last letter to his wife. She received it a week after his funeral. "I was pregnant at the time, and he said he would return home after the baby was born." Pelma said Gerry seemed to be looking forward to seeing her. He had visited her briefly only the month before and had seemed in good spirits. His letter made no reference to any problems he was having or to the De los Santos massacre. If Gerry had been troubled by the massacre, he would certainly have said something, Pelma thought. The letter, along with the contradictory explanations from Gerry's friends and commanding officers, made her even more firmly convinced that he had been murdered.

Pelma De los Santos never did learn the truth about how her husband died, and she didn't get to attend his funeral. When Gerry's body failed to arrive in Leyte, Pelma sent a telegram to Gerry's parents, who replied that they would keep their son's remains in Basud for only three days, after which his remains would be forwarded to her. When Pelma again contacted her in-laws, though, they told her that the burial had gone ahead without her. They later sent her Gerry's wristwatch as a memento. Five months after Gerry died, Pelma gave birth to their second son.

*   *   *

Pelma identified Gerry's closest friends as Virgilio Quijano and Efren Llaneta. Philippine Army records indicated that Corporal Llaneta went AWOL shortly after the De los Santos massacre, and

they located Quijano at a military camp in Catbalogan, a port city on
the west coast of Samar, not far from Quijano's hometown. In
Manila, the island is best known as a leading exporter of young girls
for the city's booming sex industry, but Samar is also a textbook
study of how rampant deforestation in the Philippines has led to the
destruction of farmland and water resources and to the creation of
massive unemployment and a formidable insurgency. The insurgency
was the reason Quijano had been sent there.

Quijano, known to his friends as Batch, met Gerry during their
initial Ranger training in 1981, and the two young men were rarely
apart for the next seven years. They ate together, often slept in the
same bed, and fought side by side against Communists in Leyte,
Quezon, Kalinga Apao, the Cagayan Valley, as well as Negros—
places with exotic names and the same mundane problems of
poverty and insurgency. To Quijano, Negros was without question
the worst. "There were encounters every week; always a lot of shooting—in Murcia, Manapla, Victorias, Sipalay, Silay, Binalbagan,
Himamaylan."

Quijano recalls his final hours with Gerry vividly. "A few hours
before he died, Gerry came to talk to me," Quijano says:

His face was very red and his eyes were misty, as if he was
about to cry. And he said to me, "Batch, please, you have to
help me. My CO [commanding officer] is going to kill me."
This was at around 3:30 in the afternoon. I told him I didn't
believe it and that he shouldn't panic. I said the CO [Lieu-
tenant Arrojado, who had replaced Captain Gutierrez two
days earlier] was a good man, and I told Gerry he should try to
talk to him. But I was also upset that Gerry didn't have a
weapon. It puzzled me that he was unarmed. So I said, "Okay,
go and see him, but take my baby Armalite [a short M-16]
with you." And I told him, "If anything happens to you, there
will always be a bullet for him."

Quijano explained that he was prepared to get revenge, to kill Arrojado if Gerry were murdered.

At around 4:00, Gerry returned. He shook hands with me,
and he said, "Brod [brother], thank you for all your advice."
And I asked him, "Is everything all right? Did you resolve the

problem?" And he said, "Everything is fine. Why don't we cook some dinner?" We had some vegetables and some coconuts, and we divided the labor—I chopped, and Gerry cooked. When I went out to a birthday party for Merle Tayaban, I remember leaving my Armalite on the bed. Then at about 5:30, Gerry and I met at the party, and he said, "Please take care of my son for me." I just couldn't believe he was saying this, asking me to take care of Gerry, Jr. I thought it was some kind of joke. So I said, "Okay, I'll look after him." I really didn't pay much attention to it. But at around 6:00, I was leaving the camp when I heard a shout, "Ho!," followed by a gunshot. There was only one shot initially, and then a burst of gunfire as some of the Rangers started shooting wildly. Nobody knew what was happening until Sergeant Montajes shouted an order to stop firing. I was about a hundred meters away when the shooting started.

Quijano moved cautiously back into the camp. "As I arrived, I saw a black Ford Fiera carrying Gerry's body to the hospital," Quijano said, taking a deep breath before continuing. "But he didn't make it. Several of the guys rushed up to me and said, 'Take it easy. Nobody killed your friend. It's a suicide.' In front of our hut I saw a puddle of blood."

After his colleagues departed, Quijano stood outside the hut by himself, the aftershock of the news washing over him. "Then, when I went into our hut, I noticed my Armalite on the bed, but it wasn't in the position I'd left it. Later on, Montajes told me that Gerry had killed himself with my gun. Of course, I had to believe him."

There was never any discussion of an investigation into Gerry's death, the weapon was never fingerprinted, and the only report on the incident was one filed with the Himamaylan police. It contained word for word the same language included in the telegram to Pelma, stating that Gerry had been killed by the NPA outside the Ranger camp at a place called Bahay, near the site of the De los Santos massacre. Quijano said he couldn't explain why Lieutenant Arrojado would have written the report and insisted it was totally untrue. "It's not accurate," he said. Gerry's death, he said, "happened inside the Army camp at Carabalan."

Quijano also said he could think of no reason why either Arrojado or Gutierrez would have killed Gerry. "I don't know of anyone who'd want to kill Gerry. There was no bad blood. Gerry was very popular, very skillful. He was a very nice guy." Quijano said Gerry mixed easily, not only with his colleagues but with civilians in Himamaylan who had played basketball with him on the plaza. If there were any witnesses to Gerry's death, they never spoke to Quijano. "No one wanted to talk about it," he said simply. Given the culture of the military, Quijano would never have dared to ask.

Quijano said he thought of Gerry as untroubled and had had no indication that he would kill himself, but he recalled that Gerry had behaved peculiarly the night before he died. "I was asleep, but woke up, and noticed Gerry smoking a cigarette under the mosquito net. He would get up, smoke another cigarette, and then go back to sleep. He did that almost the whole night. In the morning he seemed all right." In retrospect, Quijano said he thought his friend might have been distressed or "shell-shocked." He remembered several vague statements Gerry had made in the weeks immediately prior to his death.

"I think maybe he was bothered by his conscience. There had been this encounter," Quijano said, referring to the De los Santos massacre without mentioning the name of the family:

> Gerry had been tasked to go after the NPA on this raid, but he said it wasn't what he expected. He said it wasn't like the other raids. He thought they would find NPAs with weapons. He said that normally people would have been asked to surrender, to put their hands on their heads and come out of the building, but these people weren't given a chance. And he said, "If I told you any more about it, I don't know if you could take it." He told me he hoped something like this would never happen to me. He had a problem about killing these supposed NPAs. He said it disturbed him a lot. He said they were sort of helpless.

Quijano himself was not familiar with the details of the operation. He'd heard rumors, but he said it was difficult to get any hard information. "After the massacre, the military tried to muzzle the men. There was no formal order; they [the Rangers] all just denied knowing anything. If you weren't in the group, you weren't supposed to know. Nobody wanted to talk about it."

Quijano said he felt compelled to pay a visit to Our Lady of the Snows Church before the funeral to look at the coffins of the De los Santoses. He said he was curious and thought he might learn what really had happened. He remains convinced that Gerry's death was a suicide, and he has ruled out the possibility that his friend had been killed by the NPA, Arrojado, or one of the other Rangers. "I'm not a mind reader. Some people know how to deal with life; they know how to get along. Others—sometimes people just do things like that."

The evening of Gerry's death, Quijano sat on their bed cradling his rifle in his arms, disturbed by the idea that it might have been used in the death of his friend, wondering whether he himself did not somehow bear some responsibility. It was twilight, and beyond the perimeter of the Ranger camp, Quijano could still see people moving about in the soft graying end of the day. Inside the camp, nestled in a dense grove of tall *santal* trees, it was already dark. Quijano couldn't remember how long he sat silently, alone in the hut, thinking about Gerry, his death, and the times they'd spent together. He remembered getting up and looking through Gerry's meager possessions, thinking they would have to be sent to Pelma, and discovering a small bundle of letters. He began thumbing through them and removed the ones from Emerine Mabugat, Gerry's beautiful nineteen-year-old girlfriend.

The love letters were addressed to Herbert De los Santos. It was funny, Quijano thought, this girl, his mistress, didn't even know his real name. They had met at a funeral, in Cadiz, at the northern end of Negros, and Gerry had told her his name was Herbert. The funeral was for Emerine's cousin, a Scout Ranger who had just been killed in Mindanao. Emerine began dating Gerry. Sometimes they would get a room in one of the cheap Bacolod hotels. Once they went to the Santa Fe Beach Resort and spent the day talking about cooking. Gerry asked her where he could get an *anting anting,* and Emerine told him she didn't know anything about lucky charms or amulets, wondering why he wanted one. "Are you afraid to die?" she asked him. But he didn't answer. Emerine liked being with Gerry; he was different from the other soldiers: tender, quiet, serious. Quijano thought about Emerine and Gerry and Pelma and decided to hold on to Emerine's letters, that there was no need for Pelma to know about her. He sat down and looked around the spare quarters he had shared with Gerry—the bamboo floor, the nipa walls, and the ceiling, where a curtain hung listlessly in the still air, separating Quijano's half of the bed from Gerry's. Quijano examined the curtain, thought about it, and as the night closed around him, stood up, yanked it from its mooring, took it outside, lit a match, and set it on fire. Quijano said he was afraid that if he left the curtain, Gerry's ghost would come back.

* * *

Gerry's other close Ranger friend and roommate, Efren Llaneta, was supposed to be married to Jocelyn Arriola the day after Gerry died. The wedding went ahead. The ceremony was held at the home of Jocelyn's aunt, next door to Pepe Vallota's house, facing the Himamaylan town plaza. The Scout Rangers who attended dressed in black fatigues and black T-shirts, a sign of mourning for Gerry. One of them described the wedding as a "very solemn" affair.

It is customary in the Philippines for a bridegroom to seek "sponsors" for his wedding—friends and patrons who contribute money for food and other costs. Efren's sponsors included Celestino Guara, Himamaylan's chief of police, who, at Captain Gutierrez's insistence, had neglected to investigate the massacre. Guara recalled the wedding well, particularly a conversation shortly before the ceremony itself in which Efren said he believed Gerry had been murdered by one of his fellow Scout Rangers. "Efren wanted to go up to the [Army] camp to search for whoever killed Gerry. I had to physically restrain him. I told him, 'Look, this is your wedding day. Why don't you let your commanding officer settle the problem?' So the wedding pushed through." Efren's commanding officer, Alan Arrojado, a suspect in Gerry's death and the man ordered by Gutierrez to prepare the official coverup of the De los Santos massacre, was another sponsor of the wedding, which Police Chief Guara characterized as "half happy." Guara said he had not seen Efren Llaneta since the wedding but believed he had gone AWOL, moved to Manila, and eventually joined the group of Scout Rangers who tried to overthrow the Aquino government in December 1989.

———

Efren Llaneta's wife, Jocelyn, still lives in Himamaylan with her curly-haired daughter, Efrelyn (the name is a contraction of Efren and Jocelyn). The girl, who wears gold stud earrings that match her mother's, looks like her father, Jocelyn says. Efrelyn plays quietly on a couch, standing on her head, sliding onto the floor. Jocelyn's skin is almost as white as her cotton dress. Her hands are delicate. As she talked, she was joined by her friend, Joan Sian, the former girlfriend of Quijano and of Moret's brother, Dan, and, if he is to be believed, of Joaquin De los Santos as well. The two young women sat on a couch facing a wicker coffee table covered by a piece of glass. Biblical admonitions, hand-lettered on pink construction paper, were pressed underneath. "Be anxious for nothing, but in everything by prayer and supplication, with thanksgiving, let your requests be made known to God," one of them said. Outside, a long green lizard appended itself to the side of the garden wall behind a patch of pink orchids, waiting motionless for its next victim to scurry by.

Jocelyn says she and Efren exchanged vows beneath a bamboo arbor constructed specially for the wedding by the Rangers. It was a simple ceremony, followed by a small reception. Jocelyn's aunt was angry at Gerry because he was supposed to have brought several cases of beer to the wedding. Now that he was dead, she would have to buy the beer. Immediately after the reception, the newlyweds left for the Funeraria del Sur in Binalbagan to spend some time with Gerry's body. Jocelyn said Efren spent their wedding night crying. The following morning they returned to the funeral home, but Gerry's coffin had already been sealed, so they left.

Like Quijano, Jocelyn remembered that Gerry had behaved strangely just before his death. She had seen him pacing to and fro at Merle Tayaban's birthday party and recalled an earlier conversation with him that was almost identical to the one reported by Quijano. "We were all having dinner together at a restaurant in Carabalan, and Gerry told us he thought he was going to be killed, that his commanding officer was going to kill him." Jocelyn also recalled that the day before Gerry died, Efren, too, had been very agitated. "He said he felt like something was going to happen. He couldn't sleep that night." Jocelyn added that neither she nor Efren questioned Gerry about his fears. "I didn't think anything would happen." Jocelyn was busy preparing for her wedding; she didn't dwell very much on Gerry's comments until after he was dead.

Jocelyn's own life began to unravel right after Gerry's death and her wedding to Efren. She said Efren and Melanio Vinluan were both afraid to sleep in the hut they had shared with Gerry and Quijano in Carabalan, and she herself thought about Gerry almost constantly. "One night I was sleeping there with Efren," Jocelyn said. "It was two in the morning. I knew I had turned off the electric fan, but when I looked at it, I could see it spinning, and then I saw Gerry with his long straight hair, as if he was alive. I immediately covered myself in the blanket and cried out for Efren. Since then, I keep a candle lit by my bed until morning."

Jocelyn thinks Gerry De los Santos committed suicide because he believed he had murdered members of his own family. "Gerry was bothered by his conscience because of the De los Santos massacre. He was one of the ones who strafed the house, and later he realized that the victims were his relatives. He was thinking, 'I have children, too,' and he was afraid that this would happen to them. He told Efren about his feelings two days before we were married." Jocelyn said Efren related little else to her about the massacre. She said he wasn't involved but was actually with her at the time. However, an affidavit signed by Efren says that he was, in fact, one of the perpetrators. Essentially a capsule summary of the official Ranger version of events, the affidavit says that the Rangers were fired on from the De los Santos home and that during the subsequent battle, "the five members of the De los Santos family were unintentionally caught in the crossfire." The affidavit is written in English, which Jocelyn barely understands, and is initialed by her husband next to his typed name. Jocelyn said she didn't know why Efren would have signed it if he hadn't been there.

Efren Llaneta went AWOL from the Scout Rangers less than two months after the De los Santos massacre and Gerry's death. Jocelyn said she hasn't spoken with him since. She said her husband left the Rangers with Alex Bayle, who also had been involved in the massacre, that the two men found jobs at the Victorias Milling Company guarding the sugarcane trucks and rail cars on their way to the mill. She said they were disappointed with the pay at Victorias, though, as well as with the way they were treated, and quit. Jocelyn last heard from Efren in two letters he mailed from Davao City, on the south-

ern island of Mindanao. She said she didn't know what Efren was
doing in Davao, although others said he had gone there to work for
Melvin Gutierrez, who had been posted there after a short stint in
Manila.

Since Efren quit the Scout Rangers, Jocelyn has been visited by
her husband only in her dreams. "The other night, I dreamed I saw
him with a new wife, and I went to him and I had a fight with her
right in front of Efren." Jocelyn said she was growing tired of waiting to hear from Efren. "I wish something had happened to him
while he was still in the military," she said. "Then at least I would
know. Now I don't know if he's alive or dead."

Whitewash

For murder, though it have no tongue, will speak with
most miraculous organ.

—William Shakespeare, *Hamlet*

The Philippines is often described as a "tribal" culture
in which loyalties barely extend beyond immediate family members,
patrons—the employer, politician, or local thug who can give you
work, lend you money, or get you out of jail—and a few close friends
who become godparents to your children. According to this view,
commitments to society or community are deemed to be nearly
nonexistent, and "nationalism" is something reserved for students,
intellectuals, and a small segment of the urban elite. What passes
for the "nation" is little more than a pyramid of interlocking personal loyalties, grounded in debt, *utang na loob,* in which the oligarchs and politicians at the pinnacle control the country's natural
resources and industry and reap the wealth produced by those
below them. There are examples of popular nationalism—such as
the anti-Japanese resistance and the mass protests against Marcos—
but nationalism in the Philippines has never translated into a strong
sense of community.

While one might expect to find a sense of nationalism within the
armed forces, there is, in fact, probably no place in Filipino culture
where loyalties are as constricted and parochial. The U.S.-created
Philippine military, supposedly inculcated with a deep respect for
civilian rule, was from the outset a tool of the agrarian elite. It col-
laborated with the Americans during the first decades of the century,
then with the Japanese during World War II, again with the Ameri-

cans after liberation, and always with the oligarchs. Not surprisingly, it was always despised by the common people. Likewise, the paramilitary forces, which first began to service the *hacenderos* in the 1940s, were created not to serve anything even remotely resembling a national interest but rather to defend the private interests of landowners and provincial politicians.

Under Marcos, paramilitary groups proliferated, and the "professional" military was used to rig elections, arrest tens of thousands of the dictator's opponents, and protect the investments of his cronies and supporters. For their efforts, military commanders were allowed to engage in illegal logging, drug smuggling, prostitution, gambling, gunrunning, and any number of other rackets. During martial law, top officers were also given control over expropriated companies, the customs bureau, and several government corporations.

Had the military been more committed to the constitution and civilian rule, President Aquino would not have faced six coup attempts during her six years in office, and those who participated in what were, after all, acts of treason would have been severely punished. Military discipline was so poor, devotion to democracy so weak, and corruption so pervasive, though, that Armed Forces Chief of Staff Fidel Ramos, now President Ramos, barely dared to challenge his rebellious underlings. Following the first coup attempt, he punished the mutineers by ordering each to do fifty pushups.

Within the armed forces, loyalties rarely reach further than a soldier's closest comrades, typically to members of his graduating class at the military academy. "On a daily basis," said Aquino's Air Force Chief of Staff Loven Abadia, "an enlisted man's loyalties would not go beyond his immediate commander. His thinking does not go beyond survival: 'How do I eat?' " Given the meager salary of an enlisted man, his standard of living is not much better than that of the average peasant he is supposedly fighting for. Even though soldiers may recognize that fact, however, the poor generally fall outside their personal hierarchy of loyalties. By joining the military, a young man moves to a higher social caste than that occupied by the average peasant. Depending on luck, promotions, personal connections, and the degree to which he is able to enrich himself through graft, a young man may eventually aspire to move among the elite, just like his officers.

* * *

Shortly after the De los Santos massacre, Captain Melvin Gutierrez concluded that the NPA would probably try to kill him, and he requested reassignment off of Negros. Before leaving, he selected as his successor his close friend and executive officer, First Lieutenant Alan Arrojado. Arrojado's appointment over numerous older and more senior officers carried with it a set of unspoken obligations, a sense of *utang na loob*, that needed no spelling out. Most important, Arrojado would be responsible for protecting Gutierrez from any repercussions arising out of the De los Santos massacre.

In many ways, Arrojado appears to be the model soldier. A graduate of the country's premier military academy, he joined the Scout Rangers because he wanted to fight Communists, became the first member of his class to be given a company command, and received more than two dozen awards and citations before reaching the age of thirty. Unlike many of the opportunists who constitute the rank and file of the supposedly "elite" Rangers, Arrojado consistently remained loyal to the government. In 1986, he refused to participate in the coup against Marcos, and three years later, he rejected efforts to recruit him for a nearly successful coup against Aquino. Arrojado was not entirely without his critics, however. One colleague described him as a "war freak"—a guy who thrived on combat—and something of an eccentric. "He had very long hair and wore red nailpolish, and he had an *anting anting*—a small bottle of coconut oil —strapped around his waist. He claimed that if there was an enemy nearby, the oil would boil over. We have an expression for this kind of guy. We call it *utak pulbura*. It means he has gunpowder for brains."

As the chief author of the coverup of the De los Santos massacre, Arrojado seemed an unlikely source of information. Lower-ranking Rangers had refused to talk about the massacre or lied about their involvement. One who had earlier signed an affidavit owning his part in the massacre later said he'd never been to Negros. Another who signed the same affidavit said he was simply the company cook and was on base preparing breakfast for the troops at the time of the slaughter. Arrojado's role in the De los Santos case, on the other hand, was entirely after the fact, and perhaps for that reason alone, he is more candid in discussing it.

Arrojado, who decided to become a soldier when he was still in elementary school, idolizes men with extensive combat experience and, until he got married, kept a grisly pile of photos documenting his battlefield experiences. He won't say how many men he's killed and says he disposed of the photos because he didn't want his wife to see them. He describes himself as a devout Catholic, who goes to church with his family every Sunday and crosses himself before going into battle. "You have to ask for guidance," he explains.

In central Negros, Arrojado said he and his men constantly felt as if they were surrounded by NPAs. His own fears are evident in a section of the report he wrote on the massacre, "Lessons Learned." A soldier, Arrojado states, must "never trust any place, any house, any person, for anytime they can be used by the enemy." Since identifying the enemy was often even more difficult than divining the purpose of the war itself, it was not surprising that Arrojado's case against Moret De los Santos seemed to confuse hypothesis and conjecture with evidence. Thus, Our Lady of the Snows Church was "a front" for the NPA: "The church was not only infiltrated by the NPA, there was an underground within the church, and NPA commanders conducted meetings in the church. Because of that, Gutierrez prohibited us from attending church in Himamaylan." The only evidence Arrojado could cite to support his allegation was hardly a smoking gun. "Our friends in Himamaylan said they saw people coming and going from the church at midnight a lot of times." Similarly, Arrojado described parish priest Eamon Gill as "an NPA, a subversive. He was anti-military, anti-government, and we knew that he traveled to faraway barrios spreading propaganda."

Arrojado had a similar take on Moret De los Santos, whom he called "a kangaroo judge of the NPAs" and "a political leader of the NPA who ordered the killing of Serafin Gatuslao." He suggested that Moret's participation in the BCC, a perfectly legal organization, justified the massacre. "We felt sorry about the kids, but he [Moret] was a leader of the BCC. . . . After De los Santos was killed, a lot of people came to our headquarters and thanked us for killing him— not the family but the father. He had great influence in the area." Although Arrojado was able to rationalize killing BCC members, he also had an honest appreciation for why organizations like the BCC and the NPA flourished on Negros. "You can see the richest people and the poorest people on Negros," he said. "The land is controlled

by a very few; the insurgency survives because of the poverty." It was
the same analysis U.S. colonel John Roberts White had offered at the
turn of the century. Like White, Arrojado saw no contradiction in
the military's alliance with those "very few" he identified as the root
of the problem. The relationship between the military and the mon-
eyed elite has been in place so long that hardly anyone even questions it anymore.

Given his friendship with Gutierrez, it came as no surprise that
Arrojado's report on the massacre followed almost verbatim a script
Gutierrez had penned only hours after the shooting stopped. Arrojado candidly acknowledged that he did not interview a single civilian witness to the massacre. "I relied on Gutierrez's reporting to
make my own report because he had already conducted the investigation," Arrojado said, adding with just a hint of irony, "After all he
was still my commanding officer."

The Gutierrez report claims that the Rangers were on a "routine
security/combat patrol" when they "happen[ed] to chance" upon a
"number of Communist terrorists," that an "armed clash" ensued,
and that the "family of Reynaldo De los Santos with five members
were caught in the crossfire [sic]." Arrojado barely embellished this
description, adding only that the house was "noisily packed" with
NPAs, who were conducting a meeting. Gutierrez had also filed a list
of evidence collected from the De los Santos house, which Arrojado
dutifully copied word for word, as is demonstrated by the fact that
both reports present the items in precisely the same order and with
the same flawed syntax: "two fragmentary grenades" are listed,
rather than "fragmentation grenades"; "one .45 with two ammos,"
"six magazines of M-16 fully loaded," a Communist flag, and various
"subversive documents." The red flag and "subversive documents"
are a sine qua non of military reports filed after any significant encounter with the NPA.

The only surprising piece of evidence cited in Arrojado's report
was the actual corpse of "one unidentified Red fighter killed in action." Although more than a dozen witnesses saw the bodies of the
De los Santoses removed from the house, no one saw the body of the
"Red fighter," and police records make no mention of the purported
victim. Nor do the records of the Gatuslao Hospital, the only hospital in Himamaylan, which show no death certificates issued on April
6 other than those for members of the De los Santos family. While

some have suggested that the NPAs took their dead comrade with them when they fled, Arrojado's report includes a diagram identifying the exact location in the house where the body was purportedly found after the rebels had all been chased away. Thus, if the dead man's comrades did recover the body, they would have had to return to the De los Santos house after having been forced to flee and would have had to smuggle the body out in broad daylight without any of several dozen local residents noticing them. Given the fact that hundreds of bullets coursed through the De los Santos house—which was supposedly "packed" with NPAs—and given the duration of the firefight, it was nothing short of miraculous that the only casualties were civilians and that not a single Scout Ranger was wounded. Unless you believe that the Rangers were protected by powerful *anting antings*.

Another interesting bit of "evidence" is something that isn't even mentioned in the Ranger reports, a small detail not unlike Sherlock Holmes's celebrated "dog that didn't bark." Neighbors collected 247 shell casings *outside* the De los Santos house, but nowhere do the Arrojado or Gutierrez reports mention a single shell casing found inside the house or anywhere else—extraordinary, given that the Rangers reported a thirty-minute firefight with NPA rebels. Unless one believes that the guerrillas were fastidious in cleaning up after themselves as they fled for their lives through the ring of Rangers surrounding the house. Arrojado couldn't explain this discrepancy.

Arrojado's personal view of the massacre is that "nobody was to blame for this incident; you can't blame either the victims or the men." The men involved, he said, "were performing their duty." In his final report, Arrojado makes three recommendations. First, that "ammunition expenditures be replenished"; second, that the investigation of the "alleged massacre be dropped and closed"; and third, that "awards be given to the personnel involved in the operation."

Arrojado was also the author of the official report on the death of Gerry De los Santos, according to which Gerry had been killed in an NPA ambush. Arrojado met Gerry in Pelma's hometown when they were both assigned to Leyte and insists that Gerry was a close friend and one of his best soldiers. But he said Gerry's life began falling

apart right after the De los Santos incident because Gerry felt a personal responsibility for the killings. "He was mentally tortured. It
was combat stress. I didn't detect it right away. I advised him to go
to church and tell the priest in a confession what he'd done, to light
a candle for the family, for the victims."

Gerry apparently never got around to confessing to a priest. But
Arrojado said Gerry came to talk to him the night he died:

> He was drunk and he made a confession to me. He told me
> he was afraid that I might shoot him. I asked him why he said
> that, and Gerry said he thought I was angry because of the
> massacre. I told him, "It's not your fault; it was an honest mis-
> take. They were victims of circumstance." But Gerry believed
> he was related to the De los Santos family. And he asked me to
> take care of his family. It was as if there was a premonition.

Gerry's friends and colleagues were adamant that Arrojado's report stating that Gerry had been killed in an NPA ambush was simply not true, and Arrojado himself eventually acknowledged that he
had deliberately misrepresented the situation. "I know I should not
have done it. But Gerry's wife was pregnant at the time. I was in
command, and I wrote the report out of a sense of moral obligation.
It was my moral responsibility. She would not have gotten his pension benefits if I'd reported that he killed himself. So it depends how
you look at it."

One way to look at it is that Arrojado was the only one who made
good on Gerry's request to his friends that they look after his family.
Another explanation is the one that spread with the *tsismis*—that
Gerry was ready to blow the whistle on the massacre and that Gu-
tierrez or Arrojado had him killed. Arrojado vehemently denied that
Gerry had been murdered.

Arrojado said Gerry was not the only Ranger to have been emotionally affected by the massacre. "At some point, each of the men
involved discussed his concerns with me. They were afraid they
would be discharged from the service and came to me seeking assur-
ances. They were worried about their careers." Arrojado specifically
mentioned Jocelyn Llaneta's husband, Efren, and Alex Bayle, both
of whom had gone AWOL a few months after the incident. "Their
consciences bothered them because they killed innocent civilians,"

Arrojado said. He said he told his men that what they did was "part of the job" and that they should not think about it because it would "destroy their morale and their moral fiber."

*   *   *

It is a simple fact of life that a dog chained to a tree will, in due course, wind itself around and around until it can go no farther and will starve to death before it figures a way out of its predicament. Alberto Nabong was like that: not even twenty, he was already caught up in a longtime losing streak. In the aftermath of the De los Santos massacre, the military had come up with three witnesses to support its account of what happened in Mambagaton on that Easter Wednesday, and Alberto had the ill fortune to be one of them.

In his affidavit, Alberto claimed that he just happened to be wandering by the De los Santos home at 5 A.M., that he witnessed the firefight, saw a group of armed rebels retreat, and that he, too, fled the scene because he was afraid he would be "taken hostage by the soldiers and shot." That would have been extremely unlikely, however, since he and the other two men who had signed affidavits supporting the Rangers were all working for the military. According to Alberto's mother, the men belonged to a paramilitary unit operating out of the office of Police Chief Guara, Efren Llaneta's wedding sponsor and the same man who on the day of the massacre agreed to Captain Gutierrez's request that he keep his hands off any investigation.

Mrs. Nabong provided an address for her son in Himamaylan, and a young girl living there identified Alberto with a barely discernible nod. A skinny kid with closely cropped hair, he sat perched on a narrow ledge by a glassless window that looks out the front of a small wood house. The De los Santos massacre is not Alberto's favorite topic of conversation. Indeed, the subject leaves him squirming in his seat with his eyes roaming the room, as though he was plotting an escape. As he sends the girl to buy him some cigarettes, he fidgets with the frayed edge of his cut-off denim jeans just above the stain of a dark blue tattoo.

It took the Scout Rangers more than two months from the time of the massacre to come up with affidavits supporting their version of

the event. Alberto and the others signed them just two days before
Melvin Gutierrez left Negros, suggesting that Gutierrez himself was
actively involved in preparing the coverup as one of his final acts as
commander. Alberto, who calls himself a "returnee," using the term
for ex-NPA rebels who surrender to the military, talks through a
smile as tight as twisted rope. He says he recalls signing the statement but doesn't want to discuss it, that it speaks for itself. But it
doesn't. Mostly, it raises questions.

When the girl returns, she hands Alberto a half-dozen Hope
menthol cigarettes. He quickly lights one, inhales deeply, and blows
the smoke through clenched teeth.

"Immediately after that incident that I was involved in, I couldn't
understand what I was doing," he begins. "During that time I had
a lot of problems. Problems were piled one on top of the other.
Personal problems, financial problems, problems in staying alive."

When it comes to the specifics, though, such as whether Melvin
Gutierrez or someone else forced him to sign the statement, Alberto's memory disappoints. "I can't recall, because at that time I
was very worried," he says, then offers an explanation that comes as
close as any to describing his predicament. "You know, in this world,
life would be better if we had a lot of money, if we were provided for.
But I have to think about my family, my livelihood, and how to defend myself."

Alberto Nabong is, perhaps, the archetypal Negros victim: the
son of the poorest dirt farmers who joins the New People's Army,
most likely because of financial frustrations or to avenge some injustice by a landlord or a farm manager, the military, or some vigilante,
but almost certainly out of no ideological commitment; then finds
that the revolution is going nowhere or realizes that the rebels
couldn't provide the solutions he'd been looking for. So he decides
to get out and ends up changing sides, thinking he can start over. Instead, he becomes the pawn of his new patrons in the military, who
keep him on an extremely short tether. Alberto is expected to provide information about his former comrades and gains a reputation
as a snitch and a traitor. As a result, he finds it impossible to stray far
from the military's protective custody.

One time he paid a visit to his family in Barrio San Antonio in the
mountains of Himamaylan, about five miles from the center of town.
He got a ride back in a truck with a group of sugarcane workers, and

when they stopped at Crossing Calasa, directly in front of Don Serafin Gatuslao's crumbling turn-of-the-century sugar mill, they were attacked by NPA Sparrows. A witness, Angelina Llanera, who lives in a one-room shack at Crossing Calasa, said she was hit in the arm by a metal fragment when a hand grenade exploded near the truck. An animated old lady with rotten brown teeth and breasts that lick about like little tongues beneath a stained blouse as she talks, Mrs. Llanera said a half-dozen people were wounded, and one woman, Frucosa de Leon, was killed. "They found some of her flesh on the fence over there," she stated matter-of-factly, pointing in the direction of the sugar mill.

. Mrs. Llanera said she couldn't imagine why the NPAs would have attacked a truck carrying sugar workers. According to Police Chief Guara, however, the rebels had been trying to kill Alberto Nabong.

Alberto Nabong has little in common with the sugar planters or the soldiers who rely on the "intelligence" he gathers, but, like them, and like Mayor Daisy and Governor Lacson and President Aquino, Alberto feels trapped, feels he has to choose between the Communists and the military. He consumes his cigarettes, one after the other, blowing smoke on a life no longer of his own making, unwilling to say whether he was even in Mambagaton at the time of the massacre, as his affidavit states. Nor will he directly reaffirm that he actually saw rebels at the De los Santos house. "If there were, then there were lots of them. Because even here they follow me; they follow me everywhere."

Alberto doesn't know exactly how he ended up in this bind but follows his instincts and hopes for the best. He is apologetic about his inability to tell the truth about what he knows and believes he has no choice other than to remain silent. "I'm sorry," he says, "but I can't tell my story."

*　*　*

Speaking to a reporter from his home in Honolulu on April 19, 1988, two weeks after the De los Santos massacre, Ferdinand Marcos sought to dispel a rumor circulated in several Manila papers that he was brain dead. "I am very much distressed to hear this idea of my having been declared clinically dead, and I deny this absolutely." The same day on Negros, Melvin Gutierrez and his family packed their bags and flew to Manila. Father Gill gave Consoy Perez money to buy a bottle of rum so everyone could celebrate.

In Manila, Captain Gutierrez became a teacher of sorts—chief of counterinsurgency for the Army's Combat Arms School at Fort Bonifacio. But he was soon reassigned to Davao City in eastern Mindanao, the large southernmost Philippine island, where a war between the government and an armed Muslim secession movement left 50,000 people dead and more than a million refugees in the mid-1970s. Davao calls itself the country's largest city because it covers the largest area, but its population is under a million, and only a tiny section of the city even begins to suggest a metropolis. In fact, most of the city could actually pass for rural. At the time the Marcos dictatorship was toppled, Davao City was known as the "laboratory" for the Communist revolution in the Philippines and was famous for the almost daily assassinations by NPA Sparrows and a weird collection of paramilitary death squads in a barrio called Agdao, which locals called "Nicaragdao," to suggest a comparison with the ongoing war between the Sandinistas and U.S.-backed Contras in Nicaragua.

In recent years, Mindanao has been the scene of a large number of kidnapping rings, most of them run by former members of the police and armed forces. It has also received some international attention because of the monkey-eating eagle, the Philippines' national bird, which is on the brink of extinction. Once a common sight, the huge bird with its crested head and a wingspan of nearly seven feet has lost most of its habitat as loggers have pillaged Mindanao's tropical rain forests. Today there are reportedly fewer than fifty monkey-eating eagles in the wild, although a conservation program is having some success breeding the birds in captivity at Callinan, a remote corner of Davao City. Callinan also happens to be home to the Seventy-fifth Infantry Battalion, where Captain Gutierrez landed a new job as an "operations officer" in charge of training paramilitary forces.

Although it isn't the most inviting place, Callinan is no worse than the military bases at Carabalan or Task Force Sugarland. Gutierrez seems to be living quite well for someone of his rank. He owns a fashionable new house near the center of Davao, where several servants attend to his needs, and he parks a sparkling stainless-steel Jeep and a large motorcycle in his driveway. With his gold watch and gold signet ring—a large letter *M* in diamonds—he is the picture of

a comfortable middle-class suburbanite, a disappointment for anyone hoping to find a volatile, scar-faced, tattooed mass murderer.
Gutierrez's career doesn't seem to have suffered, either. Three
years after the De los Santos massacre, he spent seven months at
Fort Sill, Oklahoma, in a U.S. Army artillery training course, a highly
prized assignment for Philippine soldiers trying to move up the career ladder and one he wouldn't have received had there been any
residual fallout from the De los Santos massacre. U.S. officials were
apparently unaware of Gutierrez's background when they approved
his admission, although it's not clear whether it would have made
much difference. Gutierrez's instructors at Fort Sill were pleased
with his performance and submitted an assessment that reads like
the Sunday school report card of a model student. "He was highly
motivated toward mastering course material, and worked especially
well in small group exercises," the U.S. military commander wrote.
"He freely shared of his experience, which was always a highlight for
the junior officers." The report also praised his participation in ex-
tracurricular activities and said, "He represented the Philippines ex-
ceptionally well and made many friends." The report concluded that
he "should be favorably considered for further advanced training in
the U.S."

The webbed, deracinated stumps of a dozen coconut trees pounded
upside-down into the ground stand in the garden of Gutierrez's
home like dark, tribal idols festooned with flamboyant orchid head-
dresses. The captain's six-year-old son, Tyrone, enters the garden in
his navy-blue school shorts and crisp white shirt, carrying a clunky,
oversized briefcase. The boy greets his father silently with the *mano*,
the customary sign of respect for an elder, bowing his head and
touching the back of his father's hand to his own forehead. Tyrone
changes into play clothes and, with the plastic M-16 his father gave
him tucked into the back of his pants, heads off to hunt for friends
in the neighborhood. Gutierrez is a proud father. On the surface, he
seems at peace with himself. He has never talked publicly about the
De los Santos massacre. It's unlikely that he's discussed it with his
fellow Rangers, and he has almost certainly kept it from his wife,
Kristi. But it is with him privately.
The thirteen-year Ranger veteran is consumed by the possibility

that he might be brought to justice for what he refers to as the "incident." "After that incident," Gutierrez confides, "I was ready for any eventuality. I could see that it might work against my career. And my morale was affected. It was mental torture for me. But I kept this secret to myself." Over the years, Gutierrez has guarded his secret zealously—at the same time telling himself he has "nothing to hide" —and has defended the massacre as a regrettable but understandable occurrence, "a legitimate encounter," an act of self-defense in response to shots fired from inside the De los Santos house. "I did not murder anybody," he says, asserting his innocence time and again as if reciting the mantra for some personal rite of exorcism.

Gutierrez rearranges the pieces of the massacre in his mind like an artist working on a complex collage, shifting his elements, looking for a way to relegate that one brief but sanguinary moment to some obscure shadowed corner of a grander tableau that takes account of his numerous citations and awards, his successful encounters, his heroism and leadership, the hundreds of soldiers he has commanded and fought with, the shiny scar tissue on his thigh where an NPA's bullet brought him down. No matter how much his artistic endeavor is rewarded, though, the blood of the De los Santos massacre continues to seep onto his canvas, marring an otherwise noble self-portrait.

Gutierrez feels that the massacre has unfairly damaged his standing in the military, that it has caused delays in promotions and engendered disrespect. The more he denies any culpability, the more he seems haunted by the killings:

> I was really affected by this incident in my career. Personally, I believe I have served the military organization to the best of my ability. . . . Basically, I am oriented with the Scout Ranger type of attitude; to fight against the NPA by any and all means. It's a matter of survival. But if I remain with the Scout Rangers, I will never be able to escape these accusations of human rights violations. . . . This unfavorable experience in my military career, it actually broadens my perception. . . . Sometimes I feel very sorry about that incident. We did not mean to kill people unnecessarily. But I maintain that my men must be aggressive; they must not become weak. In 1983 I was wounded here in Davao. We were traveling in a 6-by-6, and we

were ambushed by the NPA. Only two of us survived. I
jumped into a ravine, and I was shot twice. Sometimes when
these things happen, your warrior attitude may disappear. . . .
If the NPA survives, what happens to us? If the Communists
survive, I will be killed. . . . A lot of my men have already been
killed. My mission is not to oppress people. My mission is not
to destroy civilians. . . . I had no criminal or malicious intent to
kill people. God knows, during that incident I did not intend
to kill people who might be innocent. But sometimes civilians
are caught in a crossfire, and it's also their fault, because I told
the people not to meet with the NPAs in their house. "Don't
allow your house to be utilized as a meeting place, because if
they are there, I will conduct a raid, and then I'm sorry for
you." I told the people, "I don't blame you if you talk to the
NPA. I know that you're forced to get involved. But you have
to avoid these incidents. My men have to survive. I have to survive in my own area."

Gutierrez insists that he had the highest regard for the rights of
civilians and exacted a high standard of discipline from his men.
One of his "cardinal rules," he says, is that his men never "abuse
women or kill children" and never take food from civilians, and he
insisted that his troops nearly always obeyed the rules he laid out for
them:

I get mad when my people move slowly. If you can't do the
job, you should get out. Sometimes I joined my soldiers on a
drinking spree, but those who could not maintain the proper
decorum, I told to stop, to get out. One time, one of my men
went wild; he strafed a bus carrying civilians. I used my knuck-
les against him. I beat him so much he was sent to the hospital,
and I told him, "I sent you to patrol, not to make foolishness
against civilians." I'm a disciplinarian. I've hit a lot of soldiers.
Physical punishment, that's my style. You have to do that in a
Ranger unit. I offer my men a choice: physical punishment, or
get out.

Gutierrez says allegations of wrongdoing against him or his soldiers were routine. "Most of the time when there were encounters,

there were these alleged human rights violations. If you're in the
Scout Rangers, you're very susceptible to these fabrications." Although Gutierrez might be expected to dismiss any such charges, his
version of the De los Santos massacre contains a number of surprising elements. He claims, for example, that he had actually never met
Moret De los Santos, never quarreled with him or threatened him in
the Himamaylan cockpit. In fact, he insists he had only seen photos
of Moret provided by his intelligence operatives. But Gutierrez
knew about Moret's work for the Basic Christian Community. He
must have known that Moret was part of a BCC team that had
looked into the recent Ranger attack in Carabalan and concluded
that Gutierrez's men, assisted by vigilantes, had massacred and
burned the bodies of eleven civilians, mostly BCC members. He
knew that the same BCC had asked Governor Lacson to force the
military to disband its detachment at Apin Gatuslao's Hacienda Benedicto because it had torched the homes of farmers in Sitio Baloyo.

> This incident on Negros was really quite unfortunate. The
> man involved—what was his name? Reynato? Reynaldo De los
> Santos? Reynaldo De los Santos was an untouchable in that
> area. People were very afraid of him. They could not go
> against this Reynaldo. You know he was on the payroll of the
> district engineer [Rojelio Tongson], but he was not working
> there. We had a lot of information about his involvement with
> the NPA. He was chairman of one of the legal fronts of the
> New People's Army, the Kristianong Katilingban [the Ilongo
> name for the BCC].

Gutierrez also said that the De los Santos house was used as a "ren-
dezvous point" by the NPA, a fact he claimed to have learned from
an informant named Berto—Alberto Nabong. "I had assets, including former NPAs, and one of them arrived and told me about a
meeting in that area." Curiously, Gutierrez's elaborate explanation
of the massacre made no reference to Apin Gatuslao and never
linked his murder to the massacre, a connection Lieutenant Arrojado and Colonel Cardones made a centerpiece of their respective
accounts.
    The most astonishing element of Gutierrez's defense, however, is
his claim that he actually had nothing to do with the slaughter—that

he hadn't even been at the De los Santos house but was instead part of a backup team of Rangers that stopped about a quarter of a mile away. "I could have washed my hands of this. I wasn't there; I only supported the attacking force from a distance," he says. This claim, however, is directly contradicted by eyewitness Rudi Garcia, who knew Gutierrez and said he spoke with him at the scene of the massacre. It is also contradicted by the Rangers' own reports. Even Gutierrez's handpicked coverup man, Alan Arrojado, wrote in his initial account that a single team of Rangers was involved and that it was "led by Captain Gutierrez." An affidavit signed by eight of the men who participated in the massacre also supports the single-team view with the claim that Gutierrez "organized the team, being himself the leader," to conduct the combat patrol. Arrojado and others familiar with Ranger operational procedures said it would have been unheard of for a backup team to be separated from the attacking force by a quarter-mile and to remain at that distance during a half-hour firefight.

But if Gutierrez didn't command the operation, then who did? Surprisingly, Gutierrez blames the low-ranking Corporal Gerry De los Santos, who is not even mentioned in any of the other reports on the massacre. Following the massacre, Gutierrez says that he interviewed all of the men who were directly involved and that Gerry told him: "Sir, there were civilian casualties. Sir, we did not intend to kill those people—except the ones with guns—but when the other side started firing, we had to fire also." Gutierrez insists he then told Gerry he shouldn't "feel sorry" about what happened, that it was "part of the operation," and that he, Gutierrez, would take full responsibility for it. "I told the men who were involved not to worry, that even if my career will be destroyed, I will take responsibility. I will take criminal responsibility or civil responsibility. I don't want to stay in the military without dignity."

In the final analysis, however, Gutierrez says the primary responsibility for the massacre lay not with him but with Gerry De los Santos. Gutierrez also denies that he had anything to do with Gerry's death, insisting that Gerry committed suicide.

While a plausible motive can be found for silencing Gerry, it is difficult to discern an equally powerful motive for murdering Moret De los Santos, his wife, and three children. Gutierrez's alleged humiliation by Moret in the cockpit fails to make a compelling case for revenge. True, Filipinos are routinely dispatched in disputes over matters less consequential than a chicken, but Gutierrez undoubtedly saw himself playing for higher, more "strategic" stakes, like defeating the Hydra-headed monster of communism or destroying "Communist fronts" like the Basic Christian Community. As a leader of the BCC, a thorn in the side of the military and the planters, Moret himself was a likely target, but not his family. Harassment and murder of BCC leaders began before the massacre and continued long after it, and killing Moret or making Moret "disappear" could easily have been accomplished with far less carnage. Why it wasn't remains a subject for speculation. A distinct possibility never suggested in any records or testimony is that these bloody, unnatural acts were a result of accidental judgments, that the seemingly casual slaughter was a mistake, a blunder, that Gutierrez went to find Moret and things got terribly out of hand, that despite their supposedly rigorous training, as soon as the first shots were fired, none of the "elite" Rangers really knew what was going on, and neither Gutierrez nor anyone else made any real effort to figure it out. This was, after all, the same Ranger company that started firing wildly a few weeks later, when a single bullet felled Gerry De los Santos *inside* an Army camp. In the case of the De los Santos family, the Rangers at least had the excuse of having been in what they considered enemy territory in the dark of night. It wasn't much, but if the Rangers' conduct was inexcusable, there was at least this, along with ineptitude and sheer stupidity, as mitigating factors.

Of course, Gutierrez could never acknowledge such a disastrous mistake; the careers of self-described "warriors" are not advanced by error but by heroism. Nevertheless, as Gutierrez recycles his defense in his own mind, preparing for the trial he will never face, he seems less than sanguine about vindication:

> You know, that incident on Negros really affected me so much. I had to work out a resolution of this problem myself. My image as a commander was under attack, and the higher-ups, headquarters, they could have done more to support me. Sometimes I felt neglected. You know, when you're achieving, if you're getting laurels, everyone is happy; but if things go wrong, you're left alone. I don't know if my performance affected the insurgency. I did what I needed to. Sometimes

things go wrong. Things happen that you don't intend to happen. It was really unfortunate that other members of the family were hit. I was really very sorry for that. I did not anticipate that these things would go wrong.

At the end of the day, Gutierrez pleads his own defense like an attorney who is not entirely convinced of his client's innocence. He is committed and engaged, making his closing arguments with passion and conviction, but in his heart he is removed, an outsider viewing the play of events from a distance, knowing that the final judgment is not to be his. Gutierrez may be condemned to try this case before his jury of one until the day he dies.

"You know," he mused as a purple twilight settled on his garden, "when you cry, you cry all alone. I don't cry physically, only deep inside me. But what's important is that your conscience is clear. You do not do things to destroy other people. I am not a madman, for God's sake."

Justice

Everything's got a moral, if only you can find it.

—Lewis Carroll, *Alice in Wonderland*

If you're looking for a story with a happy ending on Negros, the best place to find one is on the radio, among the dozens of serialized dramas that keep people company all day and most of the night in the bamboo and nipa cabins of isolated villages and in the lavishly appointed mansions of Bacolod and Silay. Mawkish and frequently moralizing themes run through many of these dramas. *Dabu Dabu* (Drizzle) specializes in tormented accounts of love and betrayal; the heroes of *Birtud* (Virtue) use powerful *anting antings* to work their will. In *Cristina,* young girls triumph against abusive guardians, lovers, and masters; fans of *Encantada* (The Enchanted) are carried away with the struggles of men and women victimized by witches and evil spirits.

But the program with perhaps the most pointed moral lessons is *Condenado* (The Condemned), which deals with victims of murder who return to the world as ghosts or specters. In one *Condenado* episode, the victim is a fabulously wealthy man who dies without a will, his soul condemned to the haunted mansion where he has hidden all his money. The man, that is, the *condenado,* knows that until he disposes of this wealth, his soul cannot be released, but he refuses to give his money to his avaricious relatives, the only people who visit the mansion. To frighten them off, the *condenado* pummels them with pieces of his own bloody, dismembered body. Eventually he is visited by a kindly priest, who finds a seat at a huge, candle-lit banquet table. He, too, is pelted with appendages, but when the *condenado*'s head crashes onto the table and stares at the intruder, the priest calmly uses the opportunity to engage the monstrous apparition in conversation and convinces him to cede his fortune to the church, which will use it in its charitable missions. Then, the *condenado*'s body is miraculously pieced back together, and the priest releases his soul to heaven.

Sergeant Abraham Bustamante, a former member of the Himamaylan Police Department, spends a lot of time listening to the radio dramas that issue from the open windows of the small wooden houses in his neighborhood, a short walk from the marketplace. He finds that the plays make a lot more sense than his own story, which he has never been fully able to explain. Bustamante sits in a hard-back wooden chair at the center of a broad, generous garden that overflows with tiny white orchids. His constant companions are a white dog with a patch of mange at the base of its tail, a dozen fighting cocks housed in a double tier of bamboo cages, and an ancient woman in a faded cotton duster who sucks on thick hand-rolled cigars.

At fifty-five, Bustamante is a slight man with a receding hairline and hunched froglike shoulders that bear the weight of a forlorn spirit. His face is gaunt, his left cheek marred by the shiny tissue of a thick scar where an NPA Sparrow's .38 bullet entered and lodged in his jaw. A green fishnet shirt, like a mathematician's graph paper, forms a grid over Bustamante's torso and charts the progress of a surgeon's blade from a circular bullet wound in the policeman's left shoulder down the center of his chest. On his belly is a third ragged scar the size of a beer cap.

Bustamante was born and raised in Himamaylan, became a cop, married a schoolteacher, and reared three children. He was a familiar presence in the marketplace until he and his partner, Corporal Leodagario Solina, were attacked there one morning in broad daylight. Solina died on the spot. Bustamante says he's given the incident a lot of thought but doesn't really know why he was singled out. "As long as you're on active duty, they'll go after you," is about all he has to say. The prospect of seeing his assailants apprehended and brought to trial never seems to have occurred to him. As far as he knows, there's never been a case where a policeman who was shot got any justice officially.

No one bothered to protest the attack on Bustamante and his companion—not even the priests, although they're supposed to be against killing. The *Daily Star* didn't report it, which wasn't all that surprising, since cops and soldiers are only slightly less expendable than the Communists. "The people just shut their mouths when the NPA is involved," Bustamante says. "There was an investigation, but nobody would talk—they were afraid! While the NPAs were walking away, they were still firing shots; people in the marketplace just threw themselves flat on the ground. The assailants left along the provincial road; they didn't even bother to hide."

The Philippine police have always had a rotten reputation, going back to the Spaniards and the Americans, and a half-century of independence hasn't done much to improve their image. Even the best of them are known as "crocodiles" because of the way they lurk in the shadows waiting to shake down the next innocent victim of their petty extortion schemes. If Sergeant Bustamante had been committing "crimes against the people," though, no one in Himamaylan seems to remember what they were.

An NPA political officer who uses the nom de guerre Ka Edfil remembers the Bustamante case well. Indeed, he is familiar with all of the political violence in Himamaylan, including the murders of the De los Santoses, Apin Gatuslao, and Moroy Alamon—the infamous "Moroy" of Cerila De los Santos's bloody note. Edfil is a delicate-looking Chinese mestizo with high, sharply etched cheekbones that give him a gaunt, skeletal appearance, and although he says he's thirty-six, his gray hair and weary eyes suggest a man fifteen years his senior. Edfil worked seven years for the NPA section responsible for Himamaylan and became involved with a militant faction responsible for attacks on the local police. He insists the NPA Sparrows never intended to kill either Bustamante or his friend but were only trying to steal their firearms. The Sparrows shot them when they resisted, he says.

Apin Gatuslao's murder, on the other hand, was a killing Edfil seems proud of, and he suggests that the rebels had simply rendered justice to the victims of the *hacendero*'s abuses. According to Edfil, the planter and his so-called goons were guilty of a litany of "crimes against the people." He reiterated charges made by others in the movement at the time of Apin's death, and further suggested that the planter's private army had terrorized people "in Batman country." Edfil said Gatuslao had allowed the Army to set up detachments of anywhere from forty to a hundred men on his properties; prevented the National Federation of Sugar Workers from organizing a union on any of the family's farms; owed a million pesos in back wages to more than a hundred of his workers; used the Army to force poor farmers off their land, and had built roads through their farms for his logging operations, destroying their crops in the process.

Himamaylan residents confirm many of these charges. Apin, however, was never allowed to answer them. Instead, he was tried in absentia by a people's court and received his verdict in a hail of gunfire that very nearly killed his wife. As for Apin's bodyguards, the Giconcillo brothers, who died in the same attack, Edfil said they were targeted because of their work both for warlord Armando Gustilo and for Apin. "They went around beating people up for flimsy reasons, abusing them, terrorizing them." When Gatuslao's workers complained about him, the Giconcillos were sent to shut them up.

Edfil dismissed out of hand the allegations of Colonel Cardones, Lieutenant Arrojado, and others that Moret De los Santos had been responsible for Apin's death. "Moret was a member of the Basic Christian Community. He had no ties to the movement. None. At most, you might classify him as a 'sympathizer,' but he did no work for the movement. He never provided us information, and we never gave him any assignments. We knew he wouldn't cooperate even if we asked!" Edfil insisted that it was ludicrous to suggest that Moret could have had any control whatsoever over the decision to execute Gatuslao. "Decisions to eliminate people of the stature of Apin Gatuslao come from the highest level. A section committee in a town like Himamaylan could not make a decision like that. There's simply no way De los Santos could have ordered this."

Furthermore, Edfil denied allegations that De los Santos had allowed rebels to store their weapons at his home. "It's not our habit to just leave our guns lying around. The NPA force sent to kill Gatuslao passed by the De los Santos house because it was on the way to the highway. But we never left weapons there or stayed in the De los Santos house."

That Edfil knew as much as he did about Moret and his family was a bit odd. He knew, for example, that Moret had had a personal argument with Moroy Alamon shortly before Moret and his family were killed, and he knew that Moret's stepbrother, Dan Galagpat, had already left Negros by the time Moroy disappeared, which meant that Dan could not have been directly responsible for killing Moroy to avenge the massacre, as some members of the Alamon family had alleged. But why would Edfil, a high-level political operative, be aware of the details of Dan's departure or of a petty personal feud?

Edfil said Moroy was abducted by NPA Sparrows, detained for a week, and subjected to a "tactical interrogation" in which he confessed to being a full-time military informant and admitted to having "betrayed" Moret to the Scout Rangers. The Sparrows executed Moroy both for spying and in revenge for the De los Santos massacre. It was understandable that the rebels would go after an informant, but it was not at all obvious how an informant could betray Moret to the military if, as Edfil claimed, Moret wasn't working for the movement. And even if Moroy had fabricated a story to get Moret in trouble with the Army, why should the NPA care?

Edfil acknowledged that Moret's survivors had asked the NPA to avenge the massacre but denied that this led his men to kill Moroy. "We don't accept demands for retribution from families," he said, explaining that people often make false accusations to the NPA— just as they do to the military—to try to settle purely personal grudges. "We have our own policies for meting out penalties, including the death penalty." Edfil insisted the betrayal of Moret "was just one of the reasons" Moroy was executed. "The primary reason was that Moroy was part of the military network in the area."

Nevertheless, it appeared that the NPA had at least some interest in the De los Santoses. When Moret's friend Fred Veraguas was murdered a few months after the massacre, a Communist front issued a statement condemning both killings and linking them to a broad effort to destroy the Basic Christian Community. Although this didn't necessarily mean that Moret had direct ties to the movement, it at least suggested that the rebels were protective of the BCC's leadership.

There was, however, at least one laudable reason for Ka Edfil to deny Moret's having worked for the NPA, if, indeed, he had: exposing Moret De los Santos could have put his surviving family members in peril. Certainly Moroy Alamon's family might have sought revenge. Blowing Moret's cover might have also damaged the BCC, given Moret's prominent position in the group. Despite Edfil's repeated categorical denials of any involvement by Moret with the movement, two other NPAs, now retired, insisted that Moret had indeed worked for the Communists. One of them said Moret handled finances and logistics for the NPA in three barrios, including Mambagaton. This informant's credibility is somewhat suspect, however, since she belonged to a fanatical Manila-based group of former rebels called the Red Scorpions who teamed up with a band of renegade soldiers to pull off a string of messy bank robberies and other criminal acts, including the 19°2 kidnapping of an American businessman that resulted in the death of fourteen Filipinos. All in all, not the strongest character reference. Nevertheless, it was hard to imagine why she would deliberately implicate someone like Moret if, in fact, he had had nothing to do with the movement.

The testimony of a second former NPA, who asked to be identified by the pseudonym "Ka Rene" because he feared retribution by the movement, seemed a bit more solid. Ka Rene was an NPA political officer like Ka Edfil but was aligned with moderates who were opposed to the escalating violence. Rene said he was actually sleeping in a hut in Aton-Aton when the De los Santos massacre began and barely escaped from the barrio during the fusillade. He said an NPA unit had been based in Aton-Aton as recently as three months prior to the massacre, although they had not been very well received by Moret and other residents, who were growing tired of the steady stream of killings by the military, the NPA, and the vigilantes.

Ka Rene, who knew Moret personally and considered him a friend, said he was one of the first recruits the NPA had "developed" when the party started organizing Mambagaton around 1983. Rene disputed the Scorpion's claim that Moret had handled money and logistics but said he sometimes allowed rebels, including those involved with the armed assassin units, to eat or rest at his house. Rene said Moret wouldn't allow them to spend the night because the house was so close to the main highway and wouldn't be safe. By the time of the massacre, however, Rene said Moret had broken his ties with the movement entirely.

"Tay Moret was keeping his distance from us," he said, both because of the intense military operations in the area and because "he was unhappy with the way some of the armed comrades had become lax about security; they would hold meetings in the barrio during the day and move around openly with their firearms." The former NPA also said Moret had recently received warnings from someone at the municipal hall that "he was a target for assassination."

Surprisingly, Ka Rene said Moroy Alamon had also been an NPA sympathizer and, like Moret, had allowed the rebels to take refuge in his home. Rene said that in places like Mambagaton, where the movement was strong, it was normal for people like Moroy and Moret to open their doors to the rebels; it was hard to say no. Contradicting Edfil, Rene said Moroy Alamon's murder was indeed staged explicitly to avenge the De los Santos massacre, but that Moroy had not been the one to betray Moret.

According to Ka Edfil, Moroy had been treated well by his captors, was given plenty to eat, confessed voluntarily to having betrayed Moret to the military, and died painlessly from a gunshot wound. As far as Edfil was concerned, it was revolutionary justice at its best. But Ka Rene said he had spoken with the Sparrows who abducted Moroy and learned that they had beaten and tortured him and stabbed him repeatedly until he died. Contradicting Ka Edfil once again, Rene said Moroy never made any confession of involvement with the De los Santos massacre. Rene believes the NPA executed an innocent man. If so, the bloody deathbed accusation against Moroy by Moret's wife, Cerila, may have contributed to this miscarriage of justice. Rene insists that the execution of Moroy was another case of violence-prone Sparrows getting out of control, and he cites it as one of the reasons he resigned from the NPA a few months later. He said he could no longer support the increasingly violent course on which his comrades had embarked.

*   *   *

Ferdinand Marcos spent a good part of his political career fashioning a heroic and largely fictitious autobiography that linked him to the country's ancient creation myths as well as to emotionally powerful moments in the country's history. He claimed, for example, that Gregorio Aglipay, the nationalist founder of the Philippine Independent church, inserted his own *anting anting* in Marcos's back shortly before the infamous Bataan campaign in World War II and that the talisman allowed him to become invisible. There were also the incessantly repeated and embellished stories about the Maharlika guerrilla unit. To make sure the Marcoses wouldn't be forgotten, the family erected a series of monuments as lasting testimonials to themselves. The most famous of these is undoubtedly the Mount Rushmore-style bust of Marcos carved into the side of a mountain in Agoo. But there is also a university named after Marcos's father, Imelda's Santo Niño Shrine, and the incomparable Marcos family museum at the dictator's ancestral home in Batac.

The museum, which might be described as an unintended public confessional to the banality of evil, is best known for its display of the repeatedly re-embalmed remains of Marcos's mother, Doña Josefa, who was kept in a glass-covered coffin for several years after her death. Mrs. Marcos's corpse was effectively held hostage by her exiled son, who insisted that she would not be buried until he himself was allowed to return to the Philippines, a wish only realized after his demise. Doña Josefa is no longer on public display, having been finally laid to rest beside her son, but visitors can still view a wide array of Marcos kitsch, including twenty-three life-size mannequins of the dictator in his favorite "lucky shirts," priceless collections of Marcos's golfing caps, pocket knives, and automobile license plates, a clay urn into which he supposedly vomited after nearly drowning at age twelve, a complete collection of his phony World War II medals, and copies of various books he purportedly authored, including *A Perspective on Human Rights and the Rule of Law* and the indispensable *The Marcos Wit*. Tourists can also see a curious photograph taken in 1954 of a young, smiling Marcos dressed up as a king, his head topped with a little crown, surrounded by a group of men attired in women's clothing. According to a museum docent, the picture was taken at a local festival known as Innocence Day, when people dress up in costumes and pretend to be someone they're not.

Given the embarrassment of Marcos shrines scattered around the country, it came as something of a surprise that Corazon Aquino would elect to create yet another one immediately after taking office and that she would use what is perhaps the country's greatest historic landmark, the presidential palace known as Malacañang, to house it. Malacañang, an elegant Castilian mansion erected in 1802, is perhaps the only structure in the Philippines that symbolically links the country's 400-year colonial past to its present. The palace served as the official residence of Spanish and American colonial governors as well as of six Philippine presidents before Aquino.

When the People Power Revolution swept the Marcoses from their gilded, faux Louis XIV thrones in the palace's ceremonial hall, Aquino decided to reside at the more humble suburban home she had occupied with her husband and turned Malacañang into a "Ripley's Believe-It-or-Not" of Marcos memorabilia, a vast warehouse of insipid, hagiographic portraits, gallons of perfume, piles of furs, Imelda's thousands of shoes—as well as dozens of pairs of platform shoes used by the diminutive dictator to make himself appear four inches taller—and the first lady's unique bulletproof bra.

Anyone who has toured Malacañang can appreciate how Aquino came to equate it with the vulgar extravagances of the Marcoses. After twenty years of dictatorship, exposure of the Marcoses' excesses undoubtedly had purgative, if not palliative, benefits. It gave Filipinos an outlet for their outrage and a graphic picture of how the Marcoses had squandered the wealth of an impoverished nation. In creating this museum, though, Aquino forfeited an opportunity to rehabilitate a great national treasure. In an American context, her decision would be analogous to Gerald Ford having turned the White House into a museum about Watergate, a statement about the depravity of the presidency rather than its greatness.

As public support for Aquino's administration deteriorated, the Marcos museum became the most visible symbol of her acute reliance on the dictator. Indeed, Aquino and her advisors clung to the calamitous Marcos legacy as if it were some magic voodoo doll that could immunize them from often blistering attacks. Anytime someone suggested that Aquino might not be living up to her promise, her palace guard would trot out the tattered totem and stick it with another pin, as if to say, "Look, at least she's better than that."

It was no secret that criticism made Aquino apoplectic. A disdainful dismissal early in her term—"I do not welcome unsolicited advice"—had earned her a reputation for being imperious, aloof, and humorless. On one occasion, she actually sued a journalist for libel when he suggested that she was so frightened during an attempted coup that she hid under her bed. The lawsuit led to the unseemly spectacle of having the nation's highest elected official testifying in court—and on national television—that the accusation could not have been true because she slept on a platform bed.

Aquino's allergy to criticism apparently led her to turn down a series of requests for a meeting from the country's largest organization of clerics during the first half of 1988. The Association of Major Religious Superiors of the Philippines not only represented 3,000 priests and brothers and more than 7,000 nuns but included many of the leaders and foot soldiers both in the struggle against Marcos and the military and on behalf of the country's poor. The president's snub came as something of a shock to the group's leadership, which had assumed it would have regular access to the devoutly Catholic Aquino.

The president and her advisors knew the AMRSP wanted to protest what its members viewed as a serious deterioration in the human rights situation in the countryside following the collapse of peace talks with the Communists in early 1987, and they concluded that there was nothing to be gained from a meeting. The president put the group off for more than six months until finally the AMRSP leadership threatened to go public with a statement sharply critical of her performance on human rights. Only then did Aquino relent. A meeting was set for July 7, 1988, at Malacañang, and the AMRSP designated twelve priests and nuns from around the country to present the organization's concerns. Among them was Father Eamon Gill of Himamaylan, who brought with him a stack of graphic eight-by-ten glossy photographs he had taken of the victims of the De los Santos massacre.

Aquino arrived at the meeting wearing a dark blue dress with bold white polka dots and one of the wide Victorian lace collars she fancies that draped her neck and shoulders like an antimacassar snatched from an overstuffed armchair. With her were all of her top cabinet officials responsible for dealing with individual rights, including her secretary of justice, the chairwoman of her Commission on Human Rights, her secretary of defense, and the chief of staff of the armed forces. The group gathered around a large conference table and opened the meeting with a reading from Romans which one of the priests had selected for the occasion: "For the kingdom of God is not food and drink, but righteousness and peace and joy in the Holy Spirit." Aquino offered her guests glasses of sugary orange drink.

Aquino's visitors recalled a palpable tension as the meeting got under way, owing in equal parts to the grudging nature of her invitation and the highly critical content of their agenda. Although the defamation or slander of an adversary behind his back is acceptable behavior in Philippine society, direct confrontation that may cause someone to lose face is considered the height of bad form and decidedly un-Filipino. Yet the priests and nuns had come to present the president with detailed case studies of murder, kidnapping, and four separate massacres allegedly perpetrated by Aquino's military and government-backed vigilantes.

The clergymen and women found it difficult to confront Aquino with this information, in part because none of them really believed the president condoned these crimes, but also because they'd all invested so much energy and faith in Mrs. Aquino's cause. In addition, they appreciated that they were sitting with a woman who, less than three years earlier, had dazzled the entire world when she fearlessly stood down the dictator. Aquino had inspired ordinary Filipinos like no one before her by turning the story of her life and the martyrdom of her husband into a contemporary *pasyon*. She had made people believe that the story of Ninoy's life, his stations of the cross—his incarceration, his trial for subversion, his exile, and his fateful return—were the story of the Filipino people. In this contemporary passion play, Filipinos had come to see that Marcos was the pharaoh, they were the Israelites, and Cory was Moses leading them to the Promised Land. No one was more attuned to this imagery than the priests and nuns seated with the president.

It wasn't merely Aquino's achievement that made the clerics uncomfortable, however. It was also the knowledge that Aquino had been their candidate, the candidate of the Catholic church, selected personally by the archbishop of Manila, the improbably named Jaime Cardinal Sin, to represent the Marcos opposition. Their church had intervened brazenly on Aquino's behalf in the election. The Catholic Bishops Conference—despite Imelda Marcos's personal appeal to Sin—declared the election a fraud and issued a stunning condemnation of the "intimidation, harassment, terrorism, and murder" perpetrated by Marcos supporters, a statement that stopped just short of calling on Filipinos to rebel against Marcos. "According to moral principles, a government that assumes or retains power through fraudulent means has no moral basis," the bishops declared. "If such a government does not of itself freely correct the evil it has inflicted on the people, then it is our serious moral obligation as a people to make it do so." When a small group of military reformists—who had been planning a coup for months—advised Cardinal Sin of their plans, he gave their rebellion his blessing. "Please do your duty for God," he told one of the coup leaders. After the rebels moved against Marcos, Sin told Filipinos to support them, and tens of thousands heeded his call, converging along Manila's main boulevard, Epifanio De los Santos Avenue, or EDSA, creating a human barricade around the military camp where the rebels were holed up. It was EDSA, as the nearly bloodless People Power Revolution came to be known, that brought the dictator down.

Cardinal Sin had pronounced EDSA a "miracle," and Aquino had emerged from it as the church's Joan of Arc, the fearless, transcendent crusader against the evil tyrant. No one at that table could deny Aquino this. Nor could they argue with her subsequent efforts to dismantle Marcos's authoritarian institutions: her repeal of decrees allowing for arbitrary and indefinite detention; her restoration of the writ of *habeas corpus* and a free press; and her release of political prisoners, including the heads of the Communist party and the New People's Army. The priests and nuns from the AMRSP also recalled, however, that on the day of her inauguration, Aquino had made a "pledge to do justice to the numerous victims of human rights violations." In their view, there was already voluminous evidence that human rights were no longer a priority of Aquino's government.

Certainly, Aquino had created a Commission on Human Rights. Why, the head of it, Mary Concepcion Bautista, was sitting right there in front of them. But Bautista had become a symptom of what the superiors saw as the problem rather than part of any solution. A porcine woman who wore chunky costume jewelry and squeezed into tight-fitting suits that exaggerated her already prominent cleavage, Bautista had packed the CHR with retired military men, ensuring that embarrassing cases would quickly be swept under the rug. Worse, she had become the leading civilian apologist for military abuses and had redefined human rights so broadly that her investigators rarely had time to look into the military's conduct because they were preoccupied with examining such "abuses" as auto thefts, insurance and land claims, and marital disputes.

Bautista was only a tiny part of what was wrong with Aquino's human rights agenda. Seated beside her at the meeting was Justice Secretary Sedfrey Ordoñez, a sweet, aging, gentlemanly lawyer who had helped defend Ninoy Aquino when the Marcos government charged him with murder, subversion, and possession of firearms and subsequently sentenced him to death. A personal friend of the president, Ordoñez had publicly excused his department for failing to pursue important human rights cases with the absurd explanation that it was the responsibility of the victims rather than the government to conduct investigations of abuses and gather evidence. "If we have the evidence, we prosecute, but if we don't get any evidence, what can we do?" In short, if Joaquin De los Santos and his three sisters were ready to investigate the Scout Rangers and piece together the evidence against them, Ordoñez's Justice Department was ready to prosecute.

Ordoñez and Bautista were typical of the kinds of people Aquino surrounded herself with—well-meaning, articulate, impeccably mannered, political moderates. Philosophically, they were all "anti-Marcos," and collectively they demonstrated how meaningless that approbation really was. Above all, they were members of a homogeneous class with the same self-aggrandizing economic and social interests as the comfortable elite that had sustained the dictator. Certainly they spoke out for democracy and good government, for uplifting the poor, and for human rights. But those willing to make any personal sacrifice to bring about change were few. Though Aquino and cabinet-level officials like Bautista and Ordoñez were personally honest, the sinecure- and corruption-riddled bureaucracies inherited from Marcos were now packed with Aquino loyalists who proved themselves as indolent, thieving, and paltry as their predecessors. The elected branches of government were no different. When a new Congress was convened a year after EDSA, fully 70 percent of its representatives were members of political dynasties, among them five relatives of Aquino. People Power, the pundits agreed, was less a revolution than a restoration.

The Philippines, it seemed, was stuck in the mire left by a ruinous dictatorship, an entrenched oligarchy, and years of Spanish and U.S. colonialism—"Three hundred years in a Catholic convent and fifty years in Hollywood," Filipinos quipped—and it was not about to be magically transformed simply because Ferdinand and Imelda Marcos had moved their soap opera to Honolulu. Besides, despite its se-

ductive, egalitarian ring, People Power had been as much about military power as about democracy, a fact Aquino had refused to recognize until she was nearly forced from office by a series of coup
attempts. If Marcos's own military had not revolted in February
1986, Aquino's movement would have almost certainly been
crushed. The fact that Aquino probably won the election in a landslide (the CIA estimated that she would have gotten 58 percent of
the vote had Marcos not rigged the count) would have made little
difference. The leaders of the revolt against the dictator were not
men known for their deep commitment to democracy, and the
armed forces Aquino inherited was replete with Marcos loyalists and
ambitious officers who exploited every weakness in Aquino's civilian
retinue of advisors and administrators to press the case for a military
takeover.

During her first eighteen months in office, Aquino weathered
four separate coup attempts. Each diminished her self-confidence
and public faith in her ability to govern. Sensing Aquino's vulnerability, the military increased the pressure on her, demanding that
she demonstrate her anti-Communist credentials. Aquino approved
salary hikes for the soldiers, announced a "total war policy" to wipe
out the rebels by the end of her term, endorsed vigilantes, and fired
alleged leftists in her government. The fatal blow to her human
rights policy came with the nearly successful coup of August 1987,
which left fifty-three dead and hundreds wounded. Among the
wounded was the president's only son, Benigno "Noynoy" Aquino
III. Badly shaken, Aquino came to appreciate the stakes of the game
in the most personal terms: If she wanted her family to survive, she
would have to give in to the military's demands.

A year after that coup, Senator Rene Saguisag, a prominent
human rights lawyer and Aquino's first spokesman, publicly acknowledged that the president had made a conscious decision to
abandon human rights as a priority. "This government had an obligation to survive," Saguisag said, in blunt defense of that policy. Indeed, survival became the ultimate standard by which Aquino's
administration measured its success—just as Marcos had done at the
end of his presidency. Nothing else mattered. "The battle was for the
survival of her government, and Cory was playing it all by ear," said
Paulynn Paredes Sicam, a member of Bautista's Commission on
Human Rights and a close personal friend of the president. "She had

to calibrate her moves; she had to react on a day-to-day basis. It became imperative for her to close an eye to human rights to buy loyalties—and to buy time. Every other new democracy has had to face this problem when it has taken on the military; you've won, but you still have to work with the military. So it wasn't a real revolution. The question is, at what cost do you keep democracy alive?" Aquino became convinced that if she could only hold on to her office and hand over power to a freely elected successor, her presidency would triumph, that it would demonstrate the vitality of Philippine democracy. Elevated to a point of principle, survival liberated her from attending to the nitty-gritty details of democracy, which had been the broader mandate of People Power.

The man most responsible for ensuring the survival of Aquino's democracy was seated right beside her during the meeting at Malacañang. However, he was also the man the priests and nuns held most responsible for the abdication of Aquino's human rights commitments. If Aquino had been forced into a Faustian bargain with her military, then for the president's guests, General Fidel V. "Eddie" Ramos, Aquino's secretary of defense, was the devil. In reality, however, Ramos could not be so easily pigeonholed. A West Point graduate, Ramos managed to maintain a surprising reputation for personal integrity throughout the Marcos dictatorship, despite the fact that he headed the most violent and corrupt branch of the armed forces and had personally been responsible for jailing Ninoy Aquino under martial law. Whatever his faults, though, in the minds of most Filipinos, Ramos had redeemed himself when he and Juan Ponce Enrile led the revolt that brought Marcos down. The fact that Ramos, a notoriously cautious and calculating man, had not revolted until he learned that Marcos was preparing to arrest him was quickly forgotten in the flush of victory.

Ramos was, in short, the quintessential survivor. Although he seemed genuinely dedicated to ensuring the survival of Philippine democracy, he was driven in no small measure by his own presidential ambitions. As a result, from the beginning to the end of Aquino's administration, Ramos walked a tightrope, defending against one coup after another a president who was tremendously unpopular with the armed forces while attempting to anchor his own standing with commanders in the field. Challenging them to account for atrocities they or their men may have committed would only have created enemies he didn't need—"weakened morale" was the usual euphemism. Inasmuch as the officers invariably denied responsibility for rights abuses, and the corrupt military justice system made successful prosecutions impossible, Ramos could see no reason to open this can of worms. Instead, he simply assured Aquino that progress was being made. Aquino never respected or fully trusted Ramos, but before the end of her second year in office, her presidency was largely in his hands.

The religious superiors, finally granted an audience with the president and her top aides; could not have been terribly hopeful about the outcome. The discussions got off to an inauspicious start when Aquino insisted that the meeting be kept strictly confidential, a demand that infuriated several of her guests who felt that they had come to discuss an issue of paramount importance, one that required greater public discussion, to say nothing of a firm statement of commitment by the president. The clerics presented Aquino with a list of nineteen case studies of human rights problems from around the country, but fully a third of the meeting was spent discussing the De los Santos massacre.

Father Gill, his voice trembling with emotion, described the incident in detail and presented the president with the blown-up photographs he'd taken of the victims. As the president slowly examined them, each with the distinctive string of numbers across the bottom indicating the date of the massacre, Gill and the others watched in silence. The pictures are not easy to look at. One of them shows Cerila De los Santos lying on a bed, her right hand clenched in a fist, with blood oozing from wounds in both her breasts and the lower portion of her face completely obliterated. Another shows Juvi De los Santos standing in front of a wall with bright sunlight shining through dozens of bullet holes behind her. At the little girl's feet lies her father, covered head to foot in his own blood. Other photos show Juvi standing next to the bodies of her little brother, Jun Jun, and her sister, Mary Joy, who lie side by side beneath a small crucifix of woven bamboo leaves, and with her older brother, Joenes, dead from a bullet in his head.

When Aquino looked up from the photos, Gill continued. "This little girl asked to come with me when I went into her house," he said haltingly, catching his breath as he completed each phrase. "And she asked to have her picture taken with each member of her

family. And then she kissed each of them. And then she left." After
Juvi had gone, Gill told Aquino, he just stood there, surrounded by
the dead bodies of his friends, and wept. "This was the only time
since I reached manhood that I've broken down," the priest confessed to the president.

Aquino was visibly moved as she leafed through the pile of grisly
color photographs, but her visitors said she was also angered by
Gill's presentation and lashed out at him as soon as he'd finished.
"Why is it always foreigners who bring these things to our attention?" the president snapped. "During the time of Marcos, I could
understand that Filipinos would use foreigners to speak on their behalf, but now that we have a democracy, we don't need them." Sister
Leontina Castillo, a Filipina, said the president's complaint was bol-
stered by Commission on Human Rights Chairwoman Bautista, who
accused the religious leaders of "magnifying the negative things the
military does without mentioning the good things." Aquino went on
to deride the priests' human rights assessment as no different from
what she heard "from the left," recalled Father Domingo Moraleda.
"Her reaction was not very positive. She said, 'Who says the NPAs
weren't shooting from behind the house?' To which Gill replied,
'But surely someone would have been hurt in a half-hour firefight.' "

"She took the position that we should not be so hard on the military," another priest said. "I depend on the military," she said,
adding, not quite to the point, "and, you know, some of them are un-
derpaid and underfed." Sister Teresita Alo, a Franciscan nun, said
Aquino also objected that her visitors seemed concerned about the
victims only of military abuses. "She turned to Ramos and said,
'Now Eddie, what do you say about this? They're always complaining about our soldiers, but what about the NPA?' " Ramos answered
that the military was trying to root out its "scalawags," but he allowed that they were a serious problem and that all he could do was
"plug the leaks in the dike." Armed Forces Chief of Staff Renato De
Villa went so far as to vow that the perpetrators of the De los Santos
massacre would be punished. Justice Secretary Ordoñez compli-
mented the military on its road building in rural areas and other
public works projects, suggesting that the church leaders try to look
at the positive contributions the military was making.

Sister Castillo said she encountered Aquino in a hallway of Malacañang later in the day and found her somewhat apologetic about

the meeting, insisting that she had tried to do something about abuses like the De los Santos massacre but that "something is wrong in the bureaucracy." The issue, however, was not Aquino's barely functional bureaucracy but her personal commitment. Even though she never ordered the military, her Justice Department, or her Commission on Human Rights to ignore human rights violations, the church leaders agreed that her comments sent an unmistakable message: The De los Santos case need not be pursued, and human rights matters in general were no longer a serious concern of her administration.

There followed several perfunctory efforts to look into the massacre. Sixteen months after the killings, Scout Ranger headquarters in Manila subpoenaed Joaquin De los Santos, his sister, and several other members of the family to answer questions in connection with "the alleged multiple murder and frustrated murder case filed against Captain Melvin M. Gutierrez." The wording of the subpoena suggested that there actually was a legal case pending, but the subpoena was nothing more than a formality, the Army's way of demonstrating that it had tried to pursue the matter. Franki Cruz, an attorney for the Basic Christian Community on Negros, advised the family members not to cooperate and informed the Army that the surviving De los Santoses could not afford the cost of transportation to Manila.

Officials at the CHR in Manila seemed unable to make up their minds whether to look into the De los Santos incident. Chairman Bautista had in fact requested an investigation ten weeks after the massacre but had never followed up on it. CHR officials on Negros took their first look at the case a day after they received Bautista's request. They made the ninety-minute trip from Bacolod to Himamaylan, where they interviewed Father Gill. A two-page report of the four-man "investigating team" imputes a sense of gravity and urgency to their inquiry, noting that the Negros governor's office provided a photographer, car, and free gasoline "to speed up our investigation." The investigators reported that their first order of business on reaching Himamaylan at eleven in the morning was to have lunch and to pay a courtesy call on Mayor Daisy Silverio. By the time they left, four hours later, they'd interviewed all of two people. Human rights case no. 88-600 had been officially opened.

The CHR "investigation" seemed to be mainly a means of fending off accusations of nonfeasance. The CHR's own records suggest that the regional office repeatedly tried to shift responsibility for an inquiry to the Manila office, whereas Manila passed the buck back to the region. The regional CHR did manage to conduct one interview with Gutierrez in Bacolod ten months after the massacre, but the tape and official transcript of that interview are missing, and the CHR disowns a partial transcript that remains. The CHR failed to pursue numerous inconsistencies in Gutierrez's testimony, among them a statement that he could "hear them [the NPAs] whispering" during the assault on the De los Santos home—an amazing achievement, given the fact that the captain also told the CHR he was a quarter-mile from the scene of the shooting.

No additional work was done on the case for eighteen months following the Gutierrez interview. Then, more than two years after the massacre, when the matter was called to his attention by a journalist, David Bermudo, a CHR attorney in the regional office responsible for Negros, reexamined the affidavit of Joaquin De los Santos and the report on the CHR's trip to Himamaylan. Bermudo concluded that the Rangers were "probably guilty" of murder.

Whether he was motivated by a real commitment to justice or concern that he might receive unfavorable press if he failed to take action is not clear. One month later, though, without having determined the whereabouts of any of the surviving De los Santoses, he drafted a complaint—"Joaquin De los Santos versus Captain Melvin Gutierrez, et al. (Scout Rangers)"—alleging that the Army Scout Rangers were guilty of "multiple murder." Bermudo's complaint, in effect a recommendation that the Justice Department file a criminal case, suggests several possible motives for the killings—the cockfight, information allegedly given the military by Moroy Alamon, Moret's involvement in the BCC and in human rights work—and asserts that there is "incontrovertible" evidence that Gutierrez led the mission. The document allows that there may in fact have been NPA rebels on the scene and an actual gun battle, but it offers no evidence one way or the other.

Bermudo's complaint was endorsed by the CHR in Manila, but neither he nor the CHR could actually file a criminal case. That could be done only by the Justice Department or the military's judge advocate general. Bermudo recognized that it would be impossible to get Joaquin De los Santos and other potential witnesses to testify before a military tribunal and impossible to win a conviction even if they did. If justice was to be served, he knew a case would have to be brought in a civilian court. Under Philippine law, though, cases involving alleged crimes by members of the armed forces could be removed from the military's jurisdiction only with an explicit authorization from the president. So Bermudo reinforced his complaint by getting CHR to send a letter to President Aquino that recommended indictments, pointed out that the military had already absolved Gutierrez and his men, and spelled out the fact that unless the president authorized the transfer of the matter to a civil court, there would be no chance of winning convictions. The De los Santos matter was now officially presidential business. Or almost.

Aquino's administration was notorious for its lack of organization, even on such simple matters as handling the mail, and a rubber stamp mark on Bermudo's letter indicates that the document sat around the president's office for a full month before it was "received." Then, the president apparently decided the matter was too hot to handle. Two years and four months after the massacre, Aquino referred the case back to her Defense Department, which had no legal authority over a decision that was exclusively hers to make.

The Army took three months to respond to the president. When it did, it told her that the case had been closed because the De los Santoses had failed to respond to subpoenas. Still, the president could have authorized the Justice Department to proceed with the CHR complaint in a civil court; instead, she did nothing. The De los Santos case died on her desk.

*   *   *

While CHR attorneys, Malacañang, and the armed forces were figuring out how to dispose of the De los Santos matter, a young woman by the name of Jacqueline Mejia read through the case file and began pursuing her own personal campaign on behalf of the massacre survivors. Mejia had no authority to recommend investigations or indictments, but she did run an obscure CHR office that provided small amounts of money for victims of human rights abuses. Based on her reading of the evidence, she concluded that the De los Santos children would be entitled to compensation if a criminal complaint was filed or if they had been caught in a crossfire between the military and the NPA. Although there was no substantial evidence of a crossfire, when the criminal case faltered, Mejia decided to proceed anyway, pressing her agency to make a monetary award. Three years after the massacre, the CHR granted the four surviving De los Santos children the maximum amount allowed under the law—50,000 pesos, or approximately $2,500. Roughly $500 per victim.

Kanlaon

They were nothing of their own making, they were like
living symbols of what had happened to them, living abstractions and witnesses of the absurdity of human institutions. They were not individuals like the old
adventurers, they were the shadows of events with which
they had nothing to do.

—Hannah Arendt, *The Origins of Totalitarianism*

The year is divided into two seasons, dry and rainy,
which isn't to say there aren't a dozen others—brief, whispered conversations insinuating themselves in between—only that this is the
way the world has been described for as long as anyone can remember. The monsoon climaxes the progress from the one to the other,
from clear balmy days and refreshing nights that pass without remark, then slowly bend to the sun's lengthening fury and the heated,
thickening air as heavy as soaked denim. Cirrus clouds, delicate as
maidenhair, draw little notice as they sail beneath the bright blue
dome and gather together into a pearly ceiling that smoothes the
harsh, refracting light and delivers a cooling reprieve. A drop of rain
or two may remind the sugarcane cutter of the still far-off monsoon,
but before it arrives, late-afternoon showers must first establish
themselves with clockwork regularity, promising refreshment but delivering instead a dense, viscous sweat, as if the lid had suddenly
been lifted from an enormous kettle.

Finally, the nacreous sky darkens to a monotonous, then livid
gray, and the monsoon descends upon a hollow stillness where birds,
beetles, and cicadas have found shelter, breathless as an audience an-
ticipating the orchestra's opening bars. A fierce wind churns the dust
in the streets, announcing the monsoon's arrival, and is quickly fol-

lowed by lashing rains that tear leaves from hunched bamboos and palms and lift roofs weighted with old tires from the temporary dwellings of men and women who have suffered all of this before. Deafening, repetitive thunder, joined by simultaneous flashes of light, stalls directly overhead, raindrops the size of duck's eggs pelt the corrugated tin, and the flood pours out of the opened sky for days, then weeks, endlessly.

When the storms pass, blue morning glories open up everywhere, strung like Christmas lights on cane stalks and barbed wire fences, and birds splash in puddles left behind on leathery tropical leaves. Sunlit clouds like ghostly mansions stream past Mount Kanlaon, and the patchwork skirt of farms and fields that clings to its slopes flickers in a revolving palette of charcoal, ocher, and silver, olive green, indigo, and mustard. Varied as the glass fragments in a kaleidoscope, these patterns turn, blur, and dissolve with the sun and clouds, as the monsoon moves away.

Kanlaon, the island's only active volcano and home to its ancient guardian spirit, looms over Negros. Unlike Mayon, the country's most famous, perfectly symmetrical volcanic cone, which slopes up gently from the flat plain of Albay near the birthplace of Melvin Gutierrez, Kanlaon is handsome yet imperfect, battered and rugged as an Egyptian pyramid. Having ceded ground to loggers and *hacenderos,* to the monsoons and the millennia, Kanlaon still threatens, and occasionally and unexpectedly exacts its arbitrary revenge on the coastal towns and barrios below.

Kanla, the long-forgotten rice farmer who gave the mountain its name, was a humble, accidental hero who was only trying to make his work easier by devising a simple method of husking rice. At the time, the sky hung like a ceiling over Negros, so low, in fact, that a tall person had to hunch over to keep from bumping into it. But when Kanla began using a long pole to pound rice in a bowl carved from the stump of a tree, he suddenly found that his upward motions had lifted the sky. Then one day, in a fit of pique, Kanla struck a stone with a piece of steel, igniting sparks that rose into the sky, and before he knew it, he'd filled the heavens with stars and altered the universe forever. Sadly, Kanla's contributions made some of his neighbors extremely envious, and to punish them, Lalaon, the creator, or "ancient one," took Kanla away from them, burying him alive under the volcano until such time as human cruelties ceased to exist on Negros. Negrenses have long since given up any hope of seeing Kanla again. It became a familiar story; the people's saviors snatched from their midst. Since Kanla disappeared, numerous lesser, fatally flawed Filipino heroes and revolutionaries have come and gone, each attempting to liberate what the nation's patriarch, José Rizal, called "a people without a soul." Some failed for want of money or guns. Others lacked charisma, a galvanizing message, a practical strategy—or were simply in over their heads.

Rizal, like Kanla, was punished for a crime he didn't commit, shot in the back for inciting Andrés Bonifacio's insurrection against the Spanish government, a rebellion Rizal's novels had inspired but he himself explicitly condemned as an "absurd, savage uprising, plotted behind my back, that dishonors us Filipinos." Rizal described the dehumanizing effects of both foreign and indigenous colonialism better than anyone before or since, and in his own short lifetime (he died at age thirty-five) became a figure of messianic stature. But he was, in fact, a consummate reformer.

Rizal had predicted that a military revolt against Spain would not succeed, and Bonifacio's uprising turned out to be short-lived. Bonifacio, the "great plebeian," the self-educated orphan who inspired the masses to revolt, was soon betrayed, murdered by one of the country's other great revolutionary heroes, Emilio Aguinaldo, who then reached a temporary peace with the Spaniards in which he accepted 400,000 pesos and agreed to leave the country. He subsequently used the money to arm his rebels for a second phase of the revolution, but his grandest plans for liberation of the Filipinos would also fail. When the United States refused to recognize Philippine sovereignty following the Spanish–American War, Filipinos rebelled. Thousands died in one of the most pointless and tragic exercises of U.S. military power in this century, and Aguinaldo made his accommodation with the new American colonizers.

Filipino nationalists like Bonifacio, Papa Isio on Negros, the NPAs, and dozens of lesser-known revolutionary, millenarian, and fanatical figures have proved less willing to compromise on matters of national sovereignty than Aguinaldo. However, they have met with only limited success; all have stumbled and fallen without redeeming the national soul which Rizal had struggled so hard to define.

In the shadow of Kanlaon, in the thin, stale air of Himamaylan, ambitious, determined men such as Moret De los Santos and Apin Gatuslao carved out their discrete worlds. Moret, it seemed, was destined to be remembered both as a villain and a martyr, neither of which was strictly accurate. Nor, for that matter, were the sundry explanations for his death; those for members of his family, even less so. Nobody really tried to justify the slaughter of Moret's wife and children, other than to attribute it to the vagaries of the war, which somehow excused it. A few made a case that the killings had served a purpose, sent a message, from the military or from God, depending on their point of view. No one had proved that Moret had committed a crime, though, and, in the end, the truth about whether or not Moret had had some tie to the NPA wasn't terribly important. The killing was merely rationalized in a wilderness of dubious assumptions: He worked for the NPA, for a front, was a Communist, helped to kill Apin Gatuslao. These assumptions were explained away by others: that the NPA would destroy Negros; that the military and the anti-Communists offered people alternatives, democracy, peace; that people had choices.

Corazon Aquino had brought democracy back to the Philippines and to Negros, the same democracy that had existed before Marcos. The clock had been turned back twenty years. A sign of progress. People voted. On the official ballot, sugar cutters could elect the planter of their choice; on the unofficial one, they could choose the NPA or the military. Or they could try to abstain, to mind their own business. That could be difficult, often impossible—if your community was hamleted, if the NPAs needed a place to sleep, some food or money, if the military needed information, had some point to make, if someone like Melvin Gutierrez had you on his agenda, in his gun sights. Communism was a threat, but so was democracy. Not the democracy the military was defending, the democratic shell that lent legitimacy to the Negros status quo. Rather the little working democracy one found in the Basic Christian Community, and the democracy in the hazy dreams of people like Moret: democracy that could deliver justice, that tolerated new ideas, that put the military under civilian control, that gave people power.

In Manila, the night air carries the rancid stench of smoldering garbage fires, which illuminate dark corners of neighborhoods in a vision of Hades. The city is home to an estimated 75,000 street children who scrape by as scavengers or hustlers, or by selling newspapers, penny candies, cigarettes, or their bodies in the streets. Crablike cripples and disheveled beggars tap at the smoked-glass windows of millionaires in Mercedes Benzes as they roll past vast colonies of squatters constituting over a fourth of the urban population. Designed for two million people, Manila, with eleven million in 1990, had become a laboratory of metastasizing decay, with filthy diesel-choked air, congested refuse-laden streets, poisoned water, and rivers of sewage. Behind the terra cotta–roofed presidential palace, Malacañang, the Pasig oozes its course, a reeking reminder that no one escapes the consequences of this thoroughgoing neglect.

As a matter of survival, the rich have always charted their own narrow trajectory through it all, and Aquino was no exception. The president had an astonishing capacity for obscuring, excusing, and romanticizing her country's afflictions, distancing herself to the point that the Philippines outside her prefabricated little world remained a land beyond her ken or control. It might just as well have been a foreign country. The deeply religious and fatalistic president saw her husband's martyrdom as God's way of redeeming her nation. "A country that had lost faith in its future found it in a faithless and brazen act of murder," she said in the aftermath of Ninoy's assassination. Perhaps she believed, like Negros Bishop Navarra, that the deaths of the De los Santoses and all the others were also part of God's plan for the Philippines. Certainly she allowed that forces greater than herself, beyond her control, determined much of what occurred during her six years in office.

"I did my best," Aquino said repeatedly in defense of her presidency, and most Filipinos, with their seemingly bottomless reservoir of patience, believe she did. They accepted her calculus that if she'd tried to do more, she would surely have been overthrown by her own military, or they concluded that Corazon C. Aquino simply wasn't up to the job, that her courageous performance during the 1986 election was an aberration never to be repeated during her presidency. *"Corazon, sí, Aqui, no,"* people punned on her name, pointing first to their hearts and then to their heads: "Heart, yes, but no brains." Although the constitution restricting a Philippine president to a single term took effect after Aquino's election, she agreed to respect the six-year limit. In 1992, she got her wish and transferred the mantle of her presidency following a free, fair, and, by Philippine standards, largely nonviolent election in which a huge 80 percent of eligible voters cast their ballots. Although her successor, General Fidel V. Ramos, probably had more to do with ensuring the survival of Aquino's presidency than anyone else, Aquino resisted acknowledging his contribution and endorsed his candidacy haltingly and belatedly, which very nearly cost him the election. In a seven-candidate race, Ramos won with 24 percent of the vote, whereas fully 28 percent of the voters cast ballots for either Marcos crony Eduardo "Danding" Cojuangco or former first lady Imelda Marcos, willfully risking a return to the corruption and lunacy of the recent authoritarian past. Aquino read the election both as the measure of her own success and as the all-important test of the strength of Philippine democracy. It was also a measure of that democracy's weakness, though; of the broad public disenchantment with Aquino's timid leadership, and of a peculiar nostalgia for the Marcos era, reflecting what nationalist Claro M. Recto once referred to as "a nation unique in the annals of mankind, a sacrificial race with a mysterious urge to suicide." In the span of six years, Filipinos had demonstrated not only the resolve to remove a tyrannical dictator but a deeply rooted, anarchic compulsion to undermine the very democratic government they themselves had installed. Like the victims of terrorist kidnappings who fall in love with their tormentors, the country clung to what it deplored. It was often difficult to figure exactly what people wanted.

President Aquino retired from politics to write her memoirs and spend more time with her children and grandchildren. She made news in 1995, when she boycotted the baptism for the child of her unmarried, starlet daughter, Kris—known as the "Massacre Queen" for movie roles in which she was gang-raped, hacked to death, or chopped to pieces—because the president would have nothing to do with her daughter's lover, a philandering, thrice-married actor who is twice Kris's age. Mrs. Aquino then reemerged briefly on the political

stage to campaign against two candidates: Colonel Gregorio Hona-
son, who had plotted two nearly successful coups against her, and in
1995 was running for the Senate; and Imelda Marcos, who that same
year ran for Congress. Both were elected. The president reportedly
spends much of her time playing mah-jongg with her girlfriends and
occasionally travels abroad. Sometimes she gives speeches about the
People Power Revolution and the "miracle" of Philippine democracy. She has even spoken up on several occasions about the egregious human rights situation—in Burma.

Asked about the De los Santos massacre in an interview one year
after her retirement, Aquino said she had no recollection of it whatsoever, or of the emotional meeting held in her office, or of the eight-
by-ten glossy photos of the victims, which she had studied. The
president said the entire matter had probably been handled by one
of her aides. It was the kind of unpleasant encounter Mrs. Aquino
was famous for blotting from her memory.

The war between the government and the NPA escalated dramatically following Aquino's failed attempt at a negotiated peace. During
her first three and a half years in office, more than a half-million people were forcibly evacuated from their homes by the military. A
month after Apin Gatuslao was killed, the NPA launched a campaign against U.S. citizens in the Philippines, murdering three
Americans at Clark Air Base north of Manila. Two weeks after the
De los Santos massacre, the highest-ranking member of the National
Democratic Front on Negros, rebel priest Frank Fernandez, announced a similar program. Fernandez said the rebels would attack
U.S. officials believed to be involved in counterinsurgency on the island, as well as in socioeconomic programs of organizations financed
by the Central Intelligence Agency. Although NPA leaders acknowledged privately that they had no evidence of direct U.S. involvement
on the island, a few weeks after Fernandez's threat, the NPA murdered an Australian businessman who owned a rice mill in Himamaylan, alleging that he worked for the CIA. The man was shot six
times in front of his Filipina wife.

Despite the widening carnage on Negros, within three years of
the De los Santos massacre, the rebel movement was reduced to an
almost insignificant threat due to a combination of Army offensives,

infiltration, intimidation, and what might be characterized as the NPA's self-immolation—the internecine disputes, purges, defections, criminal activities, executions of suspected spies, and a badly flawed reading of both the political and military landscape. The same period also witnessed the decimation of the Basic Christian Communities; where there had once been sixty separate BCC chapters in Himamaylan alone, only ten remained. Church leaders insisted that the groups would eventually be resurrected because the problems they were designed to address hadn't gone away. The same argument could be made for the NPA: Obituaries for the rebels have been written before, and it's a safe bet that, unless the government or private investors create work for the exploding population of impoverished Filipinos, the NPA or something similar will reemerge within the next few years. The NPA is like malaria, someone once said: It never goes away.

The church that once championed the BCCs and the poor has undergone its own transformation in recent years and seems to have rediscovered its more traditional spiritual calling. Bishop Fortich has retired, and a younger, more conservative bishop, Camilo Gregorio, has set out to depoliticize a church he concluded had been funneling money to the New People's Army and had been dominated by a Gospel skewed to liberation theology. "We must serve the poor without causing class struggle," the bishop proclaimed, suggesting a notion of service devoid of any economic element. "Naturally, I see a need to tend to the poor, but they are not my only concern. Our concept of the poor must be broader than the materially poor. There are many who are poorer; people hungering not just for bread, but for the bread of life." In recent years, the church at large has increased its efforts to ensure that a growing number of Filipinos will feast at this cornucopia for the spirit with its crusade against any and all forms of population control. On this issue church leaders had a loyal ally in Aquino, who was incapable of uttering the words contraception and family planning without blushing. President Ramos, however, a Protestant, recognized that economic recovery and the country's environment were doomed unless population growth was controlled. Should the church prevail in its efforts to stifle family planning, as seems likely, the country's population is expected to double by the year 2010 to 120 million people. That will no doubt ensure a ready supply of recruits for a new, revitalized NPA.

Scout Ranger Captain Melvin Gutierrez was promoted to major in June 1994, and it looked as if his career was finally back on track. He never did get the award for the De los Santos massacre recommended by Lieutenant Arrojado, but none of the other Scout Rangers involved got one, either, and most were just as happy that the whole matter seemed to have been forgotten. Although he feels the De los Santos incident has hurt him professionally, Gutierrez says he still dreams of becoming a battalion commander one day. "I haven't given up hope." Lieutenant Arrojado was promoted to captain and rewarded for his exemplary performance with a ten-week course in basic intelligence-gathering techniques at the U.S. Army training center at Fort Huachuca, Arizona. He returned to Manila, where he was employed at the Joint U.S. Military Advisory Group, a liaison between the Pentagon and the Philippine armed forces.

Gerry De los Santos's good friend and roommate, Virgilio Quijano, never got in touch with Gerry's wife, Pelma, and never made good on his promise to look after Gerry, Jr. Gerry's girlfriend, Emerine, was working in the intelligence office at Task Force Sugarland when she learned of Gerry's death, but by then his body had been taken to the airport, so she didn't get to say good-bye. Emerine's boss told her to keep her mouth shut about the whole affair, that "Herbert's death was 'unnatural,' and they were going to report it as something else." He told her Herbert—that is, Gerry—didn't die in the field but had been shot by one of his fellow Rangers during a drinking brawl. Yet another explanation for his death. Emerine moved to Kuala Lumpur, Malaysia, where she became a maid.

A "new breed" of planters—more sensitive to their workers' needs, the plight of the poor, and the environment—and a "new generation" of entrepreneurs who say they're committed to improving Negros have supposedly emerged in recent years. Bacolod streets are packed with new cars, and the city even has traffic jams and its first traffic lights; new restaurants, coffee shops, and boutiques have opened, and Chamber of Commerce types are boasting of an economic revival. Governor Lacson retired after one term without realizing his dream of seeing Negros become the next Taiwan and was appointed president of the Philippine National Bank.

A "sugar museum" to record the history and economic and cultural contributions of Negros's big sugar families is in the works, and oil portraits of all of the island's sugar planter governors were restored and unveiled at a ceremony in the crumbling provincial capitol building. Bishop Gregorio sprinkled them with holy water, and a talented local tenor with black greased-back hair sang Italian arias. Apin's brother-in-law, Rudi Remitio, has been promoting a vast new housing development for the elite, "Philippine Estates," which is to be built on a 2,000-acre cane field at the northern edge of Bacolod. Plans call for the Spanish-style homes to be arrayed around the edge of a new eighteen-hole golf course and for security guards costumed in uniforms modeled after those of the once detested Spanish Guardia Civil.

The little towns and villages in the countryside, places like Himamaylan, look pretty much as they did twenty or thirty years ago. Most of the island's sugar farms remain without union representation, and the only land reform taking place is the multiplication of ever smaller farms brought about through the geometry of inheritance. Many planters have invested in tiger prawns for export to Japan, but prawns have not proven to be the salvation the planters had hoped for, and most other efforts at agricultural diversification have met with failure. Although tarnished, sugar remains the golden calf of elite devotions. Meanwhile, nearly all research and development on improved sugar varieties have ceased, and degradation of both soil and water continues unabated. Planters must grow 20 percent more cane today to produce the same yields they had twenty years ago.

In local elections held in 1992, the Gatuslaos regained control of the Himamaylan mayor's office when incumbent Daisy Silverio was defeated by Hernan Gatuslao, a cousin of Apin. But Hernan died of cancer before finishing his term and was replaced by Luz Bayot Ramos, daughter of the notorious philanderer Francisco Ramos and his lunatic wife's half-sister. Then, in 1995, the Ramoses lost the mayor's office once again to the Gatuslaos, to another cousin of Apin's, Carminia Bascon. The Gatuslaos are slowly rebuilding their political base from Himamaylan. Hernan, Carminia, and her brother, Tony, have reportedly done a good deal to repair some of the damage Apin did to the family's reputation, but whether they

can reclaim the power the Gatuslaos once had in national politics
remains to be seen.

Esperanza "Panching" Gatuslao, Serafin's wife, settled in Los Angeles, where she found work doing what she described as "menial
jobs" paying six dollars an hour. "I started all over again with nothing. My son worked in a warehouse driving a forklift. I used to make
light of it; I would tell him, you didn't have to come to the United
States to drive a forklift." Panching is currently employed as a care-
giver to an elderly woman and is taking courses in pharmacy, the
profession she once practiced on Negros. Since leaving the Philippines, she has not received a dime from the family corporation that
took over her and Serafin's assets on Negros.

In 1992 Panching remarried, to a retired American policeman
who works as a security officer in a bank. She says she has tried hard
to forget about Negros and has avoided contact with the extensive
Negrense immigrant community in California. "It's not that I'm not
interested in what's happening there, but if I keep abreast, all the
heartbreak comes back. That's my reason for not knowing. I can't
explain the hurt." Mrs. Gatuslao has not, of course, stopped thinking about Serafin.

> I felt what happened to him was very unfair; it shouldn't
> have happened to a man who never had anything but goodwill
> for just about everybody. I used to joke with him that if a
> sucker is born every minute, then you are born every minute.
> The last money in his pocket, he would give it away. He had a
> very big heart. I'm not proud of the way Serafin died. It was an
> insult to him. But I'm glad that they were never able to intim-
> idate him. I don't know if I will ever get over this. Serafin Ga-
> tuslao was my friend, my husband—he was everything.

Members of the De los Santos family were completely surprised
when the Commission on Human Rights finally came through with
their 50,000 pesos, a godsend they eagerly accepted, and quickly disposed of, with no enduring effect on their bleak circumstance. The
Blessed Virgin and the Santo Niño could perform a miracle in the
cockpit, give you the winning lottery number, or send some other
bonanza your way, but mostly they offered hope, which simply gave
way to hope.

Jenelyn De los Santos had a concrete slab poured over the common grave for her family in the shade of an *ipil ipil* tree at the Himamaylan cemetery. The concrete and a small headstone at the top were painted white and inscribed in hand-painted black letters. TO OUR BELOVED PARENTS, BROS & SISTER, it read, followed by the names of Moret, Cerila, Joenes, Mary Joy, and Jun Jun, each of their birth dates, and the date they all died. Four wooden posts stand at the corners of the simple memorial; a metal chain marked the perimeter, until it was stolen. Boy Rubiato, a friend of the family who witnessed the massacre, paints the posts and a little gate at the front from time to time, but the names have weathered badly over the years and are nearly invisible now; the grave itself has sunk, the slab is cracked, and a corner of it has fallen away. An eight-foot-high banner listing the victims of military atrocities on Negros, including the De los Santoses, was hung at the front of the sanctuary of Our Lady of the Snows Church. The banner was illustrated with silhouettes of the dead family members, rifles, hand grenades, pistols, bullets, and rockets. The Negros church also designated April 6, the day of the massacre, "Martyrs' Day," to be celebrated each year with remembrances of those victimized by the war.

One month after the massacre, the De los Santos house at Aton-Aton, the one Moret first constructed at what became Ernesto Tongson's prawn farm, was dismantled again by Jenelyn and her husband, who used the materials to build a new home a mile away at Bangat Trece, along a dusty gray path that cuts through a sugarcane field.

Rudi Garcia's family sought refuge in the office of his boss, Roger Tongson, for several weeks following the massacre. When he returned to his house, he took it apart piece by piece and rebuilt it about two hundred yards east along the Mambagaton Road. Rudi said he felt safer at the new site, away from whatever spirits the De los Santoses may have left behind.

For the first month after he moved in with Father O'Brien, Joaquin De los Santos didn't leave the house even once. Slowly, however, his strength returned and his spirits improved; he went for walks, made friends, resumed playing basketball before his wound had healed and broke an arm, began drinking, stayed out late with girlfriends, and sometimes disappeared for days on trips to Iloilo or Manila. Nothing ever came of all the revenge schemes he'd so carefully plotted.

Father O'Brien said he gave Joaquin money so he could study at a computer school and found out he'd spent it on his social life instead. The priest felt Joaquin was neglecting his sisters, accused him of stealing money from the house, and said he began telling wild, unbelievable stories. "It was just too much for us to swallow," the priest said. "I told him he was involved in financial anomalies in my house and that I had the proof of it. It became very difficult having him around." It was the last time he saw Joaquin.

Joaquin made his way to Manila, where he vanished into one of the city's sprawling squatter colonies. His new residence was a tiny five-foot-high shack on a hillside above the reeking Pasig River, about six miles downstream from Malacañang. The place was furnished with a single chair and a narrow wooden platform on which he, his sister Jasmin, her husband, and an infant slept in shifts. Two small windows without glass allowed air to circulate through the box and afforded easy access for the legions of rats that infest the slum.

Joaquin's gunshot wound left him with only partial use of his left arm, making most physical labor impossible. In Manila he found work driving a tricycle, which allowed him to earn as much as five dollars on a good day. Jasmin said he got into a lot of fights, had recurring nightmares about the massacre, and would often break down in tears for no apparent reason. Joaquin fell in love with a girl named Carol, married, started a family, and moved to his wife's home province, where he somehow landed a job as a chauffeur for Senator Jovito Salonga, one of the country's most revered nationalists, a close friend and lawyer of Ninoy Aquino, and the man most responsible for forcing the closure of U.S. military bases in the Philippines.

The surviving De los Santoses in Himamaylan continue to live in fear of the family of Moroy Alamon. Jenelyn says Moroy's five sons will eventually take revenge for his death. "If something happens to us, they will be responsible."

A two-room house with a grass roof sits on a Mambagaton bluff overlooking the rice fields and fish ponds of the Gatuslaos and Tongsons. The front yard is covered by a Mediterranean-blue fishing net used for drying rice. The house itself is sparsely furnished, with two wooden benches, three cups, four glasses, and a half-dozen plates. Two cats, one gray and one white, cool themselves behind a large orange clay water vessel. Religious images adorn the walls—three color prints of saints, a three-dimensional molded plastic bust of Jesus, a *Last Supper,* and a sign that says, THE FAMILY THAT PRAYS TOGETHER STAYS TOGETHER. There is also an Añejo Rum poster—six alluring nymphs draped in transparent pink and purple gowns who look as if they never completed their religious instruction. On the bamboo-slat floor, two sacks of unhusked rice hunch beside a long wooden pole used for pounding it.

Barefoot and dressed in a blue cotton duster, Moroy Alamon's wife, Prescilla, stirs a black kettle of rice over an open charcoal hearth. She is joined by her teenage daughter, Marites, who sits lotuslike with her pink blouse open to her waist. Her two daughters in matching pink skirts periodically interrupt their games to suckle at her breasts, while a little boy walks about, chewing a three-foot stick of raw sugarcane, the candy and appetite suppressant of choice among Sugarlandia's poor.

Prescilla, fifty-four, settled on a bench, tucked her legs up against her chest, and perched her head on her knees, recollecting the events that took the life of her husband and the De los Santoses. Prescilla described her husband as "very close to Moret De los Santos," called them *kumpares,* meaning they saw each other almost as siblings. As if pleading the case for her dead husband, she denied that the stories linking Moroy to the massacre had even a grain of truth. "Our youngest daughter, Maria Cecilia, is the godchild of Moret. They were very close, Moroy and Moret. They were always together; they attended prayer services together." The two NPAs, Ka Edfil and Ka Rene, had both said Moroy worked for the military, but Prescilla denied it. In fact, she said, the main reason Moroy fled Himamaylan after the massacre was because he'd heard rumors that the military was going to kill him next. She also said Moroy had hesitated to return home because there were still other rumors of threats from the De los Santoses. "He wanted to come back here, but since the De los Santos family had a son [Joaquin] who was still alive, we didn't know what they might cook up."

Prescilla said that Moroy had warned Moret that the military believed Moret was channeling funds to the NPA. What she didn't say was how Moroy could have known this if he hadn't been close to someone in the Army—someone to whom he certainly could have betrayed Moret. Then again, her speculation about Moret's involve-

ment with the NPA may have been nothing but *tsismis*. Prescilla also
said she'd heard from friends that Moret had attended NPA seminars in the mountains. Did she think the stories were true? "Well,
yes," she said. "Possibly."

Moroy Alamon, fifty-six, had just finished his dinner with Prescilla,
their four children, and a friend, Carlito, who traveled around Negros selling herbal medicines, potions, and *anting antings,* when four
men wearing short pants arrived at their house brandishing pistols.
Prescilla said it was around seven in the evening. "They said they
wanted to talk to Moroy alone and asked us for something to eat, but
we didn't have any food to give them. They searched Carlito's be-
longings, and they warned us not to go downstairs, or we would be
shot. So we didn't go out to get help until five o'clock the next morning." As she described the kidnapping of her husband, Prescilla
cried quietly, clutching a towel. Marites watched her mother press
the towel to her face and also began crying.
      The day after Moroy disappeared, a note was found on the little
bridge over the stream just up the Mambagaton Road from Aton-
Aton, the stream where the dragonlike *halo-halo* lizards come to
drink at night, where the De los Santos children used to gather nipa
palm fronds to stitch together for roofing. Prescilla said the note
"came from the NPAs," and although she hadn't actually seen it herself, she was absolutely certain that "a lot of people did see it," including the guy who told her about it, although he didn't finish
reading it because he was so afraid that he actually tore it up, threw
it in the stream, and ran away. No, she couldn't be sure that the note
mentioned Moroy. But, yes, the NPA had boasted of killing her husband. She was sure of that.
      Prescilla said Moroy's abductors gave no reason for taking him
and never mentioned the De los Santos family or the massacre. Nevertheless, Prescilla believes the two incidents were related: "Because
the daughter of De los Santos, Nening [Jenelyn], was saying that
Moroy ordered the killing of her family. She said her mother had
scribbled a note saying Moroy ordered the killing. I think the son of
De los Santos [Joaquin] had a grudge against Moroy. He disappeared right after Moroy was killed."
      Prescilla didn't know how Moroy had been killed. The *tsismis*

she'd heard from the mountains carried two accounts: one, that he had been forced to dig his own grave and then was shot; the other, that he had been bound to a tree and burned alive. Where Moroy's body was disposed of isn't known. Ka Edfil said it was buried in Himamaylan but refused to pinpoint the actual site because of what he called "security reasons." One story had it that it's buried somewhere on Mario Chiu's hacienda. Prescilla paid a fortuneteller 200 pesos to help her locate her dead husband. The fortuneteller described a place in Himamaylan and told Prescilla that if she went there, she could find Moroy. The seeress conjured a brook, several distinctive trees, and other details—landmarks Prescilla can no longer remember, but that seemed at the time to divine a place that sounded familiar. But Prescilla said she was too afraid to go there to dig for her husband's remains, and to this day they have not been recovered.

Notes on Sources

The events chronicled in this book were pulled together from more than 200 interviews I conducted between 1987 and 1995, as well as from official Philippine government documents. At the same time, my understanding and appreciation of the culture, history, and politics of Negros and the Philippines owe a great deal to the writings of other journalists and scholars, in particular those whose works are cited below.

I. GENERAL PHILIPPINES HISTORY AND POLITICS

For those unfamiliar with the Philippines, there are several highly readable and informative overviews of the subject, notably, David Joel Steinberg's *The Philippines: A Singular and Plural Place* (Westview Press, Boulder, 1990), and Stanley Karnow's Pulitzer Prize–winning history, *In Our Image: America's Empire in the Philippines* (Random House, New York, 1989). David Wurfel's *Filipino Politics: Development and Decay* (Cornell University Press, Ithaca, 1988) is an excellent introduction to the country's national politics through the demise of Marcos, while Remigio E. Agpalo's *The Political Elite and the People: A Study of Politics in Occidental Mindoro* (University of the Philippines, 1972) is a classic study of grass-roots Philippine politics. *An Anarchy of Families: State and Family in the Philippines,* edited by Alfred W. McCoy (University of Wisconsin Center for Southeast Asian Studies, 1993), is an excellent collection of essays focusing on the enormous clout of the country's most influential families, including the Lopezes of Panay and Negros. Raymond Bonner's *Waltzing with a Dictator: The Marcoses and the Making of American Policy* (Random House, New York, 1987) is a fascinating and detailed look at the dictatorship and the U.S. role in sustaining it. Bonner's book makes extensive use of U.S. government documents he obtained under the Freedom of Information Act. More than 3,400 documents are available on microfiche in *The Philippines: U.S. Policy During the Marcos Years, 1965–1986* (Craig Nelson, Elizabeth McQuerry, eds.), a publication of the private National Security Archive in Washington, D.C. Another well-organized introduction to the country is Ronald E. Dolan, editor, *Philippines: A Country Study* (Federal Research Division, Library of Congress, Washington, D.C., 1993). Other general histories I found useful were O. D. Corpuz's *The Roots of the Filipino Nation* (Aklahi Foundation, Inc., Quezon City, 1989); Teodoro A. Agoncillo and Oscar M. Alfonso's *History of the Filipino People* (Malaya Books, Quezon City, 1967), and Agoncillo's *A Short History of the Philippines* (New American Library, New York, 1975).

A compelling account of the American takeover of the Philippines and the Philippine–American War is Stuart Creighton Miller's *"Benevolent Assimilation": The American Conquest of the Philippines, 1899–1903* (Yale University Press, New Haven, 1982). Indispensable to an understanding of the peasant culture that produced the various uprisings of the nineteenth and twentieth centuries is Reynaldo Clemeña Ileto's *Pasyon and Revolution: Popular Movements in the Philippines, 1840–1910* (Ateneo de Manila University Press, Quezon City, 1979). David Reeves Sturtevant's *Agrarian Unrest in the Philippines* (Ohio University, Center for International Studies, Athens, 1969) and *Popular Uprisings in the Philippines, 1840–1940* (Cornell University Press, Ithaca, N.Y., 1976) are superb histories of the country's peasant movements. The best works on the Hukbalahap are Benedict J. Kerkvliet's *The Huk Rebellion: A Study of Peasant Revolt in the Philippines* (University of California Press, Berkeley, 1977), Eduardo Lachica's *Huk: Philippine Agrarian Society in Revolt* (Solidaridad Publishing House, Ermita, Manila, 1971), and *Born of the People* by Louis Taruc, the leader of the Huk uprising (Greenwood Press, Wesport, Conn., 1973). Edward Geary Landsdale's *In the Midst of Wars: An American's Mission to Southeast Asia* (Harper and Row, New York, 1972) is the story of the Huk war and the years following Philippine independence from the point of view of the chief CIA operative charged with suppressing the revolt. Joseph Burkholder Smith, another ex-agent, provides a compelling tale of U.S. operations in the fifties and early sixties in his *Portrait of a Cold Warrior* (G. P. Putnam's Sons, New York, 1976).

On the American colonial period and the U.S. role after independence, see: Lewis E. Gleeck, Jr., *The American Half-Century (1898–1946)* (Historical Conservation Society, Manila, 1984); Michael McClintock's *Instruments of Statecraft: U.S. Guerrilla Warfare, Counter-insurgency, Counter-terrorism, 1940–1990* (Pantheon Books, New York, 1992); Daniel B. Schirmer and Stephen Rosskamm Shalom's *The Philippines Reader: A History of Colonialism, Neocolonialism, Dictatorship, and Resistance* (South End Press, Boston, 1987); John Rodgers Meigs Taylor's *The Philippine Insurrection Against the United States,* an unpublished manuscript available through the Library of Congress Rare Book/Special Collections Division; Leon Wolff's *Little Brown Brother: America's Forgotten Bid for Empire Which Cost 250,000 Lives* (Kraus Reprint Co., New York, 1970); and Dean C. Worcester's *The Philippines Past and Present* (Macmillian, New York, 1930).

II. NEGROS AND THE VISAYAN ISLANDS

Although there is no concise overview of the history and culture of Negros and the Visayan Islands, some excellent work is available. Historian Alfred W. McCoy's *Priests on Trial* (Penguin Books, New York, 1968) describes the history and economic context for the notorious murder trial of several Negros priests during the Marcos dictatorship. Other important essays by McCoy include: "Baylan: Animist Religion and Philippine Peasant Ideology" (*Philippine Quarterly of Society and Culture* 10:3, 1982); "In Extreme Unction: The Philippine Sugar Industry," in Randolf S. David, ed., *Political Economy of Philippine Commodities* (University of the Philippines, Quezon City, 1983); "The Restoration of Planter Power in La Carlota City," in Benedict J. Kerkvliet and Resil B. Mojares, *From Marcos to Aquino: Local Perspectives on Political Transition in the Philippines* (University of Hawaii Press, Honolulu, 1991); "A Queen Dies Slowly: The Rise and Decline of Iloilo City," in Alfred W. McCoy and Ed. C. de Jesus, *Philippine Social History: Global Trade and Local Transformation* (Asian Studies Association of Australia, Southeast Asia Publication Series, 1982).

A fascinating look at the culture of Negros during the nineteenth century is Robustiano Echauz's *Sketches of the Island of Negros* (Ohio University, Center for International Studies, Athens, 1978). Angel Martinez Cuesta's *History of Negros* (Historical Conservation Society, Manila, 1980) chronicles the history of the island under Spanish rule, while Modesto Sa-Onoy's *A History of Negros Occidental* (Today Printers and Publishers, Bacolod, 1992) covers the Spanish era through World War II. Maria Fe. Hernaez's *Negros Occidental Between Two Foreign Powers* (Negros Occidental Historical Commission, 1974) is the most detailed account of the transition from Spanish to American rule on Negros.

Some of the most important work on Negros and Visayan culture was done by anthropologist Donn Vorhis Hart, in particular his *Compadrinazgo: Ritual Kinship in the Philippines* (Northern Illinois University Press, De Kalb, 1977); "The Filipino Villager and His Spirits" (*Solidarity* magazine October/December, 1966; Solidaridad Publishing House, Ermita, Manila); and *Riddles in Filipino Folklore, an Anthropological Analysis* (Syracuse University Press, Syracuse, N.Y., 1964). An important book on the native priests of Negros is Evelyn Tan Cullamar's *Babaylanism in Negros: 1896–1907* (New Day Publishers, Quezon City, 1986). Doreen G. Fernandez's *The Iloilo Zarzuela, 1903–1930* (Ateneo de Manila University Press, Quezon City, 1978) is the most thorough study available on the theater of the Visayas, a major cultural phenomenon until the early decades of this century. Francisco Demetrio's *Encyclopedia of Philippine Folk Beliefs and Customs* (vols. 1 and 2; Xavier University, Cagayan de Oro City, 1991) is an extensive compilation of ancient and current pagan and Christian folk wisdom. Alejandro R. Roces's *Fiesta* (Vera-Reyes, Manila, 1980) is a good introduction to Filipino culture and includes a discussion of cockfighting. A more thorough examination of the national sport is Scott Guggenheim's "Cock or Bull: Cockfighting, Social Structure and Political Commentary in the Philippines," in Alan Dundes, ed., *The Cockfight: A Casebook* (University of Wisconsin Press, 1994). That book contains several comparative perspectives on the subject, including Clifford Geertz's classic essay, "Deep Play: Notes on the Balinese Cockfight."

Other anthropological studies of Negros include Jose Genova's *The Philippine Archipelago: Brief Notes on the Formation of Agricultural Colonies in the Island of Negros, 1896* (U. St. La Salle, Social Research Center, 1988); Karl L. Hutterer and William K. Macdonald's *Houses Built on Scattered Poles: Prehistory and Ecology in Negros Oriental, Philippines* (University of San Carlos, Cebu City, 1982); and F. Landa Jocano's *The Hiligaynon: An Ethnography of Family and Community Life in the Western Bisayas Region* (Asian Center, University of the Philippines, Quezon City, 1983).

Two very personal accounts of life on Negros are John Roberts White's *Bullets and Bolos* (The Century Co., New York, 1928), a personal account of a U.S. constabulary officer's life immediately after the Spanish–American War, and Nicholas Loney's *A Britisher in the Philippines* (National Library, Manila, 1964).

Negros under the Marcos dictatorship and during the early years of Aquino is covered by Fr. Niall O'Brien in *Revolution from the Heart* (Oxford University Press, New York, 1987), *Seeds of Injustice: Reflections on the Murder Frameup of the Negros Nine in the Philippines from the Prison Diary of Niall O'Brien* (O'Brien Press, Dublin, 1985), and *Island of Tears, Island of Hope* (Orbis Books, Maryknoll, N.Y., 1993); Joseph Collins's *The Philippines: Fire on the Rim* (Food First, San Francisco, 1989); and Bruce Stannard's *Poor Man's Priest: The Fr. Brian Gore Story* (William Collins, Sydney, 1984).

On the history and economics of the sugar industry on Negros, see John A. Larkin's *Sugar and the Origins of Modern Philippine Society* (University of California, Berkeley, 1993) and the work of Michael S. Billig, in particular "The Death and Rebirth of Entrepreneurism on Negros Island, Philippines: A Critique of Cultural Theories of Enterprise" (*Journal of Economic Issues* 28, September 1994, Department of Economics, University of Nebraska, Lincoln); "The Rationality of Growing Sugar in Negros" (*Philippine Studies* 40, Second Quarter, 1992, Ateneo de Manila University Press, Manila); "Stuck in Molasses: The Lack of Economic Diversification in Negros Occidental" (*Pilipinas* 16, Spring 1991, Arizona State University, Tempe), and "Syrup in the Wheels of Progress: The Inefficient Organization of the Philippine Sugar Industry" (*Journal of Southeast Asian Studies* 24:1, March 1993, Singapore University Press).

The problems of migrant workers in the Negros plantations were first

given widespread attention by Fr. Arsenio C. Jesena's "The Sacadas of Sugarland" (*Solidarity* magazine, May 1971). A fascinating look at the island
through the life on a single hacienda is Rosanne Rutten's *Women Workers
of Hacienda Milagros: Wage Labor and Household Subsistence on a Philippine
Sugar Plantation* (Antropologisch-Sociologisch Centru, Universiteit van Amsterdam, Amsterdam, 1982). Other studies of the lives of workers on Negros
and the issue of agrarian reform include: Rutten's "Courting the Worker's
Vote: Rhetoric and Response in a Philippine Hacienda Region" (Center for
Studies of Social Change, New School for Social Research, University of
Amsterdam, 1993); Filomeno V. Aguilar, Jr., *The Making of Cane Sugar: Cri-
sis and Change in Negros Occidental* (La Salle Social Research Center, Ba-
colod, 1984); *The Sugar Workers of Negros: A Study Commissioned by the
Association of Major Religious Superiors in the Philippines* (Manila, 1975);
The Sugar Workers: Two Studies (Institute of Labor and Manpower Studies,
Ministry of Labor and Employment, Manila, 1977); *Liberation in Sugarland:
Readings on Problems in the Sugar Industry,* Antonio Ledesma, ed. (Kilusan
ng Bayang Filipino, Manila, 1971); Antonio Ledesma and Ma. Lourdes T.
Montinola's *The Implementation of Agrarian Reform in Negros: Issues, Prob-
lems and Experiences* (Social Research Center, University of St. La Salle,
September 1988); and Jeffrey M. Riedinger's "Everyday Elite Resistance: Re-
distributive Agrarian Reform in the Philippines," in Kay B. Warren, ed., *The
Violence Within: Cultural and Political Opposition in Divided Nations* (Westview Press, Boulder, 1993). Violeta B. Lopez-Gonzaga, director of the La
Salle Social Research Center in Bacolod, has also published a number of useful books on the land issue, including: *The Resource Base for Agrarian Reform and Development in Negros Occidental* (1988); *The Sacadas in Negros:
A Poverty Profile* (1984); *The Socio-politics of Sugar: Wealth, Power Formation, and Change in Negros, 1899–1985* (1989); and *The Negrense: A Social
History of an Elite Class* (1991).

III. MARCOS AND AQUINO

In addition to the books touching on the Marcos and Aquino presiden-
cies mentioned above, see Lewis E. Gleeck, Jr., *President Marcos and the
Philippine Political Culture* (Loyal Printing, Manila, 1987); Reuben R.
Canoy, *The Counterfeit Revolution* (Philippine Editions Publishing, Manila,
1980); David Rosenberg, ed., *Marcos and Martial Law in the Philippines*
(Cornell University Press, Ithaca, 1979); Ricardo Manapat, *Some Are
Smarter Than Others: The History of Marcos' Crony Capitalism* (Alethia Pub-
lications, New York, 1991), a detailed look at the corruption of the Mar-
coses and their friends; and Benigno S. Aquino, Jr., "What's Wrong with the
Philippines?" (*Foreign Affairs* 46:4, July 1968). On the fall of Marcos and

the People Power Revolution, see Sandra Burton, *Impossible Dream: The Marcoses, the Aquinos, and the Unfinished Revolution* (Warner Books, New York, 1989); Lewis W. Simon, *Worth Dying For* (William Morrow and Company, New York, 1987), and Bryan Johnson's *The Four Days of Courage: The Untold Story of the People Who Brought Marcos Down* (Free Press, New York, 1987). James Fenton's "The Snap Revolution" (*Granta* 18, 1986) is also a superb account of the 1986 revolution. Robert Shaplen's three-part essay in *The New Yorker* (September 1, 21, 28, 1987) and his *Time Out of Hand: Revolution and Reaction in Southeast Asia* (Harper & Row, New York, 1970) offer consistently penetrating insights into the country, as do Ian Buruma's essays in the *New York Review of Books* and in his *God's Dust: A Modern Asian Journey* (Farrar Straus & Giroux, New York, 1989).

A superb study of Marcos's relationship with the Catholic church is Robert L. Youngblood's *Marcos Against the Church: Economic Development and Political Repression in the Philippines* (Cornell University Press, Ithaca, N.Y., 1990). Edicio De la Torre's *Touching Ground, Taking Root: Theological and Political Reflections on the Philippine Struggle* (Socio-Pastoral Institute, Philippines, 1986) is a radical priest's perspective on the issues the church confronted under Marcos. The Peruvian Gustavo Gutiérrez's *A Theology of Liberation* (Orbis Books, New York, 1988) provides the philosophical foundation for much of the church activism in the Philippines in the 1970s and 1980s.

On the Philippine economy under Marcos and the Marcos legacy, see James K. Boyce, *The Philippines: The Political Economy of Growth and Impoverishment in the Marcos Era* (University of Hawaii Press, Honolulu, 1993) and Boyce's *The Political Economy of External Indebtedness: A Case Study of the Philippines* (Philippine Institute for Development Studies, 1990); Robin Broad's *Unequal Alliance, 1979–1986: The World Bank, the International Monetary Fund, and the Philippines* (Ateneo De Manila University Press, Quezon City, 1988); Walden Bello, David Kinley, and Elaine Elinson, *Development Debacle: The World Bank in the Philippines* (Institute for Food and Development Policy, San Francisco, 1982); John Bresnan, ed., *Crisis in the Philippines* (Princeton University Press, Princeton, N.J., 1986); James B. Goodno, *The Philippines: Land of Broken Promises* (Zed Books, London, 1991); and R. J. May and Francisco Nemenzo, eds., *The Philippines After Marcos* (St. Martin's Press, New York, 1985). On the U.S. military's role under Marcos, see Walden Bello's *U.S.-Sponsored Low-Intensity Conflict in the Philippines* (Institute for Food and Development Policy, San Francisco, 1987).

There are several good books on the problems facing the Philippines during the Aquino era, including: Carl H. Lande, ed., *Rebuilding a Nation:*

Philippine Challenges and American Policy (Washington Institute Press, 1987); David Timberman's *A Changeless Land: Continuity and Change in Philippine Politics* (M. E. Sharpe, Inc., New York, 1991); and W. Scott Thompson's *The Philippines in Crisis: Development and Security in the Aquino Era, 1986–1992* (St. Martin's Press, New York, 1992). James Fallows's essay, "A Damaged Culture" (*The Atlantic Monthly*, November 1987), a provocative critique of Filipino nationalism and the national character, was the single most frequently debated article among Filipino politicians and intellectuals in the last decade.

The official Marcos biography is Hartzell Spence's *For Every Tear a Victory: The Story of Ferdinand E. Marcos* (McGraw-Hill, New York, 1964). A more critical view is Primitivo Mijares's *The Conjugal Dictatorship of Ferdinand and Imelda Marcos* (Union Square Publications, San Francisco, 1976). Biographies of the Aquinos include: Nick Joaquin's *The Aquinos of Tarlac: An Essay on History as Three Generations* (Cacho Hnos, Manila, 1983); Lucy Komisar's *Corazon Aquino: The Story of a Revolution* (George Braziller, New York, 1987); and Isabelo T. Crisostomo's *Cory: Profile of a President* (J. Kriz Publishing, Quezon City, 1986).

IV. HUMAN RIGHTS AND THE ENVIRONMENT

Western human rights organizations reported extensively on the Philippines during the final years of the Marcos regime and during the presidency of Aquino. The U.S. State Department also issues an annual country-by-country assessment on human rights, which is available from the Government Printing Office and on the Internet. Reports by private human rights groups dealing with the years covered in this book include those of the Lawyers Committee for Human Rights in New York, among them: "Impunity: Prosecutions of Human Rights Violations in the Philippines" (1991); "Out of Control: Militia Abuses in the Philippines" (1990); "Salvaging Democracy: Human Rights in the Philippines" (1985); and "Vigilantes in the Philippines: A Threat to Democratic Rule" (1988). The London-based Amnesty International has closely monitored the evolving human rights situation in a series of reports: "Philippines: Human Rights Violations and the Labour Movement" (1991); "Philippines: The Killing Goes On" (1992); and "Philippines: Unlawful Killings by Military and Paramilitary Forces" (1988). Asia Watch, based in New York, published "The Philippines: Violations of the Laws of War by Both Sides" (1990).

The link between human rights and environmental degradation is a subject of a growing body of literature. The best works on the Philippines are: Robin Broad and John Cavanagh's *Plundering Paradise: The Struggle for the Environment in the Philippines* (University of California Press, Berkeley,

1993); Marites Dañguilan Vitug's *The Politics of Logging: Power from the Forest* (Philippine Center for Investigative Journalism, Manila, 1993); Thomas F. Homer-Dixon, "Environmental Scarcities and Violent Conflict: Evidence from Cases" (in *International Security* 19:1, Summer 1994); Thomas F. Homer-Dixon, Jeffrey H. Boutwell, and George W. Rathjens, "Environmental Change and Violent Conflict: Growing scarcities of renewable resources can contribute to social instability and civil strife" (in *Scientific American*, February, 1993); Maria Concepcion Cruz, et al., "Population Growth, Poverty, and Environmental Stress: Frontier Migration in the Philippines and Costa Rica" (World Resources Institute, Washington, D.C., 1992); Wilfredo Cruz and Robert Repetto, "The Environmental Effects of Stabilization and Structural Adjustment Programs: The Philippines Case" (World Resources Institute, Washington, D.C., 1992); Gareth Porter and Delfin J. Ganapin, Jr., "Resources, Population, and the Philippines' Future: A Case Study" (World Resources Institute, Washington, D.C., 1988); and "Philippines: Environment and Natural Resource Management Study" (World Bank, Washington, D.C., 1989).

V. THE NEW PEOPLE'S ARMY AND THE COMMUNIST PARTY OF THE PHILIPPINES

Two excellent books on the New People's Army are Gregg R. Jones's *Red Revolution: Inside the Philippine Guerrilla Movement* (Westview Press, Boulder, 1989) and William Chapman's *Inside the Philippine Revolution: The New People's Army and Its Struggle for Power* (W. W. Norton and Co., New York, 1987). Richard J. Kessler's *Rebellion and Repression in the Philippines* (Yale University Press, New Haven, 1989) is a serious and detailed look at the evolution of both the NPA and the armed forces of the Philippines. Victor N. Corpus's *Silent War* (VNC Enterprises, Quezon City, 1989) presents a strategy for defeating the NPA by a man who saw the war from both sides—as a member of the Philippine armed forces who defected to the NPA and later rejoined the military. Other useful works on the NPA and the Communists include: Larry A. Niksch, "Insurgency and Counterinsurgency in the Philippines" (Committee on Foreign Relations, United States Senate, National Defense Division, Congressional Research Service, U.S. Government Printing Office, 1985); Alfredo B. Saulo's *Communism in the Philippines: An Introduction* (Ateneo de Manila University Press, Quezon City, 1990); Brig. Gen. Alexander P. Aguirre, *Readings on Counterinsurgency* (Pan-American Masters Consultants, Quezon City, 1987); and Miguel G. Coronel, *Pro-Democracy People's War* (Vanmarc Ventures, Quezon City, 1991). José María Sison, the founder of the Communist party of the Philippines, lays out the party line in *The Philippine Revolution: The*

Leader's View (Taylor and Francis, New York, 1989) and, writing under the penname Amado Guerrero, in *Philippine Society and Revolution* (International Association of Filipino Patriots, Oakland, 1979). There is also a vast amount of information available on the NPA in Western newspapers, the *Far Eastern Economic Review,* and in the Philippine press. Much of the material in the Philippine press is easily accessible through the well-indexed Foreign Broadcast Information Service's daily Southeast Asia report.

Acknowledgments

Many people contributed generously of their time, their insights, and their memories to make this book possible. I am first of all deeply grateful to everyone who agreed to be interviewed, some of whom did so at considerable risk to themselves.

Two Filipino journalists were especially helpful to me in researching *Dead Season*. Edgar Cadagat of Bacolod began assisting me on this project long before I had any idea it would turn into a book. Edgar worked as my Ilongo interpreter, guide, and all-around fixer on the islands of Negros and Cebu. He arranged numerous interviews, including those with subjects who were, shall we say, difficult to track down. He also shared his personal files and his considerable historical knowledge of Negros. Another fine journalist, Darrio Agnote, assisted me in a similar capacity in Manila and on the islands of Samar, Leyte, and Mindanao. Many of my interviews with members of the Philippine armed forces would have been next to impossible without Darrio's help.

A writer could not hope for a better advocate than Liz Dahransoff, my spirited and tenacious agent, who has believed in this project since I dropped a 160-page book proposal on her desk in the summer of 1992. The judicious and perceptive suggestions of Linda Healey, my editor at Pantheon, have contributed immeasurably to this book. I also want to thank Linda's assistant, Meredith Kahn; Pantheon managing editor, Altie Karper; Marian Schwartz in Austin, who copyedited the manuscript; Grace McVeigh at Pantheon, who was the book's production editor; Pantheon design director Fearn Cutler, who designed the book's interior; the proofreader, Edward Mansour; and the indexer, Max Franke.

I feel a special sense of *utang na loob* is owed my wife, Susan Blaustein, who lived this story with me for eight years and has been a constant source of inspiration and encouragement. I am deeply grateful for her wise counsel throughout the research and writing, her perceptive editing and re-editing of the manuscript, and for being the best partner I could ever hope to have in this or any other undertaking.

I am tremendously indebted to three friends who were kind enough to review the manuscript of *Dead Season* and to offer me countless, indispensable suggestions for improving it: historian and writer Michael Kazin of American University; journalist and author Joseph Nocera; and David Joel

Steinberg, historian and president of Long Island University. I cannot thank them enough for the energy they devoted to helping me with this book.

Thanks are also due to an invaluable organization for journalists, the Fund for Investigative Journalism in Washington, which gave me a research grant in 1991 to look into the killings in Himamaylan town. Aaron and Salome Sorbito extended their warm hospitality and friendship to me whenever I visited Negros, as did the Columban Fathers of Negros Occidental, in particular Father Eamon Gill, Father Eddie Allen, and Father Brendan O'Connell. Father Niall O'Brien was an indefatigable source of ideas and encouragement throughout my investigation into the massacre of the De los Santos family. Negros historian and publisher Modesto Sa-Onoy provided a wealth of information on the island's history. Ernesto Abaya, Leonardo Gallardo, and Enrique Rojas were particularly astute guides to the politics and culture of Negros. Violeta Lopez-Gonzaga, director of the Institute for Social Research and Development at the University of St. La Salle in Bacolod, was kind enough to let me peruse her unpublished data on contemporary land ownership on Negros, and Professor Alfred W. McCoy of the University of Wisconsin, Madison, was equally generous with his records of historic Negros land holdings. I am grateful to the late Ernesto Rodriguez, who shared his research into the history of the Ramoses and other prominent Negros families, and to his wife, the late Carolina Zayco Rodriquez, who was able to fill in the missing links of Negros genealogies where Ernie's memory failed him.

Joseph Collins of the Institute for Food and Policy Development introduced me to Negros in 1987 and worked with me on a series of interviews, several of which were used in the book. Andrew H. Neilly, Jr., of John Wiley & Sons, was a source of sage advice on getting *Dead Season* published. Thanks are also due to Rebecca Magdaluyo, my office assistant in Manila, for endless and tireless service; novelist James Grady; Attorney Francisco B. Cruz; Judge Alejandro Dinsay; journalists Jonathan Miller and Frank Browning; Josephine Castillano of the Negros Historical Commission; Zenaida LaRoque; Rolando M. Ybarzabal of the Radio Mindanao Network; Tony Gatmaitan; Candy Lehmann; Jacqueline Mejia and Pauline Paredes Sicam of the Commission on Human Rights in Manila; to Dr. John Wolff of Cornell University and David Zorc for their help with Tagalog etymologies, definitions, and usage; to R. Bruce Miller of Catholic University for clarifying some of the fine points of Catholic theology; Jeannie Blaustein and Leo Del Aguila for their translations of Spanish texts; astronomer Patrick Harrington of the University of Maryland for his reading of the galaxy; the late Louis Beltran for sharing his insights about cockfighting; Thomas Burwell of the National Peace Corps Association in Washington; and to Frank Strzelczyk.

Index